Americans Recaptured

Americans Recaptured
Progressive Era Memory of Frontier Captivity

MOLLY K. VARLEY

UNIVERSITY OF OKLAHOMA PRESS : NORMAN

Library of Congress Cataloging-in-Publication Data

Varley, Molly Kathleen Burnett, 1976–
Americans recaptured : progressive era memory of frontier captivity / Molly Kathleen Burnett Varley.
        pages   cm.
Includes bibliographical references and index.
ISBN 978-0-8061-4493-1 (hardcover)ISBN 978-0-8061-9405-9 (paper)
1. Captivity narratives—United States.   2. Frontier and pioneer life in literature.   3. United States—History—1865–1921.   4. Progressivism (United States politics)   5. Group identity—United States.   6. Indians in literature.   7. National characteristics, American.
I. Title.
E85.V37 2014
305.800973—dc23   2013050703

The paper in this book meets the guidelines for permanence and durability of the Committee on Production Guidelines for Book Longevity of the Council on Library Resources, Inc. ∞

Copyright © 2014 by the University of Oklahoma Press, Norman, Publishing Division of the University. Paperback published 2024. Manufactured in the U.S.A.

All rights reserved. No part of this publication may be reproduced, stored in a retrieval system, or transmitted, in any form or by any means, electronic, mechanical, photocopying, recording, or oth-erwise—except as permitted under Section 107 or 108 of the United States Copyright Act—without the prior permission of the University of Oklahoma Press.

Contents

Acknowledgments / vii

Introduction: Indian Captivity in the Post-frontier Era / 3
1. Small Towns Remember Indian Captivity / 25
2. The Indian and the Activist / 53
3. On Creating Americans / 89
4. Character Building and the Manly Mother / 129
Epilogue: The Captive as Conduit / 170

Appendix: Progressive Era Indian Captivity Narratives / 181
Notes / 189
Bibliography / 209
Index / 223

Acknowledgments

This book is the product of five years of research and writing, but it is actually the work of many people and many more years. It may be true that my own sense of existing in something of a cultural no-man's-land predisposed me to discover Indian captives and feel a great affection and sympathy for their cross-cultural struggles. For that, I must thank—or possibly blame—my parents for picking me out of a middle-class American life at the age of seven and plopping me down in East Africa, and then returning me several years later to rural South Carolina, a return that turned out to be far more traumatic than the initial culture shock. Although my own movement between cultures was hardly precipitated by the violent trauma that marks the start of the Indian captive's movements, it has left me somewhat disconnected from, and confused by, the culture designated by birth and time as "mine." This fact about my life did not lead me to seek out others who felt the same disconnect, but it did, perhaps, make me more likely to become fascinated by Indian captives once other circumstances led me to them.

My interest in history as an academic study began under Tom Showalter and David Bradshaw at Warren Wilson College. David provided the model of hard work, good humor, and interdisciplinary study on which I have depended ever since, while Tom taught me the invaluable lesson of how to love a great lecture, even at eight o'clock in the morning. My instructors at the University of Kent at Canterbury shaped my intellectual development and helped combine my interest in history with the study of national character development and the dissemination of our particular and peculiar national identities.

At the University of Montana my journey started with an interest in captivity as presented in films of the American West. Under the careful and thorough supervision of my advisor, Dan L. Flores, my exploration of captivity narratives in the twentieth century refocused on the Progressive Era. Jeff Wiltse in particular deserves credit as the one who first sparked my interest in the Progressive Era, and who never let me off with easy conclusions. I also wish to thank the rest of my committee, Anya Jabour, Nancy Cook, Jodi Pavilack, and Angelica Lawson, for their invaluable suggestions and patience. Department secretary Diane Rapp made my trek through graduate school easier, as she knows everything and always answers questions immediately and directly. Additional thanks are due to Linda G. Little, Curator of the Castile Historical Society; Stacey Steadham, Collections Assistant of the Indiana Historical Society; Heather Allen of the Wabash County Museum; and Jerome Thompson, the State Curator for the state of Iowa. I received much help from the interlibrary loan departments at the University of Montana and at Meredith College. I am also grateful to my colleagues in the Department of History and Political Science at Meredith College, whose good humor and support in my three years there helped keep me afloat during the last push to complete this work.

A number of people outside of academia have helped this project reach completion. Marsha Hoem and her children Inga and Walker provided friendship and a needed retreat when things got too hectic. They also provided much-needed child care at some critical moments. I must also thank my parents, whose support—financial and emotional—made this all possible. The lives of my grandmother Mary W. Burnett and my brother Karl Burnett have served as constant reminders that change is often quite necessary and welcome—a fact that has served me well over the last several unstable years.

More than anyone, I must thank my husband, Craig, and my children, Penelope, Madeleine, and Tilden, who have sustained me during these long years and who patiently waited for me to come back to earth. Craig has taken care of me in times of crisis, has listened to my endless babble about my research and my project, and has loved me in spite of all of it. For that alone, and for so many other reasons, this work is his as well. Penelope, Madeleine, and Tilden have reminded me that history is important only if it leads to something, and for me, that something is them. Their presence has changed the way I understand the lives of the people of the past—perhaps making me more sympathetic to the problems and irrationalities of others. I credit them with my sanity and with my education in life, which has proved far more valuable and fulfilling than my education in history.

Americans Recaptured

Introduction

Indian Captivity in the Post-frontier Era

On October 26, 1916, Theodore Roosevelt delivered a speech entitled "True Americanism and National Defense." Roosevelt asked his audience to "visualize just what I mean when I speak of Americanism. It does not depend upon the man's birthplace, it does not depend upon the man's creed." Rather, he went on, it lay in "the man's soul, and upon his possession of single-minded and wholehearted loyalty" to the United States.[1] As the country plummeted toward entry into the Great War, which would happen less than six months later, Roosevelt echoed the French philosopher Ernest Renan. Renan wrote three decades earlier that "the essence of a nation is that individuals have many things in common, but also have forgotten many other things." A nation may have race in common, for example, and perhaps language, religion, geography, and commercial or cultural interests, yet these do not by themselves make a nation. In order to form a nation, the population needs a collective identity made of up many individual identities, all based on a common history. According to Renan, "a nation is a soul" consisting of two parts: the past and the present. A nation must look to its collective past and present if it is to have a collective future. The violence that often accompanies nation building must be replaced by a story of heroism, and individual family stories must be inserted into the national history in order to create continuity between the collective long ago and the now.[2]

White Americans in the Progressive Era (roughly 1890 to 1916) looked for their collective "soul," and often found it in the history of Indian–American contact. The great brutality of that contact appeared to these "modern" men and women as the story of the development of the collective national "soul," that process when the "first Americans" (Indians) met Europeans in the wilderness. Through that contact with supposedly wild people and wild land, Europeans dropped their first identity and became, as Roosevelt would have it, "single-minded[ly] and wholehearted[ly] Americans." The main voice behind this interpretation of American history was historian Frederick Jackson Turner, who in 1893 declared that the frontier experience was the primary process in creating Americans out of Europeans. After the 1890 census stated that the frontier no longer existed, what mechanism would turn new immigrants into Americans, and by what means would current Americans retain the qualities their ancestors had developed on the frontier? Many Americans, especially on the local level, found the answer in tales of colonists or white Americans held captive by Indians. These histories provided a national identity that many people, including Roosevelt and Turner, feared they were losing.

Progressive Era Americans turned to tales of captivity by Indians (usually referred to, somewhat confusingly, as "Indian captivity" or "Indian captives") to prove that their violent national development had been just, that their individual suffering had been nationally heroic, that their contact with Indians and wilderness still characterized the "soul" of their nation, and that those people who actively remembered captives served as the vital link between the frontier past and the modern future—the link that would ensure continuation of frontier qualities in the twentieth century. Commentators commemorated real local Indian captives in order to include themselves in national "soul" development: a statue commemorated and preserved the story of the captive and the history of the white communities linked to the captive, but it also commemorated those people who formed the commissions to appropriate funds, design the monument, and organize the unveiling ceremonies. The commemoration of Indian captives in the late nineteenth and early twentieth centuries, then, can be read as an equation: historical captive plus active local citizens equals Americanism.

Progressive Era Americans used captivity by Indians as a lens through which to view certain "modern" problems: the place of small towns in the increasingly urbanizing society; how conservation could be used as a way to create a national cultural landscape; what role Indians and Indian qualities—which were viewed as primitive—would have in the modern national identity; and how women and men could and should relate to each other and to their society. This book argues that Americans, looking backward through Indian captivity, used the vision of the nation's "soul" that they found in a remembered frontier experience to advise their fellow citizens on how to construct their country in the future. Captivity narratives, then, were a means of planning for a national future by looking to the national past. They presented a concrete way to define "Americanism" and renew those frontier qualities that many deemed vital to the survival of the nation in the post-frontier world.

In Puritan captivity narratives, for example, authenticity sprang from the narrative's recounting of spiritual "truth." Yet scholars have systematically ignored the religious aspects of the narratives, choosing instead to focus on issues of race or gender, often claiming that religious significance died out almost completely after Puritan texts, or that authors who claimed to be speaking from religious conviction were instead unthinkingly following a formula.[3]

On the other hand, captivity narratives in the seventeenth and eighteenth centuries consistently sought to instruct their readers in proper moral behavior and religious interpretation of affliction, just as Puritan narratives did. Nineteenth century narratives generally emphasized sexual or cultural sensationalism, but the influences of early religiosity and moral instruction can still be seen in them. Although maybe not explicitly religious, the later sentimental narratives reflect moralistic stances that cannot be separated from a dominating religious worldview. In the Progressive Era, those who republished, memorialized, or in other ways remembered Indian captives did so in part because they took their cues as to the purposes of the stories from earlier phases of the genre. Earlier narratives offered religious moral instruction; post-frontier retelling of captivity provided nationalistic moral instructions. Such tales spoke about the heart of the American experience and could spark a nationalistic imagination.[4] Images of Indian captivity, whether in true accounts, fiction, or painting, served to unite Americans as Christians in their collective hatred of Indians while justifying America's anti-Indian policies.

In this work, I have focused only on tales of captivity of British colonists or citizens of the United States by American Indians. I have not included captivity tales of other types—prisoner-of-war narratives, slave narratives, or European tales of captivity by Moors—because in the United States, Indian captivity has defined and dominated the genre for five centuries. Moreover, in the Progressive Era, Americans looking to define their national "soul" in tales of captivity turned for a number of reasons to colonial tales and tales that focused on people of northern European descent.[5]

There are, of course, many ways to categorize captivity narratives. Because I focus on the use of these tales in the Progressive Era, a specific historical period, it is most logical to look at how historical phases of Indian captivity narratives developed. Other methods of categorizing the genre—by location, thematic elements, truthfulness, or captor group, for example—are fascinating and interesting, but in this case, historical periodization can best explain how the function of the genre has changed over time, and therefore how it comes into the Progressive Era.

In the sixteenth and seventeenth centuries, narratives written for European audiences aimed to support the colonization project of European nations; their portrayals of Indians differed based on the different aims of the home country. These are the first "American" tales of captivity (as opposed to British tales of captivity by Moors, for example), but their cultural center was usually still in Europe.[6] Late in the seventeenth century and into the eighteenth, Puritan narratives, the two most famous of which were Mary Rowlandson's *The Soveraignty* [sic] *and Goodness of God* (1682) and John William's *The Redeemed Captive, Returning to Zion* (1707), envisioned the experiences of the captives as tests sent by God. These tales were written as proof of God's mercy and to describe the captive's spiritual journey; they also established the redeemed captives as moral guides. During this "religious" phase, Indian captivity narratives were incredibly popular. Between 1680 and 1720, the best-selling book in the British colonies was *Pilgrim's Progress*, but the next three were captivity narratives.[7]

The "religious" period phased out in the mid-eighteenth century. In the third phase of captivity narratives, British colonial and Early National U.S. captivity narratives directed anger at the French, the British, and the Indians, who together seemed bent on preventing American westward expansion. During this time, narratives appeared more often as part of national history almanacs or as cheap pamphlets than as free-standing books, thus placing captivity in the broad American story and reflecting a growing sense of national identity. These narratives "degenerate[d] . . . into pulp fiction . . . for the purposes of propaganda and sensation," taking on the qualities of and becoming part of the rising tide of sentimental novels and domestic fiction.[8] In this phase, the Indian captivity narrative as a singular and unique genre might be questioned, as these works often seem to fit into other genres as well.

The female captive (in Mary Rowlandson's narrative, in *Uncle Tom's Cabin,* and in other sentimental novels) has held a distinct place in American literature across several genres. Far from resulting in "degeneration" of the genre, the inclusion of sentiment in Indian captivity narratives inspired the "sympathetic identification" between the reader and the narrator, a step necessary if we are to honor and emulate the female captive.[9] Moreover, because they were linked thematically and sometimes stylistically to a highly popular literary form, captivity narratives retained their popularity into the 1800s. In the late 1820s and early 1830s, the captivity tale *A Narrative of the Life of Mrs. Mary Jemison* (first published in 1824) joined James Fenimore Cooper's *The Pioneers, The Last of the Mohicans,* and *The Prairie*—novels that also had captivity as a central theme—as the top four best-sellers in the country.

Finally, in the late frontier period, between the Civil War and the end of the Indian Wars in 1890, captivity narratives became increasingly bloody and less reliable, their main purpose being the justification of U.S. expansion and the subjugation of "savage" Indians. In the second half of the nineteenth century, however, captivity narratives also began to focus on ethnographical accuracy and historical detail—a shift in focus that was seemingly in conflict with their simultaneous anti-Indian agenda. They started to function as laments for, and documentation of, the "vanishing" "first Americans." While the narratives might include "highly evocative descriptions of Indian brutalities" in order to "engender as much anti-Indian hostility as possible," they also included statements by experts attesting to their ethnographical accuracy, and often put the captivity in the context of local or regional history, thus justifying Indian removal while stimulating local pride and nationalism.[10]

Throughout their history, captivity narratives had two cultural purposes. First, they provided support for the "Anglo-American project[s]" of cultural and political expansionism and the "Americanization" or elimination of non-Anglo groups.[11] At the same time, they offered readers a vision (from a safe distance) of social structures, domestic organizations, and worldviews dramatically different from their own.[12] Progressive Era narratives, coming at a time when a growing interest in the value of other cultures paired with increasing expansionism and periods of almost hysterical nativism, created an odd cultural juxtaposition similar to that which scholars have argued was present in frontier-era captivity narratives.

Throughout American history, captivity narratives established standard cultural interpretations of nationhood and identity, while at the same time allowing both readers and narrators to break away from restrictive cultural norms and imagine a different way of living.[13] In the Progressive Era, captivity narratives and monuments certainly also helped shape and reflect the national character, but they did not center on Indian-hating. Rather, they advocated usurpation of elements of Indian culture and characteristics to define a unique post-frontier Americanness that still sprang from the frontier experience. Captivity narratives, and the celebration of historical Indian captives, advanced often contradictory visions of how the American national "soul" (in the terms of Renan) developed, and suggested ways to defend and develop that national "soul" in the future. Far from having descended into juvenile, sentimental fiction, or unconsidered repetitions of previous publications, captivity narratives in the Progressive Era took their national captive history with great seriousness and manipulated those stories quite intentionally.

Captivity narratives spoke to the national identity in part because they justified the violent extermination of Indians; after all, Indians in these tales violently attacked white settlers, and by doing so gave up any claims to innocent victimhood. In order to prove the point, no narrative of captivity could be complete without reveling in the death and dismemberment of at least a few relatives of the captive, including mutilated infants and grandmothers left to die alone in the woods. The captives themselves could be honored as heroic ancestors in part because of their status as the victims of, rather than the perpetrators of, national violence, and their very status as victims justified other Americans in becoming perpetrators of violence toward Indians.

But tales of captivity by Indians spoke to something else in the Progressive Era imagination as well: readers and audiences at memorial celebrations were reminded that frontier violence was only the first step in Indian–white relations. Regrettable as it was, that violence (either by Indian or white hands) had a happy side; eventually and inevitably, whites would win, the violence would end, and Indians would assimilate into the superior culture, thus ceasing to exist as recognizable Indians. Indian captivity, then, was a story of immediate hardship and suffering but also of the ultimate triumph of progress and white "civilization" over red "savagery." In the process, valuable Indian knowledge would be absorbed into white society, and a single new people would arise from the mix, confirming what many Progressives believed about the United Sates as a melting pot. White captives served as the contact point between two cultures in conflict, and later became the "filter through which knowledge of one culture was passed to another."[14] Captives—particularly those who fully assimilated into their captors' societies (like Frances Slocum and Mary Jemison), but even those whose captivity was short and who told graphic tales of Indian barbarity (like Abbie Gardner-Sharp)—demonstrated that frontier violence was not just the clash of different and opposing peoples but was the necessary, if regrettable, step in the creating of a new and superior nation.

In chapter 1, "Small Towns Remember Indian Captivity," I examine just how Americans placed their small communities in the center of American history by celebrating the link between themselves and their captive ancestors. Small towns, feeling particularly under threat by rapid urbanization and industrialization, looked to historic Indian captives to reaffirm their importance in the development of the nation and its unique people. Indian captives could establish both the longevity of important local families and the role of these families in turning European settlers into Americans. Captivity narratives gave these small places an opportunity to preserve that history for the future. Public commemoration demonstrated both the important history of these local families and places and their modern importance as their efforts at commemoration were celebrated with as much nationalist enthusiasm as the captivity itself was.

Frances Slocum, captured by the Miami Indians in 1778 at the age of 5, lived the rest of her life as a Miami. She became the ancestral connection to frontier early American history for boosters in Wyoming Valley, Pennsylvania (from where she was taken), and Wabash County, Indiana (where she lived most of her adult life and where she died). Residents of these areas focused on their genealogical link to Frances Slocum. She also became the mechanism by which families and boosters substantiated their national value to the modern, post-frontier present in which the national dialogue was dominated by cities.

One did not have to be the descendant of a captive, though, in order to develop an interest in a particular captive. Some people developed an interest in an Indian captive because of a geographical, rather than a genealogical, tie to the captive. This geographical tie allowed authors and their audiences to envision and develop a particular place as a "cultural landscape" that served as a means to investigate "Americanness" and disseminate its qualities to modern visitors. Chapter 2, "The Indian and the Activist," investigates how William Pryor Letchworth, founder of Letchworth Park in Upstate New York, incorporated the history of the colonial Shawnee captive Mary Jemison into his efforts to conserve and restore the area that became the park. Although he had no family link to Jemison, Letchworth used the captive to give this wilderness a cultural significance that "empty" land itself did not have. Letchworth became the quintessential Progressive activist who entrusted government apparatus with protecting the combined cultural and natural heritage of (and therefore the national value of) a particular place.

The interest that audiences had in tales of Indian captivity came in large part from the fact that the very space and process they memorialized—the frontier—no longer officially existed. The 1890 census had declared unequivocally that the frontier line was so broken by areas of settlement that it could no longer be called a frontier. Homesteading—the act of "frontiering"—continued and expanded in the twentieth century as settlers moved onto increasingly marginal lands, especially after the Enlarged Homestead Act of 1909. Not until 1934 did homesteading decline, when the Taylor Grazing Act led to its effective end.[15]

Despite continued homesteading and the existence of open land after 1890, the census announcement of the end of the frontier caused concern and permeated the American imagination. It created a sense of cultural insecurity that Progressives spent much time grappling with. In his iconic 1893 essay, "The Significance of the Frontier in American History," the until-then-obscure historian Frederick Jackson Turner stated that "four centuries from the discovery of America, at the end of a hundred years of life under the Constitution, the frontier has gone, and with its going has closed the first period in American history."[16] As if to emphasize the fact that modernity had arrived, the 1890 census was the first U.S. census to use distinctly modern data collection and recording techniques, including a method of electronically tabulating data on punch cards. The age of the axe and the woodsman was gone. The age of electronics had arrived.

Americans could point to other events in 1890 that symbolized the end of their "first period." In May of that year, the Church of

Jesus Christ of Latter Day Saints terminated its practice of polygamy, effectively ending large-scale western experiments in societal structures and practices that stood in opposition to, or at least outside of, mainstream Protestant American culture. The frontier, at least for some, was no longer a place where one could go to escape conforming to American mores.[17] That year also saw centuries of armed conflict between American Indian and Euro-American forces end in a bloody field beside Wounded Knee Creek in South Dakota when, on December 28, the U.S. 7th Cavalry Regiment slaughtered a group of Miniconjou and Hunkpapa Lakota. The end of U.S. military hostilities with Indians could also be seen in the death of Sitting Bull, the famous resistance leader of the Hunkpapa Lakota. Lakota policemen sent to arrest him on December 15, just thirteen days before the Wounded Knee Massacre, shot and killed him. Indians were not gone from the United States, but their military opposition to U.S. power was neutralized. The age of captivity by hostile Indians, a possibility that had been considered so much a part of the American experience since Pocahontas "saved" John Smith in 1607, was over too.[18]

In addition, Chicago was chosen in 1890 to host the World's Columbian Exposition, which would open in 1893. The heart of the fair was the great "White City," so-called because all the classically inspired buildings were made of white stucco. Among the celebrated electric lights, the Ferris Wheel (intended to compete with the Eiffel Tower in grandeur), Eadweard Muybridge's photographs of horse locomotion, Scott Joplin's performances of a new musical style called ragtime, and new products like Shredded Wheat, Juicy Fruit, and the country's first official serial killer—all of which, in retrospect, can symbolize the coming new century and the end of a previous era—at least two people at the fair looked back to the frontier period with great nostalgia.[19] The first, Buffalo Bill Cody, brought his Wild West Show to Chicago despite having been denied an official place in the fairgrounds, and set up shop just outside the sparklingly modern White City.

Frederick Jackson Turner also came to the fair as a young historian from the University of Wisconsin. It was at the meeting of the American Historical Association, held at the fair, that Turner read "The Significance of the Frontier in American History" (soon dubbed the "Frontier Thesis"). Although the two men did not meet at the fair, their very presence there together serves as a reminder that the frontier past and the act of remembering it were an intractable and acknowledged element in the modern national story and its future.

As historian Richard White has pointed out, the two men did not tell the same story. One (Turner) envisioned the filling of empty land by peaceful farmers; the other (Cody) envisioned the snatching of land from violent Indians. But the similarities *and* the contradictions between the two stories of the settlement of the West combined to reveal the very composition of the American westering myth. Many Progressive Era Americans believed in that myth without question—that violence was justified because it eventually allowed for a peaceful settlement. Frontier violence, then, while regrettable because of the terror it brought to individuals and communities, was necessary. An easy settlement of the continent would have resulted in nothing besides Europeans transplanted into a new place. Hardship and suffering on the frontier had turned Europeans into Americans. The modern country, so the myth went, needed to remember and replicate that experience. Both Turner's and Cody's versions of the "first period" came to the same conclusion: the frontier was gone and Americans needed to remember it in order to retain the national soul they had developed there.[20]

Captivity narratives, historian Richard Slotkin has argued, were part of the myth Americans created about themselves as a unique people formed on the frontier. The frontiersman served as a middleman between the civilization of white settlement and the wilds of Indian country. The captive of Indians became the ultimate frontiersman, always superior to the Indian captors because of his or her "white blood," but able to incorporate and utilize vital parts of Indian psyche and culture.[21] The Indian captive became, in some sense, an improved European through contact with Native Americans. As English literature and ethnicity scholar Shari Huhndorf has explained it, the process of "going native has served as an essential means of defining and regenerating racial whiteness and a racially inflected vision of Americanness." Huhndorf described a process of "going Indian" in order to "regenerate and to maintain European-American racial and national identities."[22] Arriving at a similar conclusion, cultural historian Philip Deloria outlined the less permanent, though no less persistent, ways that Euro-Americans adopted Indian identities in order to discover a "deep, authentic, aboriginal Americanness."[23] Americans have used captivity tales to reclassify violence directed at or coming from Indians, not as the account of the struggles between individuals and societies in conflict, but as a national creation story. In the early twentieth century, people who remembered Indian captives—whether the protagonists "went" (permanently) Indian or "played" (temporarily) Indian—placed themselves, through ancestral or geographic bond with the captives, in the center of that creation and as the vital carriers of that story into the future.

It is appropriate to take a moment to explain that this study focuses mainly on the captives of the old British colonies. There are two main reasons for this. First, those narratives attracted attention in far greater numbers than, for example, narratives of the far West, Rocky Mountain West, and the Southwest. For one thing, more recent tales of captivity would hardly serve the purpose of proving the captive and his or her family as members of what Theodore Roosevelt termed the "frontier gentry," for the actual captivity often took place far too recently to be used to establish that kind of longevity (see chapter 1). It is, after all, one thing to discuss how one's great-grandmother took on Indian characteristics and even possibly had Indian children, and to glorify that action, but it is something else altogether to discuss how one's mother or aunt or even sister did so. Freestanding narratives of captivity in the far west simply did not appear in any great numbers during this time.[24]

Of course, captivity by Indians also took place in the colonies of other countries whose territories eventually became part of the United States, such as the Mexico-U.S. borderlands. Several scholars have recently addressed the topic of captivity in this complex area, although no one has yet made a systematic study of French or Spanish captivity narratives in the context of growing *American* nationalism. The assumption, of course, has been that French and Spanish colonial tales of captivity were products of the French and Spanish for French and Spanish readers, rather than of colonial Americans speaking to later national Americans. In the Progressive Era, those narratives did not take on the nationalistic aspect that British colonial tales did, precisely because at that time Americans tended to think of themselves as having British ancestry, rather than Spanish or French ancestry.

For example, because of the historical and contemporary existence of Spanish ancestry and culture in the areas that became the American Southwest and northern Mexico, Indian captivity in those regions was not viewed as an aspect of nationalistic identity so much as an "intercultural exchange . . . [in] a borderland political cultural economy." While northeastern native groups generally took captives primarily to adopt or to hold for ransom, Indian and New Mexican societies took captives as slaves and later converted them to kin. These differences, along with the fluid intermingling of Spanish and native cultures in these regions, meant that while captivity in what was once Mexican territory was an experience that helped build and shape American society and history, it was not used by Progressives in their search for a national "soul." As historian James Brooks has so clearly stated, "native American groups went about the pragmatic and often violent business of mingling families and producing hybrid cultures."[25] Cultural commentators like Theodore Roosevelt and the scores of others less famous drew on a "hybrid culture" produced by such captives as Mary Jemison and Frances Slocum, and they even included and honored the Indian offspring of those women in their celebrations. But the national "soul" they sought to define, control, and save had no room for cultural hybrids, especially those as obvious as could be found in Arizona or New Mexico.

Tales of Indians and white captivity by Indians has helped delineate "American" as separate from both "European" and "Indian" and yet springing from both. Prior to the Revolution, *American* had meant only *Indian;* the colonists, after all, were British. But by the eve of the Revolution, *American* had come to mean "separate and different from European," with "American Indians . . . seen as free from the feudal heritage of Europe." In the context of that etymological shift, Indians were something admirable, having qualities of political independence and loyalty that Americans wanted to develop in themselves. Anglo-Americans who began to envision themselves as something different from their British parents saw American Indians as the embodiment of the two values of "life and liberty."[26] Early twentieth century Americans found those same values exemplified in captivity narratives. They used the narratives to remind themselves of what the country gained on the frontier and to teach those values to newcomers to American shores. They looked back to this colonial and Early National understanding of Indians, overlooking the slaughter and exploitation and bloodshed on the frontier, and turning to a bond between "red" and white Americans to find their collective and unique national character

Indians, whether envisioned positively or negatively, had always been judged necessary to an American history and, indeed, to an American present and future.[27] In the early twentieth century, Ernest Thompson Seton, cofounder of the Boy Scouts of America, saw Indian knowledge and behavior as the way "into" Americanness.

He argued that "America owes much to the Redman," because the help and wisdom that the patriots gained through Indian contact allowed them to best the British. But, according to Seton, "the Redman can do a greater service now and in the future" by "teach[ing] us the ways of outdoor life, the nobility of courage, the joy of beauty, the blessedness of enough, the glory of service, the power of kindness, the super-excellence of peace of mind and the scorn of death."[28] Seton's rival, "Uncle Dan" Beard, on the other hand, founded the Sons of Daniel Boone in 1905 and stressed pioneer knowledge, and pioneer Indian-hating, as the way to develop a genuine American character in young boys.

But Seton's and Beard's visions of Indians and their place in American history were, in fact, not contradictory at all, just as there was no contradiction between Frederick Jackson Turner's and Buffalo Bill's visions of frontier history. Seton "feared the alienating effects of the machine and [modern] system," while Beard welcomed a technological future "that took its vigor from a nostalgic frontier past," but both looked to the presence of historical (i.e., not living) Indians to teach boys how to be American men.[29] Seton's vision of America's future responded in fear to the industrialization and urbanization that had occurred in the late nineteenth century, and Seton used Indian knowledge as a link to a safer, preindustrial way of life. Beard, meanwhile, looked with excitement to America's industrial present and future. Beard used Indians as the mechanism by which to teach white Americans how to behave.

A positive American future required the inclusion of Indian history and Indian knowledge. Just as "earlier Americans [pre-1890] had all focused on developing an identity that was explicitly American," early twentieth century Americans sought to preserve and strengthen that identity in the face of the "historical chasm" that was modernity.[30] Progressive Era Americans used historical Indians to define the "authentic" American for their children and for the masses of immigrants now streaming into their cities. In

INTRODUCTION

this way, Indians moved from being envisioned as "inauthentic Americans" (opposed to and in opposition to pioneers, as Beard would have it) to "first Americans," destined to give way to civilization but vital to its creation. "Historical" Indians (memories of premodern Indians) at the turn of the twentieth century, like Indians during the Revolution, symbolized positive characteristics Americans wished to replicate, while "modern" Indians (those individuals actually alive in the twentieth century) represented a "degraded primitive" that needed erasure through allotment, boarding schools, and Americanization.[31] Thus, perceptions of Indians allowed for two conflicting yet complementary visions of Indians in the United States: one used the memory of Indians to create and maintain an "authentic" American identity while the other sought to remove their "Indianness" with as little guilt as possible.

As described in chapter 3, "On Creating Americans," Indian captivity tales often celebrated the contact between the two races, using narratives or memorials to emphasize the stages that took the captive from European immigrant to full American; at the same time, tales of captivity emphasized ties between the captive and the Indian captors in order to establish the captive's position as an authority on Indians and to justify and support federal allotment and Americanization policies. By fixating on tales of Euro-Americans who "went" or "played" Indian in captivity, post-frontier Americans could renew their "frontier" qualities. They gained these frontier characteristics, both individually and collectively, through suffering and privation or through contact with Indians. Captivity narratives had both. Those qualities—ingenuity, inventiveness, materialism, practicality, enthusiasm—were not necessarily permanent, and many believed that each subsequent generation needed to renew them or suffer the decline of their democratic, individualistic way of life. Indian captives, especially those like Mary Jemison and Frances Slocum, who had Indian children and lived and died as Indians, proved that the active "civilization" and "Americanization" of Indian groups would not degrade white Americans but would instead renew white frontier qualities and, in effect, save the country from a decline into European decadence.[32]

In order to use the stories and images of Indian captives to national ends, early twentieth century Americans navigated a complex set of images and contradictions. By studying and incorporating the characteristics they believed they had developed on the frontier, Americans assured themselves that they could enter the new century with confidence that they would produce a uniquely American future that drew its strength from the past. As with the link to ancestors and historical Indians, Progressive Era narratives looked back to the "first period" to find answers to confusions about gender as well as about the position of Indians. Before the end of the frontier, captivity narratives focused on women because of the tantalizing prospect of the female captive becoming defeminized. She might fall into male behaviors because of her time away from civilization and because of the lack of men to perform male tasks like hunting or defense. The very heroic acts or attributes that might save her life might also make the female captive so masculine as to become totally unappealing. She might also be raped by or married (usually by force) to an Indian. And, perhaps worst of all, the female captive might become "Indianized," in which case she would willingly accept an Indian spouse and Indian cultural practices, and produce Indian children. Readers would find this last possibility particularly disturbing because it suggested failings in white civilization and also implied that Indians might be sexually and culturally superior to white men.[33] In chapter 4, "Character Building and the Manly Mother," I argue that turn-of-the-century captivity tales envisioned women rather than men as the ideal embodiment of American "manliness" because women in captivity exhibited masculine qualities such as independence and self-sufficiency in addition to their natural female roles as community caretakers.

I believe that the three problems of female captivity did interest both writers and readers, and while they were not absent in post-frontier narratives, they actually served to strengthen a nationalized "manly" femininity that I call the "Manly Mother." This woman, personified best in Abbie Gardner-Sharp, was traumatized by her captivity experience but also used the distinctly male trait of independent thought and action to survive her captivity and often to better her post-captivity life. She was "feminine" in her frailty and the ease with which she could be psychologically damaged, and also in her fixation, sometimes obsession, with the concerns of the community over her own well-being. She was also "masculine" in her independence and strength. She exhibited the best qualities of both sexes and used those qualities to defend the community's interests and future. Likewise, "Indianized" female captives combined Indian and white traits in a way that proves the superiority of American civilization. The Manly Mother, then, personifies the act of looking backward in order to address the issues of the future.[34]

The danger of captivity by Indians might have ended by 1890, but captivity narratives did not die with the official closing of the frontier. Between the end of the Indian Wars in 1890 and U.S. entrance into the Great War in 1916, publishers—most often local publications—issued forty-nine narratives of white captivity among Indians. Most were revisions, republications or reissues of material published earlier in the nineteenth and sometimes the eighteenth centuries. The 1906 narrative of the burning of Royalton, Vermont, and the captivity of Zadock Steele, for example, first published in 1808, was republished in 1908 under the auspices of the Royalton Woman's Club and the Royalton Historical Society. Sometimes, as in the case of Martha Bennett Phelps' *Frances Slocum: The Lost Sister of Wyoming*, editions of which appeared in 1905, 1906 and 1916, the individual author published the narrative in small, local print runs.

The Progressive memory of Indian captivity, unlike many of the other major movements of the era (such as urban reform and populism), was a small-town story. Neither urban nor fully rural, local boosters, historical societies, and history buffs deemed those captives to be important to their towns' histories and to the role those towns would be able to claim in a post-frontier American culture increasingly dominated by industry and urban space. With a few exceptions, such as narratives published by major publishing companies (e.g., the 1898 and 1910 editions of the Mary Jemison narrative edited by William Pryor Letchworth, both published by G. P. Putnam's Sons), captivity narratives in the Progressive Era were local productions intended for local consumption. But, like most other captivity tales during these years, Letchworth intended the tale of Mary Jemison to convince a local population of the central position that small places held in the development and continued defense of the national "soul," which they called "Americanism" and "national spirit."

During the Progressive Era, in addition to the publication of printed narratives, a number of communities commemorated historical Indian captives in stone, erecting monuments to them with great seriousness of purpose and pomposity of spirit. Many times, in fact, the monument ceremony inspired the republication of a particular narrative accompanied by a full transcript of the monument dedication ceremony. The monument ceremonies were well planned, sometimes taking years to develop, and were well attended on a local scale. Perhaps four hundred to six hundred people attended the Slocum memorial dedication, and a slightly smaller number went to the Jemison ceremony. They attracted mainly family and community members with some nationally known speakers.

Yet captives themselves had little say in how post-frontier readers would interpret their stories. On the whole, early twentieth century captivity narratives were written by someone other than the captives themselves, and those that were authored by the captive were reissued from documents often 100 years or more old. John Leeth's narrative first appeared in 1831, Nehemiah How's in 1748, and Zadock Steele's in 1818. Those captives, being long since dead, could not shape the way modern editors and publishers presented their stories. Reuben Gold Thwaites, author of the 1904 introduction to Leeth's narrative, told readers that even after Leeth "regained his liberty through white supremacy," he "nevertheless considered himself and thenceforth was considered by them a passive member of the tribe."[35] But of course Leeth himself could not speak about his own relationship with his captors or explain to a modern reader how to interpret his story in a post-frontier context. Other captives, like Frances Slocum, who died in 1847, had simply refused to participate in explaining what readers should get out of her story.[36] Whether because they were dead, or because they did not author their narratives themselves, those captives who caught the imagination of Progressive Era readers (again, with the exception of Abbie Gardner-Sharp) had little or no say in the way their stories were interpreted in a culture that was struggling to adjust to a post-frontier, industrialized world.

The foremost means by which we define ourselves—as belonging to a particular family, a particular place, a particular race, or a particular sex and gender—combined in captivity narratives to allow Progressive Era Americans to recapture something of the nation's "first period" and use it to shape their second. Renan's two-part national soul, made up of the past and the present, became a three-part soul, consisting of the past, the present, and the future.

Despite the official closing of the frontier and the corresponding unease that announcement brought with it, tales of captivity by Indians remained quite tangible for people entering the twentieth century. It was through such tales that readers, audiences, authors, and speakers at memorial celebrations brought frontier characteristics they believed vital to the American national soul into a modern, post-frontier world. The Puritan Indian captivity narrative, in addition to its religious message, had spoken to emerging national sensibilities in the same way that tales of captivity by British forces during the Revolutionary War engendered a sense of collective captivity by a tyrannical king.[37] In the post-frontier era, captivity narratives likewise revealed the worries and anxieties that accompanied the creation of Roosevelt's "single-minded and wholehearted" national "soul." That "soul" depended upon adequately carrying the qualities of the past into the future. The act of remembering the Indian captive located the men and women who worked to enact the commemoration at the axis of that moment when "then" met "yet-to-be." The years around the turn of the century served as a hinge, and in that transition, the commemorators of captives—not the captives themselves—served as the vital conduit through which the frontier past could communicate with the post-frontier future.

CHAPTER 1

Small Towns Remember Indian Captivity

Frances Slocum and Maconaquah

Late enough in the evening that the only light in the house came from the flickering hearth fire, the Miami Indian widow Maconaquah sat in silence. It was January of 1832, and her houseguest, Colonel George W. Ewing, had found himself traveling and without a white home to stop in for the night. Conveniently, Ewing spoke Miami and chose to pass the night in this, the house of a "better sort of Indian." As the evening wore on, he tried three times to leave the room, for although the widow had asked him to sit up with her long after the rest of the family had gone to bed, she had not spoken of anything of significance for more than an hour. But when Colonel Ewing again said he would retire for the night, she told him to stay. "I shall not live long," she said, "and I must tell it. I cannot die in peace if I do not."[1]

Although Maconaquah's great-niece, Martha Bennett Phelps, would write 84 years later that Ewing knew Maconaquah was no Indian, Ewing told others that he "could not of course divine what her secret was."² In the dim firelight, after all, she must have seemed wholly Indian, even if, earlier in the day, a certain lightness to her hair and a glimpse of the pale skin under her sleeve may have hinted at her secret. When the Colonel rose to leave the room for the third time, telling her that she could speak to him later if she preferred, the elderly woman resisted. "No," she said, and, again, "I may die, I may die; and then I will have no rest in the Spirit World."³

Maconaquah told Ewing a shocking tale. Captured by Miami Indians in the aftermath of the Revolutionary War Battle of Wyoming, Pennsylvania, on July 3, 1778, the five-year-old white child Frances Slocum ceased to exist. That night she told Ewing all she could remember of her former life. She had been taken as a girl from a family she thought perhaps Quaker, from a homestead in a valley whose name she could not recall. Maconaquah, as she came to be known, had hidden from her white relatives for her entire life as an Indian, although she admitted knowing that her white brothers were hunting for her. She had no interest in returning to the white world or in finding her lost family. She had a family; she had an identity, and she did not need to resurrect a dead one. But for the sake of her peace of mind in the afterlife, she believed she needed to tell the secret of her identity to some representative of the white world. Colonel Ewing was white and he was at hand.

To Martha Bennet Phelps, writing of her great-aunt in the early twentieth century, it might have been comforting to think that her relative could not have truly passed as Indian, but to Ewing at the time, in the half-light of the fading fire and the stillness of the house, the tale of the captured child must have seemed extraordinary. Ewing was impressed enough to repeat the story to his own mother, and her sympathy for Maconaquah's brokenhearted white mother prompted him to begin a three-year search for her lost white family, one that ended in precisely the way Maconaquah had feared it would: with hopeful white relatives on her doorstep begging her to return to their world, expecting so much of her, expecting her to be five. And white.

Indian Captivity in Small Towns

Small town Americans around the turn of the century sought to define and perpetuate their own importance in the development of the national character by symbolically joining themselves to their settler history through ancestral ties and family history. An Indian captive in the town's history could serve as the point of proof that this town, and the people who inhabited it, played a vital and necessary role in the creation of a single American character through contact with the wilderness and its inhabitants. The story of the Pennsylvania Slocums reuniting with their lost sister in Indiana in 1837 attracted some local newspaper attention at the time, both in Pennsylvania (where she was captured) and Indiana (where she then lived). A series of accidents, coincidences, and letters lost and found delayed the reunion of the Slocums and Maconaquah—so longed for by the Slocums, so dreaded by Maconaquah—by several years. When the Slocums did find Maconaquah, she did not speak English and could not remember her Christian name (Frances), and, although she did not deny her kinship to the Quaker Slocums, she seemed hostile to their presence and skeptical of their motives. She was 64 years old and had lived as an Indian for 59 years.

Starting in about 1890, a group of local boosters and historians from both Wyoming Valley, Pennsylvania, and Wabash County, Indiana, took a renewed interest in Maconaquah's history. Her story was republished five times by several different authors between 1891 and 1916, and in 1900 historians and family from both states joined forces to erect a memorial to her in Peru, Indiana. White descendants also dedicated the "Frances Slocum Playground" in Wilkes-Barre in 1907. This sudden curiosity about the history of Frances Slocum, or Maconaquah, might be attributed to the personal interest of a few relatives searching for an unexpected family connection created on a porous frontier, except for the fact that others less directly connected to any particular captive shared a fascination with such tales. The Slocums might have represented an early example of this kind of revived interest, but they were hardly alone.

Beginning in about 1890, after the U.S. census declared the frontier closed and the tragic episode at Wounded Knee, South Dakota, signaled the end of the Indian wars, and well after the genre might have been thought dead, American publishers and readers developed a renewed interest in tales of Americans who had been captured by Indians on the frontier. Scholars of captivity narratives have outlined several phases of captivity narratives, including Puritan narratives that served the religious and colonial project of earlier American settlers; Revolutionary-era narratives that linked Indian captivity to national captivity under the English crown; early national narratives that justified national expansion and the subjugation of Indians; and narratives that appeared between the Civil War and the end of the frontier that legitimized increased violence against Indians and the project of "Americanizing" them. Moreover, in each period, captivity narratives established standard cultural interpretations of nationhood and identity, while at the same time allowing both reader and narrator to break away from restrictive cultural norms and imagine a different way of living. Scholars have drawn a connection between rising national and imperial identity and captivity narratives, and have emphasized that captivity narratives allowed experimentation within cultural standards of gender and racial roles.[4]

In the Progressive Era, captivity narratives likewise became one vehicle by which Progressive Era Americans sought to preserve and renew those national characteristics many feared were on the verge of extinction: independence of spirit, love of hard work, and an amorphous thing many called "manliness." Americans in the early twentieth century looked in earnest for ways to maintain their status as a frontier nation. They might, for example, sustain the farmer legacy of the Jeffersonian ideal through irrigation of the arid West; they might gain new frontiers overseas.[5]

Americans might also define and perpetuate their national character by symbolically joining themselves to their settler history through ancestral ties and family history. This act of joining present to past (albeit a past often obscured by myth or perhaps made up altogether) took place in many ways. Buffalo Bill's Wild West, for example, allowed audiences to relive the settling of the West. Ancestor-based organizations such as the Daughters of the American Revolution (and its progeny, Children of the American Revolution), the Sons of the American Revolution, the Colonial Dames of America, the Mayflower Society, and United Confederate Veterans, all founded in the last 12 years of the nineteenth century, provided members the public opportunity to display and celebrate their link to America's past. Other Americans turned to historical pageantry or to the building of monuments to assure themselves that the American past was not forgotten and remained important. Artists like Charlie Russell painted the West of the 1880s, rather than the West of the twentieth century in which he lived, because, in his own words, he was "dedicated to the West of his youth." In doing so, this "least progressive" of men became "astonishingly up to date," as Americans since the Civil War had been searching for ways to cling to and perpetuate the frontier, which they believed had created them as a unique people and as important individuals.[6] By the 1890s, and particularly by the turn of the century, with the frontier at least theoretically closed and Indian foes vanquished and vanishing on their reservations, Americans looked in all directions for their source of national identity. At the 1910 unveiling of the memorial to the Seneca captive Mary Jemison, Dr. Edward Hagaman Hall reminded his audience that the statue would "remind us of our debt to that hardy race of pioneers who, driven by a Destiny more powerful than human will, subdued the wilderness to the beneficent uses of a higher civilization." Later that day, Dr. Charles D. Vail read a letter from sculptor H. K. Bush-Brown, stating "Everyone is interested in history for it is the only means of understanding the present or providing for the future."[7] In this milieu, tales of Indian captivity gave meaning and importance to contemporary family histories as well as to current actions to remember the Indians.

Progressive Era Americans were particular in their choice of which Indian captives deserved their attention. They did not turn to the most sensational or graphic stories. In fact, they turned most often to those captives with the strongest connections to the Indians who captured them. Mary Jemison and Frances Slocum, whose stories were the most reprinted captive stories of the era, both "became Indian," refusing to return to white society even when begged to. Cynthia Ann Parker, on the other hand, famous and historically significant, was only briefly mentioned in Texas histories. Theodore Roosevelt dedicated his history *The Winning of the West* to Comanche Chief Quanah Parker, but the story of the Chief's mother, the captive Cynthia Ann Parker, saw only one retelling between 1886 and 1934.[8] Perhaps Cynthia Ann's "recapture" by whites, as well as other aspects of her story, as outlined below, made her a less appealing figure to Progressive Era Americans seeking to find importance for themselves in captivity stories.

Progressive Era readers did not look just to the most popular or most well-known captives and repeat their tales. Indeed, several of the most well-known stories of Indian captivity earned little print attention in the Progressive Era. This lack of interest in the more notorious captives signals that it was not just Indian captivity alone that grabbed the imaginations of so many readers in the early twentieth century; rather, readers wanted a personal connection, in the form of a local community link, to the captive individual.

One explanation for the lack of interest in Cynthia Ann Parker is the importance of her child, the Comanche Chief Quanah Parker. His notoriety overshadowed her importance. Moreover, other whites in the Parker family left their mark on Texas as well; the Parker clan had any number of connections between themselves and frontier history and to captivity by Indians. At 11 years of age, Cynthia Ann was taken by the Comanche from Fort Parker, Texas, on May 19, 1836, along with John Richard Parker (her brother), Rachel Plummer (her cousin), James Pratt Plummer (Rachel's son), and Elizabeth Duty Kellogg. Fort Parker still stands and is joined by Fort Parker State Park, the town and county of Parker, the city of Quanah, Quanah High School, Quanah Memorial Cemetery, and Quanah Parker Park in Fort Worth. The pedigree of the Parker family in the Texas Revolution, in the Mexican-American War, and in the early national and state political and cultural development of Texas can be well established without depending on the story of Cynthia Ann to prove the connection. Quanah Parker commanded much of the public attention in the Progressive Era, as he lived until 1911 and the family bickered for many years over his property. During the Progressive years, Quanah—not Cynthia Ann—was the primary cultural middleman to emerge from the massacre at Fort Parker. It fell to Quanah, not the white Parkers, to locate Cynthia Ann's remains in Texas and rebury her closer to him in Oklahoma in a small ceremony in 1910.[9] The Indian Quanah, not the white Cynthia Ann, captured Progressive imaginations.

Moreover, there is the problem of the miserable quality of Cynthia Ann's life after recapture. Frances Slocum and Mary Jemison, Indian captives who chose to live permanently with their captors and later drew the attention of Progressives, largely controlled their own fate after captivity. The primary difference, then, between Cynthia Ann Parker and Slocum and Jemison was that the former suffered recapture by the American army at the age of 34, followed by deliverance to her white family and separation from her Indian sons, while the latter two, although they considered returning to white society, were allowed to remain with their Indian families when they decided not to. The rather pathetic end of Cynthia Ann's story, which included being passed from one white relative to another, escape attempts, and the death of her young daughter in 1864 and herself in 1870, probably made her tale less appealing than the stories of Slocum and Jemison, who remained in control of their own fates—quite frankly, they probably seemed stronger and more admirable than Cynthia Ann. Her lack of control over her adult fate, and the fact that the Parker family could prove its frontier pedigree without her, combined to make her less appealing to Progressive Era audiences than other assimilated captives like Slocum and Jemison.[10]

The difference between Parker's family and the Slocum family may have come as well from their Progressive sentiments. Did these families see their connection to an Indian captive as primarily a personal family matter, or did they—as the Slocums certainly did—understand that link as a way to connect themselves to an elite, old-stock American heritage? Most of the Indian captive narratives reprinted or memorialized in the early twentieth century came from Northeastern or Midwestern old-stock families who took great pride in their pre-revolutionary ancestors. As Richard Hofsteader famously stated, many supported Progressivism because it sought "to restore a type of economic individualism and political democracy that was widely believed to have existed earlier in America . . . restoration [of that old world would] bring back a kind of morality and civic purity that was also believed to have been lost."[11] Small communities, and the middle-class men who ran them, experienced an "upheaval in status" as the newly rich eclipsed their power in their communities and on the national stage.[12] The "aristocratic local gentry" longed to remind both themselves and the changing country around them that they were still important members—indeed, leaders—of American culture.[13] Residents of smaller towns assumed that the rapidly industrializing cities were poised not just to eclipse their national importance but possibly to wipe them out altogether. In response, they found that they could use historical captive figures to justify their very existence, and certainly to argue for their cultural significance. Possibly the Parker family, having never exactly been part of the old gentry of the colonies, but rather frontiersmen and Baptists in the West, simply did not feel that their position in society was in danger and so did not focus on defending it.

But many Americans did defend their old-stock credentials. To this end, many narratives published in this era start with a long history of the family involved and sometimes the geographical place. Martha Bennet Phelps's tale of Frances Slocum, for example, starts with a chapter on the Slocum family's genealogy prior to Frances's captivity; likewise, it ends with appendices tracing the family genealogy since her rediscovery. As Minnie Buce Carrigan put it in the preface to her narrative, modern Americans owed their comfortable lives to the old-stock frontiersmen. Carrigan hoped that her "little book" would "instill . . . a true appreciation for the pioneers" and "a like appreciation for the manifold comforts and advantages which are ours to enjoy at present."[14] The 1906 retelling of the Burning of Royalton, Vermont, published after a monument was erected in the town, included the captivity narrative of Zadock Steele, and reminded its readers that the citizens of Royalton placed a special value on their collective history. When local citizens remember and celebrate their past, they find "in the glimpses into the life of the valley is seen the progress of a strong, able, people—the kind who make America the power it is in the world today."[15] In other words, tales of captivity would engender admiration for those who suffered, as well as appreciation for modern comforts, and, by connecting the two, would further the understanding that the latter would not have developed without the former.

As articulated by historian Frederick Jackson Turner in his 1893 article "The Significance of the Frontier in American History," and by Theodore Roosevelt in such works as *The Winning of the West,* many Americans believed that their unique place in the world and distinguishing characteristics sprang from national experiences on the frontier.[16] Although immigration was primarily an urban problem, small town boosters believed that they could help solve the immigrant dilemma in part through emphasizing captivity history. Moreover, immigrants would be more likely to assimilate if they moved to those small towns or to the country, and raising the cultural status of small towns (as historical preservation supposedly did) would attract people to them. Proof that active and intentional "Americanization" of foreign groups could be successful was imperative because of the necessity of Americanizing the large groups of "new" immigrants from southern and eastern Europe, immigrants who seemed shockingly unlike the "old" Protestant immigrants from northern and western Europe. Russians and immigrants from the Baltic states swelled to more than a million between 1901 and 1910, up from fewer than half a million only ten years earlier. Similar numbers, although not usually quite so dramatic, exist for Japanese, Irish, Polish, and Mexican immigrants.[17] Fears over the ability of these new groups to assimilate into democratic, capitalist, Protestant America permeated cultural dialogue. Therefore, it is intriguing that the particular captivity stories popular at this time emphasized the "Americanizing" of Indian groups that many assumed were in the process of culturally, and possibly physically, dying out.[18] Martha Bennet Phelps's tale of Frances Slocum's captivity and life ends with several appendices that examine the conversion of Slocum's Indian children to Christianity, her missionary work among other Indians, and her English language skills. Frances

Slocum's children and grandchildren, moreover, all intellectually "soared far above mediocrity."[19]

Perhaps even more troubling to small-town and urban leaders was the fact that immigrant groups increasingly chose to settle in cities rather than the unsettled territory in the West. In 1860, only 13 percent of Americans lived in cities; the arrival of the new century saw that number climb to 40 percent, and the majority of Americans lived urban lives by 1920.[20] Without the frontier experience, how would foreign immigrants, who made up a vast portion of the new urban population, become Americans? And with a new, urban, immigrant foreign population coming to dominate the American cultural landscape, how would the old-stock Anglo-Americans continue to assert their cultural and political dominance? In the national arena, the old-stock Americans became bulwark supporters of Progressive Era reform movements to preserve middle class power and prestige. On the local front, they began erecting monuments that would allow the new immigrants to see "the timeless virtues of [American] ancestors . . . represented symbolically before their eyes" while "testify[ing] to future generations the present residents' dedication to the timeless moral principles they associated with generations past."[21] As Dr. Charles D. Vail stated in his speech at the Mary Jemison memorial ceremony, "America, or the United States, has always stood for progress because we have ideals to live for and courage to strive. Let us hold on to and glorify our ideals, for they are the only vital things of life."[22] In his 1913 undergraduate history textbook, Carl Russell Fish of the University of Wisconsin argued that, although the country was "becoming crowded with Russians, Jew and Gentile, Italians, Poles, Bohemians, Austrians and Greeks," these new immigrants would, when they "reached the soil . . . speedily become a part of the community . . . and lines of nationality . . . [would] disappear."[23] But when they settled in the cities, as was increasingly more common, immigrants lived primarily in separate neighborhoods and actively resisted assimilation. "The energy and self-reliance developed by the conquest of the continent remain as a heritage for the nation in solving its new and more humdrum problems," Fish went on.[24] The expanding inequality between the native-born populace and the slum-dwelling immigrants strained democracy and required an immediate solution to replace the one provided by open land beyond the frontier line.[25]

Encroaching modernization in the early twentieth century was epitomized by immigration, domestic migration to national and regional urban centers, and industrial growth that led to changes in the nature of business and competition. In response, some Americans turned to a nationalist tradition to both preserve and extend their sense of global exceptionalism. Theodore Roosevelt summarized the link between a frontier nation, its citizens' personal characteristics, and its global importance:

> The men who with ax in the forests and pick in the mountains and plow on the prairies pushed to completion the dominion of our people over the American wilderness have given the definite shape to our nation. They have shown the qualities of daring, endurance, and far-sightedness, of eager desire for victory and stubborn refusal to accept defeat, which go to make up the essential manliness of the American character.... We have but little room among our people for the timid, the irresolute, and the idle; and it is no less true that there is scant room in the world at large for the nation with mighty thews that dares not to be great.[26]

Belief in an area of unsettled, free land held great implications for the country and its possibilities, and the loss of that free space seemed downright dangerous for several reasons. Even people in cities sought to regain their contact with nature and "let off steam about being trapped in urban areas."[27]

The Progressive Era saw a clash of optimism for, and fear of, the future that led to a preoccupation with the frontier and the values believed to have developed there.[28] On the one hand, frightening and apparently out-of-control changes befell economic and social structures. Big business appeared to dominate the individual, leaving men feeling decidedly out of control over their economic lives. White, educated, wealthy young women came into public and economic life in the form of the independent "New Woman" and as reformers epitomized by Jane Addams. These women openly used their traditional role as moral guides to justify their attempts to reform the sordid lives of poor immigrants and to fight unfair social condition.[29] At the same time that new immigrants swarmed into American cities, blacks moved out of the South and into northern cities. The combined presence of immigrants and blacks in cities exposed the white women who insisted on working and living in those cities to the moral and physical dangers associated with close contact with unsavory strangers on street corners or streetcars.[30]

But social changes were not the only changes. Economic realities seemed to be changing as well. The economic successes of a few well-publicized individuals such as actor Charlie Chaplin, bicycle mechanics Orville and Wilbur Wright, and self-taught inventor Thomas Edison seemed to prove that the United States did indeed provide opportunities unavailable in the rest of the world. Yet the increasing, or at least increasingly obvious, gulf between rich and poor, and the inability of the vast majority of Americans ever to rise out of abject poverty, threatened that assumption of American opportunity, while at the same time changing cultural assumptions about the sources of poverty. Accordingly, Progressive reformers, and particularly women, who maybe more than others knew at least some of the obstacles to the "self-made" ideal, began to argue that poverty and its associated problems (alcoholism, domestic abuse, crime, disease) sprang from social rather than personal failings. Increasingly violent labor unrest fed fears about the economic divide and the possibility of revolution from below or tyranny from above. The new century appeared unsettled at best, and despite the new efforts of social and political reformers to address the forces that threatened to decay American culture and society, many remained convinced that the primary problem was the disappearance of open land beyond the frontier line. Many people shared Dr. Fish's concern that a new, decidedly un-American mentality would come to overshadow the American virtues created during what Turner called the "first period of American history."[31]

Indian Captivity as Justification for Rural Life

In the face of growing social and economic change, Americans still believed that the United States as a nation, and its people as individuals, occupied an exceptional place in the world. This belief was combined with growing faith in science. Many became convinced that the host of problems facing the country at the turn of the century would be solved by American ingenuity and stick-to-it-iveness, and that in addressing those issues, Americans would bolster their collective assets and correct their failings, thereby increasing their national and individual strength and virtue. The rise of the social sciences in this era is no coincidence. Assuming that they could discover the direct causes of the ailments of modern society, experts in the new fields assumed it only logical that they could then find solutions. But while New York City became the center of both education and field practice in social and economic science, the eulogizers at captivity memorials believed that future national successes lay in marrying the modernization of the cities to the traditions that were inherent in rural life.[32] A rather pretentious letter from H. K. Bush-Brown, art historian and sculptor of the Mary Jemison statue, which was read at the 1910 dedication of the statue at Letchworth Park, New York, made this connection between past virtues and future greatness explicit:

> Everyone is interested in history, for it is the only means of understanding the present, of providing for the future. . . . We can no more separate ourselves from the responsibility of our opportunity than we can change the color of our skin or increase our stature. America, or the United States, has always stood for progress because we have ideals to live for, and the courage to strive. Let us hold on to and glorify our ideals.[33]

If the ideals and the freedoms afforded by the frontier could not be continued, perhaps Americans, both native-born and newly arrived, could discover them in tales of frontier conflict and bravery.[34] "An elite," writes Kevin Mattson—and, I would argue, a local elite who sponsored publications of captivity narratives and memorials to Indian captives—"would create . . . safety valves so that the working masses would not boil over."[35]

Horticulturalist and Dean of the New York College of Agriculture L. H. Bailey also spoke at the Jemison ceremony, emphasizing the value of country life and its link to the memory of Indian captivity:

> The general tendency of the civilization of our time is to dump everything into the cities. . . . The time must come when a real economic and social co-ordination must be found between the city and the country. Our civilization depends on finding it. One means of bringing this about is to record the episodes, the events and the persons who have figured in the history of the open country, before their memories shall have been forgotten.[36]

According to Bailey, then, American life depended not on returning to a frontier society, for that was of course impossible, but rather on valuing the country (i.e., the rural areas) and the city equally, and allowing each equal participation in national development. However, Bailey believed that the city was becoming dominant and the country forgotten. He worked to correct that imbalance.[37] Theodore Roosevelt set up the Country Life Commission in 1908, headed by Bailey and with members including conservationist Gifford Pinchot, and charged it with studying rural life in the modern era. This commission discovered that farmers were failing to change with the arrival of modern conditions. Historian Steven J. Diner writes of the Commission's findings that farm families, "suffer[ed] from land speculation, poorly managed natural resources, inadequate roads, schools and sanitation, labor shortages, and deplorable conditions for farm women."[38] The Commission's report declared that agriculture in the United States was "prosperous commercially" and that "country homes are improving in comfort, attractiveness, and healthfulness." With that general positive outlook, the Commission concluded that "prominent deficiencies" in the country sprang generally from the fact that the farmer "stands practically alone against organized interests" and so "suffers most" in the national "readjustment of modern life." Those deficiencies required government action, not just because they were issues of human rights, but because "in the supply of independent and strong citizenship, the agricultural people constitute the very foundation of our national efficiency."[39] Moreover, President Roosevelt declared to the Congress "the great recent progress made is city life is not a full measure of our civilization; for our civilization rests at bottom on the wholesomeness, the attractiveness, and the completeness, as well as the prosperity, of life in the country." The President went on, "to supply the city with fresh blood, clean bodies, and clear brains that can endure the terrific strain of modern life[,] we need the development of men in the open country, who will be in the future, as in the past, the stay and strength of the nation in time of war, and its guiding and controlling spirit in time of peace."[40] The very security of the nation, then, was at stake.

In response to these findings, Progressive Country Life reformers declared rural public schools, child labor practices, farming techniques, churches, and social structures as backward and regressive. Much of the rural population resisted the interference of urban middle class reformers, arguing that even attempts to increase farm productivity were little more than a blatant attempt, in the words of Gifford Pinchot, to "help the city man . . . [by] inducing the [farmer] to grow cheap food."[41] Farmers and rural populations held to a traditional notion of personal freedom provided by the Jeffersonian yeoman ideal, and resisted the concept that the "new era of global markets" no longer "guaranteed either autonomy or economic security" to landowners.[42]

Rural Americans refused much of the help offered to them by Progressive reformers because they believed that the values of their families, developed during the settlement of their small towns and villages, would provide them with methods for addressing the issues brought on by modernity.[43] An ancestral tale that at once articulated what it meant to be "American" and at the same time suggested that their rural values afforded them a greater ability than urban reformers to tackle modern problems—*and* served to prove their ancestral connection to those people whom they believed originally developed those values—could prove very valuable to a small town's sense of worth.

Indian Captivity as Part of the Historical Pageantry and Monuments Trend

The captivity narrative, and especially the captivity memorial, gave small towns national importance in the face of overwhelming urbanization. In response to rapid and unprecedented urban growth and immigration, a national near-obsession with the historical pageant developed in small towns (and indeed in large cities) across the country. William Chauncy Langdon, prominent historical pageant organizer in New England, explained their importance, saying, "the pageant is a drama in which the place is the hero and the development of the community the plot."[44] In a similar way, the captivity memorial, itself a kind of permanent historical pageant, and the dedication ceremony that went along with it, reminded audiences and visitors that these seemingly unimportant, often remote villages were, in fact, places of great historical action. They assured residents that their family histories held contemporary and future value; in addition, they provided much-needed tourist dollars.

Many captivity memorial ceremonies, in fact, noted the trend of building historical monuments. R. A. Smith, superintendent of the Spirit Lake Massacre Commission (Abbie Gardner-Sharp was captured at the Spirit Lake Massacre), mentioned the "awakened interest in history" in his speech at the dedication of the Spirit Lake memorial in 1895. "This spirit is manifesting itself," he went on, "by the erection of memorials and monuments." The State of Iowa should, "in her sovereign capacity, give recognition to the smaller and less pretentious, though no less deserving band of patriots and heroes." He justified the expense by stating that even God himself memorializes in the form of the rainbow and the Sabbath, so the Commission chose an obelisk because "it points toward heaven and fitly expresses the hopes and aspirations of untold generations yet to come."[45]

Theodore Roosevelt himself, so often a weathervane of national mood, articulated what many wanted to hear about their ancestors when he described the settlers who came to Kentucky and Tennessee in the early national period:

> They were of good blood . . . generations of self-restraint and courage and hard work, and careful training in mind

and in the manly virtues. Their inheritance of sturdy and self-reliant manhood helped them greatly . . . they were strong in body and mind, stout of heart, resolute of will. . . . They realized that the qualities they inherited from their forefathers ought to be further developed by them. . . . They knew that their blood and breeding, though making it probable that they would with proper effort succeed, yet entitled them to no success which they could not fairly earn in open contest with their rivals.[46]

Roosevelt described what he called the "gentry" of early permanent settlers, those who sought not simply the roving life of the frontiersman, going always from one wilderness to the next, but who rather wished to settle permanently and establish homes and communities, and to create permanent social standing. These settlers often "crowded out" earlier frontiersmen who, although a necessary stage, generally moved further west, having accomplished the "roughest of the pioneer work." Linking a modern family or community to an Indian captive, then, proved for many that their ancestors were of this gentry, those "better" settlers, rather than of those transient "lower" frontiersmen, because it provided concrete proof that ancestors of current residents had come to that place and stayed rather than quickly moving on as early frontiersmen did. Because, however, those ancestors came at a time when Indian captivity was still a danger, their frontiersman credentials were satisfied along with their qualifications as local "gentry," thus giving them the best of both types or credentials: they came of the preferable gentry stock but settled the area early enough that they went through the Turnerian "Americanizing" process. Could a more perfect American exist?

Although most captives were of frontiersman stock, they could, if using Roosevelt's logic, be seen as better than the average early frontiersman, since their ancestors were not transient. So, although the captives were settlers during the first wave of frontiersmen, their descendants sought to prove that they were of "higher" settler stock, and thus prove their inheritance in the face of foreign immigration. The settler gentry, according to Roosevelt, deserved its success both because of its bloodline (the proof of which came in the family's presence in the same area for several generations) and by individual hard work and personal virtue, also proved by familial longevity.[47]

Mary Evelyn Wood Lovejoy's 1911 *History of Vermont* reminded readers that a commemoration of the 1780 Raid of Royalton took place on April 1, 1863 with 4,000 people present. It was put together by the Royalton Soldiers' Aid Society "in its efforts to raise money to send to the boys in blue. . . . A fourth of a century after this . . . Royalton's loyal and distinguished sons" determined to erect a monument that was unveiled on May 23, 1906, by Max Bliss, David Wild, and Helen and Gertrude Dewey, all great-great-grandchildren of victims of the massacre.[48] At that 1906 ceremony, the great-grandson of another victim of the massacre read a lengthy poem that ended with the lament

> Ah, Royalton, old Royalton
>   The stately centuries glide by!
> Yet hearts will never cease to turn
>   Back to the dire calamity
> Which tried thee as the gold is tried,
>   Nor in the furnace found thee dross,
> But of true worth and purified—
>   That crucible thy lustrous cross![49]

The suffering, then, of the collective citizenry of Royalton in fact actually created a worthy and "purified" people.

For those Progressive Era Americans who celebrated their captive ancestors, the survival of a captive not only proved the personal strength and virtue of the individual captive, but also reinforced the importance and merit of local families in both the national story and the local one. "Some families," Roosevelt asserted, "were of course continually turning into permanent abodes what were merely temporary halting places of the greater number."[50] Local communities eagerly drew connections between themselves or members of their town and early settler families in order to prove that they belonged to one of Roosevelt's permanent families or communities. While Roosevelt and others celebrated frontiersmen, prominent small town citizens wanted to connect themselves to that settler gentry outlined by Roosevelt, both because it proved their ancestors to be of a "higher sort" and because it proved that modern families, individuals, and towns were "real" (that is, long established) American places rather than the more suspect abodes of recent immigrants. Abbie Gardner-Sharp, for example, brags in her 1910 narrative that her father "was the first white man to establish a home in this section of Iowa," and there she was in 1910 living in that very same house.[51]

Historical Fact Reveals Solutions for Present Problems

In 1947, Roy Harvey Pearce, founder of the University of California at San Diego's department of literature, outlined several stages in the development of the genre of captivity narratives. The first captivity narratives from the late seventeenth and early eighteenth centuries were generally Puritan religious documents, straightforward in style and honest in content. Style may have varied, but their intent, to demonstrate God's goodness and mercy, remained consistent. But by the middle of the eighteenth century, Pearce claimed, captivity narratives began to focus more on the cruelties captives suffered at the hands of their Indian or French captors than on the religious merits gained in the experience. Authors of these narratives, either journalists or sensationalist propagandists, intended to engender hatred for Indian enemies on the part of a population still struggling for control of the American landscape. According to Pearce, the narratives began to focus so exclusively on Indian barbarity that they had become, regardless of basis in actual events, untrustworthy and historically useless. By the 1780s and '90s, authors used their narratives to call directly for the annihilation of Indians.[52] Because of this shift in focus, the captivity narrative had, in Pearce's judgment, "all but completed its decline and fall" by 1800. Readers no longer took these stories seriously, he said, although they devoured them for the same reasons that readers would later consume pulp or dime novels, or frequent slasher films today. Readers assumed, and authors began to state explicitly, that captivity narratives had more in common with sentimental novels and fabricated romance than with true events.[53]

If, by 1800, readers distrusted captivity narratives, they had certainly not ceased to read them, for these narratives remained one of the most popular genres throughout the nineteenth century. By 1900, however, the form had circled back to the more straightforward style of the early captivity narratives. Many scholars have noted that the captivity narrative formula starts with a bloody attack on a settler family, resulting in the gruesome death of several people and the captivity of the story's protagonist.[54] In the Progressive Era, however, most captivity narratives began with an often disproportionately long section describing all known ancestors of the captive, the geographical importance of the area where the captivity took place, or even, as in the case of the Zadock Steele narrative, "Royalton [Vermont] Today."[55] The first chapter of the Phelps Slocum narrative, for example, is entitled "Frances' Ancestors Come to Wyoming Valley," and Abbie Gardner-Sharp does not get around to describing the actual Spirit Lake Massacre and her captivity until chapter 8, a full 69 pages into her narrative. She spent the first 7 chapters giving a full biography of her father, describing every family involved in the massacre, and providing a fairly detailed history of "Ink-Pa-Du-Ta and His Band."

Indian atrocities, then, did not appear in these narratives until well after the historical importance of the event or captured person had been established through connection to a contemporary place or community or family. Therefore, Pearce's assertion that readers did not trust narratives simply does not hold water in the Progressive Era. Historical fact, rather than sensational violence (whether true or not), had become the central feature of the narratives, and authors went to great lengths to prove the authenticity of their stories. The American Scenic and Historic Preservation Society's report on the unveiling of the Mary Jemison memorial included a lengthy discussion of the proper spelling of the captive's Indian name, and a statement from Arthur C. Parker, then archeologist in the New York State Museum, attesting to the historical exactness of the statue. "Your Mary Jemison," he assured the sculptor H. K. Bush-Brown, "is one of the most accurate, if not the most accurate, studies of New York ethnology which I have ever seen."[56] Likewise, Abbie Gardner-Sharp included in her narrative five testimonials confirming the historical accuracy and the current value of her work. Those providing testimonials included two former governors of Iowa, and the Iowa Superintendent of Public Instruction.

Moreover, threatening Indians had disappeared by the turn of the century, with Indians contained on reservations, the Indian wars over, and assimilation now official Federal policy through the actions of the Dawes Allotment Act. Indians simply had ceased to scare white Americans, so the message contained in captivity narratives also changed, with most writers arguing for understanding and Christian charity. As the Slocum saga suggests through its emphasis on events after the reunion of the Slocums to their lost sister and her relatives, the tale of the actual captivity itself had become almost secondary to the tale of kinship between contemporary families and historical captives. Ivah Dunklee's edition of the captivity of Zadock Steele, for example, presented Steele's story as it was written in 1818, but Dunklee adds a first chapter on the state of "Royalton Today," a chapter describing the "unveiling of the monument" to the victims at Royalton, Vermont, on May 23, 1906, including the entire text of a poem recited at the event and the keynote address by the Reverend William Skinner Hazen.[57] The crisis of Indian threat was over, and those who remembered Indian captives now focused on other elements, especially on the value of remembering national historical suffering.

Although they claimed to contain the solutions to modern problems, and sought to connect history to contemporary people, Progressive Era Indian captivity accounts were not modern stories. They were, by their very nature, conservative. At the 1906 ceremony unveiling a monument dedicated to the victims and survivors of the 1780 burning of Royalton (at which Zadock Steele was captured), Reverend William Skinner Hazen, former chaplain to the Vermont Senate, then age 70, stated:

> In this time of commercialism and modern thought, when men are 'hurrying to and fro' . . . there is a great danger of drifting away from the ideals of fathers, of lowering the standard of manhood and the plane of action of men in their dealings with one another and management of the affairs of State. . . . To check this downward tendency, this apparent drift away from the lofty principles and high ideals of the fathers, it is well to pause and recall the foundations laid by the fathers, the principles that actuated them, the character they developed and the work they accomplished, their vital service to freedom and the State, when they fought valiantly and with singleness of aim for the truth and would not compromise or equivocate or in the slightest degree tone down their righteous indignation at evil. . . . The most worthy tribute we can pay those whose virtues

and labors we commemorate this day is by dedicating ourselves anew to the principles for which they stood.[58]

The Reverend Hazen articulated the same fears that Roosevelt, Bailey, and Bush-Brown had voiced: that the nation would decay as its citizens settled into decadent, corrupt city life, where food came in packages and free time was spent in mindless entertainment in movie houses or amusement parks. Indian captivity stories, in other words, were emerging as a cornerstone of a new, anti-modern narrative of American history in which progress required looking back as much as it required looking forward.[59]

The Frontier Voice in the Modern Era

Authors of many early narratives hoped that the reader would learn a new devotion to Christ. Twentieth century reprints of these narratives, ones newly written during the Progressive Era, as well as memorials dedicated to captive individuals, were also intended to inspire and instruct the public, this time to balance the convenience of modern life with a dedication to traditional values and standards of behavior.[60] Recent scholars of captivity narratives, especially Rebecca Blevins Faery, have focused on searching for the "subtext" of the narratives, some forgotten or ignored thing that will finally explain them. Faery calls this the "illicit or disqualified knowledges" present in the texts.[61] Like Gary Ebersole, I believe that authors were generally accurate in stating why they were writing or what they concluded from their experience. Captivity narrative authors did not simply repeat cultural formulas; they wished to understand their experiences and spent many hours, days, or in the case of Abbie Gardner-Sharp, many years agonizing over the meanings of their experiences. Likewise, those in the Progressive Era who were drawn to celebrate and remember Indian captives spent many years convincing themselves and others of the value of their project and the messages contained in tales of captivity. The first concrete evidence that William Pryor Letchworth had discovered the story of the captive Mary Jemison and found it interesting came in 1871, when he moved her remains from near Buffalo, New York, to his land on the Genesee River, yet it was not until 1911 that Letchworth managed to erect a monument to Jemison on the same spot. Likewise, the Slocum families in Indiana and Pennsylvania joined forces in 1890 and worked together for 10 years before erecting a monument to the captive in May of 1900.[62]

Turn-of-the-century interpreters of these stories, including editors, authors, publishers, and eulogizers, created meaning by framing the tales as moral directives. As the storytellers struggled to defend the importance of small towns in the new century, in which there was an increasing gulf between cities and farms, the focus of the captivity narratives took an explicitly nationalistic rather than religious direction. "First period" Americans, those who lived with and within a frontier, spoke to modern Americans through the memory of Indian captivity, reminding modern folk what it meant to be American, reiterating those qualities without which the country would surely decay and destroy itself.[63] Progressive Era Americans used tales of Indian captivity to confirm the national significance of their small-town and rural values, and to emphasize their own importance on the national stage. As if to demonstrate that the ceremony dedicating the Frances Slocum memorial in Peru, Indiana, drew national attention, author Martha Bennett Phelps emphasized the great geographical variety of speakers: "Mrs. Lurena King Miller, of Washington D. C., read an original poem . . . Col. Richard DeHart, of Lafayette, Ind., made an excellent address . . . the benediction was pronounced by Rev. William F. Slocum, A. M., B. D., of Montour Falls, N. Y. . . . Major McFadden, of Logansport, Ind., . . . gave his recollections of her." In addition, Phelps mentioned the presence of local Slocum family members and prominent citizens such as George

Slocum Bennett of Wilkes-Barre, Pennsylvania, Charles F. Slocum of Defiance, Ohio, and Arthur Gaylord Slocum, President of Kalamazoo College, among several others.[64]

Captivity narratives, monuments, and ceremonies allowed families like the Slocums to emphasize the place of their personal histories in the national story, while at the same time proving that small towns would have a role in saving the United States. "Every new memorial in the open country," Liberty Hyde Bailey stated at the Jemison memorial ceremony, "is one additional reason for people to live in the open country."[65] The turn-of-the-century captivity narrative, then, had a fundamentally conservative message, in that it looked back to some imagined past when people were morally better, but it also had a decidedly progressive intention to understand, to address, and ultimately to solve modern problems. Small-town boosters who remembered Indian captivity, then, were participating directly in the Progressive reform mentality of the time, but they did so by looking back in order to find solutions for the future. At the Jemison ceremony Bailey went on to explain that making the countryside and small town more appealing by beautifying them, in part through memorials, would help solve the problems of over-urbanization and rural population decline. "I want to see the open country so attractive," he said, "that an energetic and forward-looking young man may express himself as completely on a farm as in [any other profession].... [Drawing young people back to the country] is a contribution to our general welfare."[66] Moreover, the early twentieth century captivity narrative reflected the Progressive faith in government legislation and committee action to address those problems.

The captivity of the child Frances Slocum in 1778 was, perhaps, the best thing that could have happened either to Wyoming Valley, Pennsylvania, from which she was taken, or to Wabash County, Indiana, where she resided when discovered by Colonel Ewing. Slocum remains the most notable figure in the stories these two places tell of themselves. Today, Indiana boasts the

Maconaquah School Corporation (home of the Braves), the Frances Slocum Elementary School, the Frances Slocum State Forest, Maconaquah Park, the Frances Slocum neighborhood in Fort Wayne, the Frances Slocum Cemetery, and the Frances Slocum Bank, while Pennsylvania holds the Frances Slocum State Park, created in 1968. Indeed, her presence remains strong throughout northern Indiana and northeastern Pennsylvania, and the white world in these two areas continues to claim her as one of them in their stories, despite the fact that she hid from white Americans and claimed an exclusively Indian identity for almost all of her life. Small-town Americans of the early twentieth century found, in the tales of captive ancestors, moral guides and hope for the future of their country. These Americans celebrated their local Indian captives with no subtlety, and memorialized them on the landscapes and in the history books of their towns. In a real sense, they were attempting to use Indian captivity accounts to shape the national narrative as it would be written in the post-frontier period.

CHAPTER 2

The Indian and the Activist

William Pryor Letchworth

The story of the creation of Letchworth State Park, which lies on the Genesee River in upstate New York, unites the history of two wholly disconnected persons: Quaker Progressive William Pryor Letchworth and the Seneca Indian Dehgewanus. The life of William Letchworth represents the dramatic alteration that the United States underwent in the period we now call the Progressive Era.

William Pryor Letchworth, who by his mid-twenties had become wealthy in the malleable iron business, combined what appears to have been a genuinely good heart with Quaker-bred instincts of service to become a quintessential Progressive activist. In addition to his work to improve the lot of orphans, epileptics, criminals, and the insane, he chose to protect a section of the Genesee River. The famous Seneca captive Mary Jemison, or Dehgewanus, became a symbol of Letchworth's love for, and protection of, the land he bought with his own money, restored through his own authority, and finally trusted to the State of New York. The name Mary

Jemison remains connected to the place, not because of anything she did, or even because she spent much of her life there (although she did), but simply because William Letchworth chose that it should be.

William Letchworth left little record of why he was so drawn to Mary Jemison's story, stating cryptically in his edited introduction to a new edition of Jemison's narrative, "The fact that this biography is out of print . . . is deemed sufficient apology for presenting this edition to the public," and "it is my intention and desire that this bronze statue of Mary Jemison shall always remain where it now is placed."[1] But we can surmise from his actions that he found in Mary Jemison a lost soul who took comfort in the area he would name Glen Iris, and that he intended to use the historical importance of her tie to the place to help him legally protect it from developers. In this case, the needs of the Erie Canal would have destroyed the place had he not taken steps to legally protect it, in part by linking it to Mary Jemison's history and the monument celebrating her life. Letchworth, then, tied his progressive land restoration and conservation to frontier history in a way that allowed him to dictate the terms under which the state of New York inherited Glen Iris, thus guaranteeing that both the land and the memory of Jemison be protected under his stipulations. Whatever personal interest he might have taken in Mary Jemison, his actions served to protect her memory in connection to a particular place, and to keep Jemison and Glen Iris under the control of his estate's directives even after it passed to state ownership.

While we have little record of Letchworth's personal motivations, his concrete accomplishment reflect a conscious linking of the past—in the form of a frontier captive and in the form of undeveloped land—with the present needs of those escaping the oppressive city. Like other Progressive Americans, particularly the old-stock gentry that felt their power diminishing, Letchworth used a connection to local history to link himself and the place that he loved to the larger national scene.

Letchworth's concern about the welfare of those who were often forgotten was evidenced by his study of new theories of the treatment of epileptics, the insane, and criminals in Europe In 1900 he published *Care and Treatment of Epileptics*.[2] In addition, he financed and built several homes for delinquent children and the insane, and he served as president of the New York State Board of Charities. The basic premise of almost all of his work was that, first, you took the suffering person to the country. Remove the unfortunates from the city and put them to some kind of productive work, and you will elevate their condition and alleviate their suffering. The happy side effect was that Letchworth's estate would be protected from purchase or use by developers.

To this end, Letchworth attempted first to protect Glen Iris through the creation of a charitable boys' home on the property. When that failed and Glen Iris came under threat from developers, he turned to Mary Jemison—his success in that regard apparently proving that the lives of past individuals had more power and longevity than the needs of present-day individuals. Letchworth's interest in Mary Jemison, then, came in part from the fact that he linked land conservation with historical preservation: connecting Glen Iris to a well-known Indian captive justified the protection of the estate. If charitable works could not save his beloved home, perhaps he could accomplish the same thing by linking the area to the national frontier history. Letchworth, as historian Jared Farmer put it, "understood a geographic principle: great landmarks are storied landmarks."[3] Mary Jemison was the "story" of the place that Letchworth loved and sought to protect, and he used her story quite consciously to that end. The landscape of the middle falls of the Genesee River, the history of the captive Mary Jemison, and the legend of William Letchworth as the great protector of both intertwined to become Letchworth

State Park, a place that reverberates with the dual story of Letchworth's benevolent actions and Mary Jemison's poignant life in the place. As Charles M. Dow, the chairman of the Letchworth Park Committee of the American Scenic and Historic Preservation Society, put it so neatly at the unveiling of the Jemison statue in 1910, "to understand the statue one must understand the park."[4]

Letchworth Discovers the Genesee

Nothing in William Letchworth's early life suggested that he would become a Progressive activist: his early life was spent as a successful businessman, and his early activism followed a decidedly self-sufficient track. Both his industry and his charity he accomplished independently, showing little intention to join with others in his work, and even less inclination to trust government to help him with any of it.

When he was just 25 years old, Letchworth wrote to his younger sister that his attention to the malleable iron business, while successful, had left him with few social connections or outside interests, and had strained his health. Another sister had been warning him for at least two years that too much work would make him "an old man before" he had been "a young one half long enough." Over the next near-decade, Letchworth continued to dedicate his energies to his company, Pratt & Letchworth, taking winter trips to Florida in an attempt to sustain himself for the ten months at his office in Buffalo, New York. Finally, at the age of 33, Letchworth took a year-long tour of Europe. Upon his return in 1857 the direction of his life changed dramatically.[5]

Whatever happened in Europe, Letchworth returned convinced that a combination of city life and overwork were killing him. He began spending as much time as possible away from Buffalo, traveling in the wilds of upstate New York. In early 1858 he stopped on the Portage Bridge overlooking the Upper and Middle Falls of the Genesee River and fell in love. As he strolled about the area, he noted a dying sawmill that had, although "in a feeble way," significantly damaged the "ancient forests," and only a little timber that "would pay" remained after it closed.[6] Perhaps this was the same sawmill from which Dehgewanus supposedly carried wood for her house.[7] Horrified by the destruction of the sublime for the sake of profit, and convinced that man's "vandalism" was thoroughly reversible, Letchworth purchased the area in early 1859 with the intention of preserving and restoring it. He named it Glen Iris after the ubiquitous rainbows caused by the falls.

William Letchworth spent the rest of his life plotting ways to protect the Genesee River falls and Glen Iris from developers. He had "sought a place close to Nature where he could withdraw from the cares and distractions of business," and he found inspiration there that changed the direction of his life. At the Mary Jemison memorial celebration in 1910, Charles M. Dow, chairman of the Letchworth Park Committee of the American Scenic and Historic Preservation Society, explained William Letchworth's reaction to the falls:

> Sitting under the rainbow [by the falls] . . . he found the quiet and repose in which he developed those broad ideas of philanthropy which led him eventually to withdraw from business altogether and to devote his life to that noble work for the unfortunate which is his greatest monument.[8]

Because of his questionable health, Letchworth stayed in Buffalo during the Civil War and watched as many friends left for military service. But Glen Iris seemed to do for Letchworth what doctors, work, and vacations had been unable to do, and he regained his health. He also changed his life and work fairly dramatically. He left Pratt & Letchworth and dedicated himself to philanthropic works, reorganizing state juvenile reformatories, almshouses, orphanages, and insane asylums, improving care and treatment for the insane and epileptics.

Dehgewanus Discovers the Genesee

In the process of restoring and preserving Glen Iris, Letchworth discovered Dehgewanus, the "white woman of the Genesee."

Born in the crossing from Ireland to Philadelphia in 1743, Mary Jemison went with her family to the western frontier of the English colonies. Jemison was captured in the French and Indian War in 1758 at the age of fifteen by French and Shawnee forces. These captors sold her to a group of Seneca Indians who adopted her and named her Dehgewanus, "Two Falling Voices," a name that suggested the double identity she would carry for the rest of her life. Dehgewanus married a man named Shenijee a year later, gave birth to a girl who lived just two days, and then to a boy whom she named Thomas after her father. In 1762, with Thomas just a few months old, the couple traveled from their home south of Pittsburgh, Pennsylvania, to Beardstown in modern Leicester, New York. Shenijee died on the journey, leaving the young white widow alone in a strange land. She sought the protection and care of Shenijee's relatives and soon remarried, settling near modern Cuylerville, New York. Seventeen years later, the family fled the violence of the Revolution and settled again near present Castile, New York. In 1797, at the Treaty of Big Tree, the Seneca sold the land west of the Genesee to the U.S. government in exchange for ten reservations, one of which, the Gardeau Reservation, contained Dehgewanus's two-square mile plot near the Genesee River.[9] The Senecas left the Gardeau Reservation in 1823, but Dehgewanus stayed until 1831. She sold her plot and moved to the Buffalo Creek Reservation just south of Buffalo, New York, to join the rest of the tribe. She died there just two years later, having spent more than thirty years in the area that would become Glen Iris. She was buried on the Buffalo Creek Reservation. Like William Letchworth, though, it seems she did not belong on the banks of Lake Erie; he would rescue her from the growing city just as he had rescued himself. In 1874, Letchworth saved her bones from destruction as the city of Buffalo expanded, and had her reburied on a bluff overlooking the Middle Falls of the Genesee, only a few miles from her old home on the Gardeau Reservation.[10]

Whose Glen Is This, Anyway?

Of the addresses given during the memorial ceremony at Glen Iris that unveiled a statue of Mary Jemison on September 19, 1910, three spotlighted the connection between William Letchworth, Glen Iris, and the American Scenic and Historic Preservation Society (ASHPS). Two of the speeches (and one of those incredibly brief) focused on Mary Jemison in particular, while the third, by Arthur C. Parker, discussed Seneca society in general. The audience at the event, and readers of later versions of the Jemison story that included transcripts from the ceremony, might have thought it odd that a ceremony commemorating one person (Mary Jemison) spent so much time honoring someone else (William Letchworth). Clearly, however, the organizers of the ceremony (William Letchworth; sculptor H. K. Bush-Brown; chairman of the Letchworth Park Committee of the ASHPS Charles M. Dow; Arthur C. Parker; and secretary of the ASHPS Edward Hagaman Hall) found an important connection between the Indian captive and the activist.

As Henry Kirke Bush-Brown put it, the Jemison monument provided a chance "to show that everyone, no matter how lowly, [could] lead a noble life, a life full of ideals and happiness."[11] Although Bush-Brown meant Dehgewanus, he might well have been discussing Letchworth. One of eight children of Quaker parents, Letchworth had made the conscious choice to move from businessman to philanthropist; in Dehgewanus's case, she had made the conscious choice to stay with her Seneca captors, even given that she missed her white family so terribly that she named all her Indian children after them.

If we compare the photograph of the young businessman William Letchworth and the statue of the young widow Dehgewanus, we see a similar sadness; both convey a sense of loneliness and isolation, a longing that seemed to find some fulfillment in the Genesee River Valley. Perhaps because of his Quaker roots, his early ill health, or a lingering isolation that drove him to good works rather than family (he never married), or because of his sense that Jemison's history would help him protect his beloved glen, Letchworth linked several Progressive ideas together. He associated historical and wilderness preservation, land restoration, the city park movement, and a contradictory understanding of the place of Indians in the modern United States with the Progressive faith in the ability of organizations and the power of government to understand, address, and solve modern problems.

In true Transcendentalist form, Letchworth, who was quite literally working himself to death, appears actually to have saved his own life through the purchase and restoration of Glen Iris. Although he turned the estate over to New York in January, 1907 (with the provision that he could continue living there and make such improvements as he saw fit), the bequest received public attention not at its own ceremony but at the Mary Jemison statue dedication in 1910. Thus, Letchworth connected his attachment to the land with the memory of the Indian captive Mary Jemison, and, by doing so, he claimed what he acknowledged to be traditional Seneca land for white America. Colonists claimed land by way of military, economic, and "geographic" power (wielded often by renaming places). Letchworth added historical power to that control by transforming Indian history into white history while still celebrating the Indians.[12]

From Individual Action to State Protection

In 1859, when William Letchworth began his crusade to protect and preserve Glen Iris, the federal government was not the customary place to seek wilderness protection, especially for useable land. The government of the nineteenth century was involved in a "virtual giveaway of public land to the railroads" and others.[13] When the federal government did involve itself in land management in the years after the Civil War, it was in the form of land grants to private corporations under the Pacific Railway Acts, or in the shape of homesteads. Many people in the antebellum age, like Henry David Thoreau, were, in the words of historian Douglas Brinkley, *contemplating* nature preservation, but it was not until the 1870s at the earliest that private hunting clubs began actually creating reserves, and not until the Forest Reserve Act of 1891 that the government became involved in wilderness protection.[14]

Presumably ascribing to his society's standard beliefs, Letchworth approached no organization whatsoever. He did not turn to federal or local government. He did not set up a society. But whether or not he had actually read Ralph Waldo Emerson's *Nature*, Letchworth proved himself to be in love with the idea of wilderness as both the source of his own spiritual renewal and of the "country's cultural greatness."[15] Letchworth, though, like Emerson, worried that Americans' "relation with nature" hinged entirely on their "power over it," either through industry or in science.[16] Horrified as he was over the destruction of the falls by a lumber company, Letchworth set about preserving the wilderness he loved through his own means, expending his own energy and financial resources.

Although his charitable work with the ill (especially epileptics), the insane, and the needy (especially orphans) absorbed the bulk of his time, Letchworth's most lasting legacy was his work in natural and historic preservation, particularly the gift of Glen Iris and the Mary Jemison grave and monument (and several other Indian artifacts) to the state. This gift came about because, by 1906, Letchworth believed that he needed help in protecting the glen, and he apparently came to believe that authorities could be trusted to continue protecting the valley he had come to love. It was a sharp change from his attitude in 1858, when he had described the government's relationship with the wilderness as "vandalism," and as grasping for anything that would make a profit.[17] By 1907, Letchworth had changed his opinion almost completely, and in that year he gave Glen Iris to the state of New York, although he "remain[ed] as much its master as ever" until he died on December 8, 1910.[18] Between 1858 and 1907, Letchworth tried several different ways of protecting Glen Iris, but the method that finally proved successful involved bringing the history of Mary Jemison to the middle falls of the Genesee River and making the bequeath dependent upon state protection of both the land and the history (including the monuments).

Letchworth began exploring possible ways to expand the protection of his estate in 1879, when he formed the Wyoming Benevolent Institute. This institute was to be a home "for the support and education of indigent young persons," and Letchworth intended it to be always connected with Glen Iris—thus, he hoped, protecting the area from expansion and industry. The plan never progressed beyond incorporation of the institute, however. Letchworth's resources had become increasingly strained from his charitable works and from buying as much of the land surrounding Glen Iris as he could. Worried that his estate would be destroyed by the unregulated actions of others, he began in 1900 to attempt to prevent the damming of the upper falls of the Genesee River. But by 1902, "these kindly attempts to make some beginning of the benevolent uses of Glen Iris . . . were soon brought to an end." Letchworth was horrified to find that men in the twentieth century loved development more than they loved "cascades and cataracts," which developers saw "as exhibitions of an idly wasted force."[19]

Letchworth was responding to what he saw as an ongoing threat against his beloved river, and he was right to be concerned. Throughout the 1880s and 90s, several companies attempted to dam the Genesee River. When Letchworth first bought Glen Iris, the threat was from logging, but in the last decades of the nineteenth century the threat came from "the menace which electric science had inspired."[20] In April of 1898, the Genesee River Company formed with the intent of building a power and storage dam for the Erie Canal at Portage, the very place where William Letchworth had first stood and looked over the valley. The Genesee River Company appears to have lied its way into the good graces of public opinion by presenting its business as almost wholly benevolent.[21] The company's charter stated that its overt goals consisted "of improving the sanitary condition of the Genesee Valley, of checking floods . . . of supplying necessary water to enlarge Erie Canal, and of furnishing pure and wholesome water for municipal purposes." The happy side effect for the Genesee River Company came in its exclusive "right to utilize all the water power *incidentally created*" (Larned's italics) by the dam.[22]

In the face of the threat from the Genesee River Company, Letchworth abandoned the plan for the Wyoming Benevolent Institute and decided to give the estate directly to the state of New York, in part because he was running out of money. In 1906, he wrote to the trustees of the Institute that "the original purposes of [it was] now utterly impracticable. Not only has the capital that I intended for this work become so lessened as to greatly reduce my income, but the expenses of carrying on the work here are greatly increased."[23] In leaving the estate to the government, Letchworth would find the solution to his problem. Needy youth had failed to protect Glen Iris, as demonstrated by the fact that Letchworth first set up the Wyoming Benevolent Institute in 1879 and the Genesee River Company got its first legal right to build its dam ten years later in 1889. Letchworth turned, then, to the most famous person connected to the area, Mary Jemison, and ensured that his estate was legally connected her history. Six years later, in 1906, he gave the estate and its history to the state, leaving a visible testimony to his own benevolence and a reminder of the importance of the area's history. He created his legacy by consciously choosing the Indian captive as the mechanism by which he accomplished it all.

Historical Places and Historical People

William Letchworth did not make the leap from private action to government ownership alone; rather, he enlisted the help of the American Scenic and Historic Preservation Society. Prior to his bequeath to the state, Letchworth had joined the American Scenic and Historic Preservation Society. It was an exploratory step to see if any organization could better serve the needs of his estate than he could. The ASHPS proved more than capable. Andrew Haswell Green, a New York lawyer and city reformer, incorporated the ASHPS in 1895 under the name Trustees of Scenic and Historic Places and Objects; members included John Pierpont Morgan and John D. Rockefeller. The incorporation of this society followed the general trend of historic and land protection and restoration that took place in the late nineteenth and early twentieth centuries. Green explained that "the memories of [historical dramas] are fast fading . . . to preserve them is a sacred duty, akin to that of teaching. . . . Where there are no such existing memorials, we believe in fostering patriotic sentiment by the erection of monuments."[24] The ASHPS created a "marriage of 'historic' and 'scenic,'" presenting the two to the public as if they were inseparable. In the Progressive outlook, "historical landscapes" held cultural significance because they combined those things that many men like Letchworth and Theodore Roosevelt believed made the country unique: uncontaminated land and historically important human action.

Tales of Indian captivity fit perfectly into that definition, as they included the meeting of both "first" (native) Americans, Euro-Americans, and the American wilderness. Author James Everett Seaver described Letchworth's reasons for removing Dehgewanus's remains to Glen Iris:

> The spot selected for the final resting place . . . is a high eminence on the left bank of the Genesee River, overlooking the Upper and Middle Falls. The point is one commanding the finest views of the picturesque scenery of Portage—including both the Upper and Middle Falls and the railroad bridge. Upon this eminence and quite near to her present grave is the ancient Seneca Council-house, removed a year or two since . . . within which it is believed Mary Jemison rested for the first time after her long and fatiguing journey . . . from Ohio.[25]

Seaver connected industry (in mentioning that from her grave could be seen the railroad bridge), sublime landscape (in the views of two falls), and human history (in the form of the council house and Jemison's presumed sheltering there) in one description of the scene from the new grave. Indian history, Euro-America technological ability, and natural beauty, then, all combine in a single spot. This fact might have gone unnoticed were it not for the Indian captive and Letchworth's conscientious remembering of her.

According to an address at the 1911 annual meeting of the Livingston County Historical Society, the main reason tourists visited the park and the Portage Falls was to see the statue and the Jemison log cabin, which Letchworth had also moved to the site. Another address at this meeting stated that "to Letchworth Park . . . with just pride we may point as presenting one of the most wonderful of nature's scenes, as well as one of great historical interest."[26] Arthur C. Parker's address at the monument unveiling in 1910 focused on the role of women in Seneca society, but he ended with a tribute to the falls and a connection between the way Indians saw the falls prior to white arrival, what they may have meant to Dehgewanus, and the way the audience in 1906 saw them:

> Amidst . . . her life, her sorrows and her smiles, she gazed forth into the beautiful valley. A legend of old tells that the Sun God in passing over this spot always paused to view these wondrous falls, to watch the play of the rainbow and to inspect the mighty seam in the rock. Who knows but that, as the ancient story tells, the Sun Spirit lingers again with us in this rare spot to look upon this fitting tribute of an appreciative heart to a noble woman, Mary Jemison, the White Captive of the Genesee![27]

In this speech, Parker, part Iroquois himself, equated Mary Jemison overlooking the falls with an Indian god, although he does not openly state that the spirit was Seneca, or more broadly connected to the extended Iroquois nation. He spoke of some Indian god, vague though it was, and used that god to claim Seneca approval for the statue (the "fitting tribute"), Letchworth (the "appreciative heart"), and the land itself. That the "Sun Spirit lingers again" in this instance demonstrates that the Indian presence, now "vanished" in daily life, had returned to bestow its blessing upon this white ceremony.

The very gods, then, approved of Letchworth's purchase of the land that had in former times belonged to the Iroquois, as well as his efforts to protect and restore it, and his use of the Iroquois captive to do so. Thus, by imagining what the Sun God thought of the whole proceeding, Parker assuaged any white guilt connected to the removal of the Indians and the acquisition of their land and story into this piece of the American national myth.[28] That message was made all the more poignant by the fact that it was delivered by Parker, speaking apparently from both the white and the Iroquois perspectives, and thus presumably a legitimate voice from each side. In other words, the white Progressive Americans at the dedication, as well as the Indians still living and present at the dedication, saw that the combination of Glen Iris, William Letchworth, and Mary Jemison came together to create a place of national importance that required active conservation—and the Indian gods themselves saw that very significance as well.

The American Scenic and Historic Preservation Society

Early conservationists assumed that efforts to protect and restore land of historic and scenic significance were "civic achievements in themselves." The civic worth of those places came not only from their historical connections and natural beauty, but also from the fact that powerful people deemed them important. Cities, counties, states, and individuals across the country began, in the 1890s, to seek historic preservation opportunities. The ASHPS declared preservation in New York State a "very holistic idea" that consisted of "the combination of natural and cultural resources" that we now call the "cultural landscape."[29]

William Letchworth joined the ASHPS to investigate the ability of an official organization to preserve both the historical and the scenic import of Glen Iris. He was clearly worried that a single individual, even one as willing as himself to expend the necessary money and energy, would fail against the next threat by another Genesee River Company. At the 1910 dedication of the Jemison statue, George Frederick Kunz, then president of the ASHPS, argued that the purpose of the Society centered as much around educating "the public, the corporations and the legislators" to the value of land and historical preservation and restoration as it did in actually carrying out such activity. "Scenic and historic preservation" encompassed many things, according to Kunz, including "eventually obtaining for every little community a school garden, a school playground, and a school park . . . [and] the preservation of our cemeteries . . . in preventing them from degenerating into hog runs and going to wreck and ruin." In addition to such little local projects, the ASHPS successfully defended and protected the Palisades, Niagara Falls, Watkins Glen, and Stony Point Park, and, of course, Letchworth State Park.[30]

Whatever governmental aid might have been forthcoming later, William Letchworth bought, restored, and protected Glen Iris in a period when federal assistance for the cause was neither sought nor offered. Letchworth protected his valley by his own efforts and with his own resources, having spent at least $500,000 on the land by 1907.[31] And when general opinion and political will caught up with his own, Letchworth handed the land, and the responsibility for it, to the state of New York, under the supervision of the ASHPS. At the unveiling of the Mary Jemison memorial in 1910, Charles M. Dow, the chairman of the Letchworth Park Committee, read a letter from Letchworth (who attended the event and had been scheduled to speak but found himself too unwell), in which he expressed his "intention and desire" that the statue and Indian relics should pass to the state along with the land, to be protected and preserved in the same way. Hence, Letchworth assured that both the scenic and the historic value of the Glen would remain intact, intertwined and protected by the state. His will bound together the protection of both, and required that New York maintain and care for the two as one. If the state failed in either, ownership of the glen and its historical relics would transfer to the ASHPS. Letchworth, like the ASHPS, valued scenic and historical space equally and used the combination to protect each.

Landscape Architecture and Scenic Parks

The estate that Letchworth gave to New York was hardly a Muir-esque wilderness, for while he had first been entranced by the wild ruggedness of Glen Iris, his protection and restoration of the area did not have room for an untouched, unmanaged wilderness. He hired landscape architect William Webster to design the estate. A former student of Frederick Law Olmsted, Webster agreed with Letchworth on most of the plans for the restoration of the estate, although Letchworth did have to expressly forbid Webster from destroying the old buildings that Webster found unsightly. Letchworth found in those abandoned buildings part of the charm and history of Glen Iris, and Letchworth, who unlike Webster thought beyond the landscape alone, believed that the sublimity of the land and the magnitude of the area's human history combined to create its ultimate value. This was another way that Letchworth connected history to wilderness. Proof of human occupation, he believed, gave value to beautiful space.

Letchworth and Webster agreed, though, that the estate, about 200 acres in total, should "adhere to the natural style." To that end, "no leveling [was] attempted," except for the installation of a driveway; all other additions were "all executed in the rustic style."[32] While both Letchworth and Webster agreed that the estate required as many "natural" elements as possible, the fact remains that they both envisioned a park designed and managed by a landscape architect, not a forester. In this respect, William Letchworth's cultural preservation of Glen Iris coincides with yet another Progressive Era trend: the park movement.

In 1897, John Olmstead, the nephew, protégé and adopted son of Frederick Law Olmstead, and a respected landscape architect in his own right, told the first meeting of the American Park and Outdoor Art Association (APOAA) that the "true purpose of a large public park is to provide for the dwellers in cities convenient opportunity to enjoy the beautiful natural scenery and to obtain occasional relief from the nervous strain due to the excessive artificiality of city life."[33] Olmstead insisted that small city parks would not accomplish this goal; rather, the parks should be "so remote that the roar of street traffic is less noticeable than the rustle of foliage stirred by the breeze or than the songs of birds or sounds of insects."[34]

But Olmstead also explained that even a natural or wild public park must be "properly fitted for and used as a public park." Therefore, although the landscape architect of a large public park must be concerned first with the wild appearance of the place, alterations were not only necessary but also often required in order to make its natural qualities welcoming and comfortable.[35] Olmstead focused on large parks in urban centers as part of the City Beautiful movement, such as New York's Central Park, but Letchworth's Glen Iris combined an interest in wilderness preservation, historic preservation, and the park movement in one property. Like another landscape architect, Jens Jensen, Webster and Letchworth emphasized the value of large parks as sites of both historical memory and cultural renewal. According to Jensen, large parks provided "wildlife habitat and often integrated other forms of art—sculpture, drama, song, and poetry—with nature and conservation themes."[36]

In the case of Letchworth State Park, the historical memory that Letchworth wished to associate with the park was not just that of brave pioneers conquering the wilderness, but a more complex one in which two people, one white and one Indian, came together in a place of scenic beauty and, by their connection to each other, created a place of historical importance. A space may be beautiful, and some will declare that to be reason enough to save it. The combination, however, of historical importance *and* scenic value, makes a space into a particular *place*—a place of national cultural meaning and, therefore, a place that demands protection. In the preface to the 1898 version of Mary Jemison's narrative, Letchworth wrote that the "strange events in her life," including her birth at sea while coming to America, being "carried a lonely captive into the depths of the American forest," and her alliance "to the Indian race," made her life "a history so extraordinary."[37] Jemison's time in the forest, her time with Indians, and her coming to America all made her significant.

Speaking to the Livingston County Historical Society about a year after the Jemison memorial ceremony, J. D. Lewis, board member of the historical society, while standing on the banks of the Genesee, referred to the river as the "noted spring of Mary Jemison." Lewis praised Letchworth for preserving for the rest of us "those beautiful trees on his park that he has spared from the woodman's ax," and the "beautiful Indian relics" in the museum on the land that "must have cost much time and money," including Mary Jemison's hand-built cabin. Lewis, then, in speaking to a local historical society, praised Letchworth for the joint protection of Indian relics, Jemison's memory, and the landscape itself. For Lewis, as for Letchworth, the three things intertwined into one wonderfully significant place.[38]

Likewise, in reporting on the unveiling of the Jemison statue, the Albany *Knickerbocker-Press* told a brief history of Jemison's captivity, the main unveiling ceremony, and the Indian closing ceremony witnessed by "only a dozen people" which used Iroquois funeral traditions "now being known only to the Canadian Iroquois." The short article goes on, without a single word to transition from the Jemison ceremony, to describe Letchworth's preservation of the park and its "great natural beauty." The article called the forest as Letchworth found it in 1858 "a crude scar," and praised Letchworth's work "in beautifying it" by protecting it from "the ravages of commercial interests" and by adding the statue of the captive as "his latest effort to beautify and add interest to it." The article implies that Letchworth's acts to conserve and protect both the land and the history will carry the meaning of the place to subsequent generations, as "Mary Jemison in bronze gazes forth into the future which none of us may know." The Indian history, Mary Jemison's particular story, the beauty of the park, and Letchworth's benevolence are united by this article into one supremely satisfying vision of a place made central to the American story by the layers of people attached to it.[39]

As if he were describing Letchworth's own life and his retreat from business in Buffalo, Olmstead declared that "there are many workers in a city who suffer more or less from nervous strain, though often they are not fully aware of it." Those who worked for public welfare often testified that the public was "not fully aware" of their urban troubles; they needed men like Roosevelt, Olmstead, and Letchworth to fix their lives, whether or not they wanted them fixed. Olmstead believed that landscape design could in fact save democracy by giving Theodore Roosevelt's hated urban "polyglot boardinghouse" a "common ground." Large naturalistic parks, Olmstead believed, would help "civilize America . . . [and] make democracy work" by "providing outdoor spaces where people of all classes could come together."[40]

Thus, "the quiet and seclusion obtainable in the middle of a large park is necessary in affording opportunities for occasional relief from the nervous strain of our artificial city life," just as Letchworth found his own relief at Glen Iris. The functioning of American democracy demanded such relief, especially now that the relief afforded by the frontier was gone. The value of open space, though, could be expanded if that relief from strain was mixed with a message of what it meant to be American. Mary Jemison's statue and the Indian artifacts that Letchworth gathered together in his park helped build a scaffolding of historical and cultural meaning in the place. The park itself was just a space; the addition of the relics of human interaction in that space made it a "hybrid creation" of Letchworth's mind.[41]

According to Olmstead, for a park to accomplish its goal, not only should the landscape be as natural as possible, but "noisy and dangerous occupations and amusements should also be kept out of, at least, the middle portions of a large park."[42] A large park, then, should not provide active amusement but rather should afford a space for quiet contemplation and spiritual renewal. Even if the public preferred "some Coney Island pleasure resort," city planners, park commissioners, and landscape architects should expend their energy and resources creating quiet natural spaces. One can imagine that Olmstead would exclude the hunting enthusiasts of the Boone and Crockett Club, with their guns, as well as the revelers and baseball players who would disturb nature's spiritual qualities. He might also have objected to activities such as snowmobiling that visitors may now participate in at Letchworth State Park. "A great many" people, Olmstead claimed, "do not know what is good for them when they go to a park to look for more exciting pleasures. They should be gradually and unconsciously educated to better uses of large public parks and not have their crude demands alone catered to."[43] Entertainment and amusements, if they had to be included, should be isolated on the edges, and "great discrimination" should be used in their selection. Olmstead apparently meant for the public to be forced into spiritual renewal through a combination of boredom and clandestine education, which usually took the form of appropriate artistic installations that would instruct visitors in what it meant to be American. Well-known historical heroes and "unsung" pioneers provided good material for that instruction. In response to Olmstead's comments, Warren H. Manning, fellow landscape architect, argued that even monuments of historical importance or those to "the memory of noted public men" should be excluded from large naturalistic parks because they interrupted personal spiritual renewal.[44]

An Indian captive could serve quite well as the medium through which this double message of spiritual renewal and national identity could be transferred to the public in a park. After all, Indians, supposedly vanished or vanishing, might inspire the visitor to quiet reflection rather than raucous recreation. Images or relics of Indians, who were believed to be more spiritual than whites and deeply connected to the land, might also inspire the visitor to look at the landscape in a supposedly "Indian" way—as a place of peace and religious meaning. Moreover, a white Indian captive like Mary Jemison, who chose to remain Indian even when she was given the option to return to white society, would remind the visitor that whites could incorporate Indian characteristics, in this case a pious connection to the land, an internal quietness, and an anti-modern mentality. Therefore, despite Manning's rather extreme objections to the use of *any* monuments, the choice of Mary Jemison and her Indian family as the main link to pioneer history in Letchworth Park is a surprisingly adroit one. It is hard to imagine an historical figure who would better embody the multiple layers of historical and natural significance of the area.[45]

On the Uses of Monuments

Like Olmstead, sculptor Henry Kirke Bush-Brown was also adopted and trained by his uncle, and he also attended the 1897 Park and Outdoor Art Association meeting. He must have been slightly offended by the suggestion that monuments to notable historical figures sullied the value of naturalistic parks. A sculptor by training, Bush-Brown produced statues for the Gettysburg Battlefield, including sculptures of Abraham Lincoln, Washington Irving, and Ulysses S. Grant. Among many other projects, he also created a Civil War memorial for the Union League Club of Philadelphia.[46] In 1910 he created the Mary Jemison statue erected at Letchworth Park in September. Although he made no rebuttal to Olmstead and Manning at the 1897 APOAA meeting, he did speak to the power and importance of public sculpture throughout his life. "We erect monuments," he wrote in 1901, "to keep alive in the mind of the community the ideals that have moved the souls of men in the past.... Public monuments, then, are intended to have a sacred moral influence, which, if properly expressed, will endure so long as bronze and stone may last, and the soul of man remains responsive to eternal love."[47]

To be clear, Bush-Brown did not suggest that monuments should be randomly chosen "to have no other object than to fill in the vacant spaces."[48] But as an architectural sculptor rather than a landscape architect, Bush-Brown understood the moral uplift of the public (even if forced upon them) differently than Olmstead and Manning did. It would come, he argued, as much from the allegorical or historical messages of artistic installations as from the proper placement of trees. William Letchworth clearly sided with Bush-Brown on this issue, combining, as he did, human and natural history into a managed cultural landscape. At the Jemison memorial dedication, Dr. Kunz pointed out that the "charm" of Glen Iris came not just from its natural "beauty" and "grandeur," but also from its "historic associations" that "conspired to make this a place of universal interest."[49]

Olmstead, Bush-Brown, and Letchworth did agree on two things: first, the general public did not know what was good for it. The "misdirected good intentions" of most reformers had done more damage than good because those in charge of committees to raise funds or run public areas were "in no way capable of judging" what would benefit the public most. Indeed, the reformers listened to the seemingly idiotic demands of the public, who kept insisting that parks provide them with fun things to do. The common people needed experts like Olmstead and Bush-Brown. Letchworth's actions demonstrated that he also agreed with the need to guide the public: he did, after all, rescue Glen Iris from the actions of his fellow businessmen; he also brought in experts like William Webster and Bush-Brown to guide the improvements made to the estate.

Olmstead and Bush-Brown also agreed that "every American citizen has a right to expect the Government to secure," and indeed pay for, the best in art and landscape design to preserve the nation's cultural landscape and to transmit that heritage to future generations.[50] It is not obvious that Letchworth held a natural sympathy with them on this issue, as he owned and renovated his land without the help of any organization for many years; yet in the face of the Genesee River Company he came to believe that the government was more capable than he was in protecting his estate.

At the 1910 dedication of Bush-Brown's Jemison statue at Glen Iris, Dr. George F. Kunz pointed out that the statue, and its placement in Glen Iris, would "not only serve to perpetuate [Jemison's] memory, but also add a beautiful object of art to the manifold natural beauties of the park." Kunz also cited Ostrogoth king Theodoric the Great that "public respect, rather than compulsion and force, must be the safeguard of the monuments and beauty" of cultural relics. Madison Grant, wildlife conservationist, member of the Boone and Crockett Club, father of the modern eugenics movement, and a man who held a decidedly low opinion of the value of public sentiment, once stated that "the law itself must be in advance of public opinion."[51] One can imagine that Olmstead would have agreed, and he and Bush-Brown believed that when the public saw how preferable the plans of the experts were to their own desires, they would come to defer to the experts with thanks. Kunz, on the other hand, believed that the public should be *taught* rather than *forced* to love and care for their natural and historic treasures. Letchworth appears to have combined the two beliefs to create a kind of "serenity prayer" of preservation and restoration that we must educate where we can, legislate where we must, and have the wisdom to recognize the difference.[52] Before public opinion coincided with his own, Letchworth simply took matters into his own hands and did the work himself, and his sincerity and apparent likeability won many people to his cause.[53]

Historical Indians in the Woods

Letchworth saw Glen Iris as a holistic cultural landscape consisting of both the land itself and the human history (both white and

Indian) associated with that land. Along with land conservation and restoration, Letchworth began to work to preserve the history of the Genesee Valley area, and especially the history of the Seneca Indians. He found that, like the trees in the forest, "relics and mementos of the aboriginal possessors of the valley, still existing, were treated with neglect and were fast disappearing."[54]

Soon after buying the land, Letchworth set about acquiring as many of those relics as he could and bringing them to Glen Iris. These included a Seneca Council House, a "small fireproof museum containing several thousand Indian relics and a fossil head of a mastodon," and eventually the bones of Dehgewanus.[55] He also organized the "Last Indian Council on the Genesee," with nineteen men and "several" women of the Seneca and Mohawk nations coming together on October 1, 1872. Two of those present, Thomas Jemison and James Shongo, were grandsons of Mary Jemison, the "White Woman of the Genesee." Nicholas H. Parker, brother of brigadier general Ely S. Parker, also attended. Thirty-eight years later, Nicholas's grandson, Arthur C. Parker, would speak at the dedication of the Mary Jemison statue just a few feet from the Council House.

At the council, most of the speeches lamented the lingering hostility between the Senecas and the Mohawks and wept for the "vanished" Indians. Poet David Gray recited a poem that, although Letchworth's biographer Joseph Larned called it a "requiem of the Senecas," spoke almost not at all of the Indians themselves, but rather focused mainly on describing Glen Iris. Gray's poem speaks to the estate rather than to or of the "vanished folk" themselves:

> Sweet Vale, more peaceful bend thy skies,
> Thy airs be fraught with rarer balm!
> A people's busy tumult lies
> Hushed in thy sylvan calm.
> Deep be thy peace! While fancy frames

Soft idylls of thy dwellers fled;—
They loved thee, called thee gentle names,
In the long summers dead.[56]

Here landscape served as a stand-in for Indians. When Letchworth connected Indians with land, he followed a long Euro-American tradition of seeing the "Noble Indian"—the native in his natural state unmolested by Europeans—as essentially *of* the land. Barely human in the sense of being separated from nature by layers of culture, the "Noble Indians" were viewed by many conservationists and self-named friends as little more than walking, talking trees who communed with natural elements and beings because they themselves were natural beings. John Muir commented that it "seem[ed] strange" that Indians had made no "heavier marks" upon the land they had populated for centuries, but explained that they "hurt the landscape hardly more than the birds and squirrels."[57]

Indian populations throughout the Americas have indeed had relationships with the land that many non-Indians found strange—from dependence upon it for day-to-day survival to religious beliefs in which the lines between human and animal blurred or disappeared altogether. Euro-Americans have used that relationship as evidence to conflate Indians and nature. "The connections between Indians and nature," Shepard Krech explained, "have been so tightly drawn over five hundred years . . . that many non-Indians expect indigenous people to walk softly in their moccasins as conservationists and even (in Muir's sense) preservationists."[58] Charles Eastman, who came from mixed Santee Sioux and white ancestry, wrote that during his 1910 attempts to collect Indian artifacts for the University of Pennsylvania Museum, he found very few Indians living after the traditional fashion until he came to Rainy Lake in Ontario. "Remote and solitary," Eastman wrote, "I found the true virgin wilderness, the final refuge, as it appears, of American big game and primitive man."[59] Eastman, then, like so many others, linked wilderness, big game animals, and "real" (historical) Indians, as if not one of the three could exist without the other two.

Letchworth's focus on historical Indians, then, put him in good company. Although Seneca descendants of the captive were present at and participated in the September 1910 Jemison ceremony, its main message was that Indians had given way to white Americans. "Here a race, now nearly extinct," said Charles Dow (chairman of the Letchworth Park Committee of the ASHPS), "once had lived in undisputed proprietorship." Later in the day, Edward Hagaman Hall stated that the Indian artifacts "remind us of the vanished people among whom [Jemison] lived," despite the fact that her great-granddaughter joined Arthur C. Parker (also part Indian) in pulling the cords that unveiled the monument.[60] Speakers of the day happily acknowledged that the land had once belonged to the Seneca people, and that Seneca people were present at the ceremony, but they did not assume it should be returned to the Seneca. Rather, they praised Letchworth for having saved it and restored it, not to its historical owners but to the government of the country that had ousted those historical owners in the first place.

The Dangers of Contemporary Indians in the Woods

But we should not confuse the value Letchworth and others had assigned to "real" historic Indians, or to white women who lived as Indians, with their attitude toward actual living Indians. Many conservationists in the late nineteenth century, like Philetus Norris, the second Superintendent of Yellowstone Park, thought that Indians in wilderness would "annoy" both game and tourists.[61] Historical Indians, by implication, trod softly like squirrels, while living ones apparently stomped about like so many elephants.

By the end of the Civil War, Mark Spence has explained, most Americans believed that Indians belonged in reservations, not in the wilderness. The memory of Mary Jemison and her Indian family proved to be an exception to that view of Indians, probably because, of course, she was not Indian. Indeed, when the rest of the tribe left the banks of the Genesee for the Buffalo Creek Reservation south of Buffalo in 1825, Mary Jemison remained in her little cabin by the water and did not follow her friends until six years later.[62]

The twentieth century American national story of nation building and continental conquest required a story of both a "vanishing" (or vanished) frontier and a native population. Likewise, even as many Progressive minds began, in the late nineteenth century, to see reservations as detrimental to Indians, they did not intend to correct the wrongs brought about by reservations by allowing Indians back into the wilderness.

Civilization, which was as disconnected from wilderness as possible, would be the only possible way to save Indians. Mary Jemison, as the source of "white blood" injected into an Indian family, was, then, the first source of the process of "civilizing" that family.[63]

The American concept of wilderness, then, that developed in the late nineteenth and early twentieth centuries envisioned a "primitive" state free of living people but filled with the evidence of dead ones. Historical Indians belonged to the land, so when envisioning them, many people, like poet David Gray and Charles Eastman, talked about land as much as about humans. But modern Indians presented a problem, and wilderness protection, either for spiritual or recreational purposes, necessitated their removal. If the Indians remained, they ruined the recreational uses of wilderness by killing or frightening the big game. They also ruined the spiritual uses of wilderness by infesting it with a "dirty" foreign presence that would make the public quite incapable of enjoying any transcendental experience. John Muir, after all, who so loved wilderness and Indian woodland skills, sarcastically commented that the Indians he found in Yosemite were covered in "dirt . . . old enough and thick enough to have a geological significance." They were a "dismal" people who accosted Muir, and he "prefer[ed] the society of squirrels and woodchucks," however "unnatural" it might be to be revolted by one's "own species."[64] "Nothing truly wild," Muir said, "is unclean."[65]

Modern Indians currently living in the woods, then, had been degraded so as to be quite repellent to civilized men and quite unnatural.[66] Because historical Indians belonged in the wilderness and modern Indians did not, men like William Letchworth began collecting Indian artifacts to preserve and display along with their land. Although they might quibble about the definition of wilderness and whether people of any kind belonged there, and what those people should be allowed to do there, America's Progressive Era conservationists saw land conservation, removal of living Indians, and protection of the memory of the historical Indian as one and the same thing.

The Last of William Letchworth

Letchworth agreed with his fellow Progressives that historical Indians should be connected with the land he sought to protect. It is not clear exactly when the Indians of the region caught Letchworth's imagination, but he went to great pains to preserve as many of their antiquities as possible. The person who engrossed him most was the white woman, captive at age 15, who lived with the Seneca people as an adopted member of the tribe for the rest of her life.

As early as 1871, Letchworth had set about collecting Mary Jemison artifacts, and when developers threatened her grave near Buffalo, New York ("relic hunters" had already damaged the tombstone), Letchworth worked with Jemison's grandson James Shongo and other relatives to bring her remains to the Glen Iris estate. The solemn re-interment ceremony in March, 1874, included readings from Scripture, prayer, and descriptions of Jemison's life before a "large concourse of people."[67] Just three years later, Letchworth edited James Seaver's narrative of Jemison's life. The greatest evidence of his lifelong fascination with Mary Jemison is that the unveiling of her statue served as the capstone event to both his life and to the Glen Iris estate. The dedication of the Mary Jemison statue (on her second and final grave on the banks of the Genesee) took place just months before Letchworth died and was, although he had officially given the estate to New York several years earlier, the main public announcement and celebration of his bequest.

William Letchworth, perhaps because of his philanthropy, but perhaps also because he had experienced the regenerative and restorative qualities of wilderness himself, decided well before many other Americans that wilderness and historic preservation were connected and necessary to personal and national well-being. The fragile, tired young Letchworth lived to be eighty-seven and worked until his last month to improve the lot of epileptics, the insane, orphans, and criminals, as well as to expand and protect Glen Iris and the memory of Mary Jemison. His life served as the perfect example to modern Americans of the need for protected natural spaces, and the celebration of Mary Jemison, which was also really a celebration of William Letchworth, honored him first for his work protecting Glen Iris and the Jemison history, and only incidentally for his work with epileptics, criminals, and the insane.

L. H. Bailey, head of the Country Life Movement, reminded the audience at the Jemison statue dedication that although "it is the habit of the time . . . [for men to] establish themselves in the city or a suburb of the city," Letchworth took a different (and Bailey suggested preferable) path. After he got rich in the city, he "went back to the country," which he proceeded to "rescue

... from vandalism." "It is an example worth of emulation," Bailey went on, "for he has accomplished much for a quiet countryside." Certainly Letchworth's life provided proof that country living could provide as much personal satisfaction and fulfilling "means of self-expression" as the city could—indeed, perhaps more. The restoration and continued cultural development of the countryside, Bailey believed, was necessary to national survival, just as it was necessary to Letchworth's own well-being.[68]

Toward the end of his life, and in tributes after his death, those who honored William Letchworth for his preservation of Glen Iris, or for his work for the needy or sick, often linked him to the estate in a spiritual sense. In the 1910 reprinted and expanded edition of *Voices of the Glen*, several poems dedicated to William Letchworth described the land rather than the man, just as other poems, such as those of David Gray, focused on land in order to memorialize Indians. For those who admired William Letchworth, their love of Glen Iris sprang from his affection for it. He became, like Dehgewanus, like her adopted Indian people, part of the land, at least in the image the public held of the area. After his death, Letchworth became part of the historical significance of the place and its cultural landscape. Mary Percival described the tribute paid to the man by Glen Iris itself:

> The trees are blossoming again
>   And all the birds are singing,
> To him [Letchworth] who loves both flower and song
>   Their yearly tribute bringing.[69]

In another poem, Amanda T. Jones attributed Letchworth's greatness to a divine hand:

> God said, 'As living springs his life shall be,—
> Even as rivers in a thirst land
> That make men glad!—I putting forth the hand

> To lead the under-currents of the sea
> Through mountains where the great rocks wait for Me . . .
> . . . How would My palm-trees perish where they grew!
> For his delight, in whom I find no fault,
> Still for his poor, the streams I will renew,—
> Howbeit, among My sons, I him [Letchworth] exalt.'[70]

Letchworth's niece, Sara Evans Letchworth, combined the two sentiments in "From Inspiration Point, June 8th, 1909."

> Where, free at home, the woodland bird did flit,
>   Thou wert supreme in august majesty—
>   All, all was thine as far as the eye could see—
>   God wrought for us this scene beyond compare,
>   But one man's loving hand protected it
>   And gave it to his fellow-men to share.[71]

In "To Glen Iris," James N. Johnston noted that he did not love Glen Iris just because of its woods and streams, but because of

> Thy master's weary years of ceaseless care
>   To aid the sick, the hapless one to seek;
>   His voice of mercy pleading for the weak;
> His word of hope to brighten dark despair;
> His potent message helpful everywhere,—
> For these I love thee [Glen Iris] most and these
>   forever speak.[72]

Letchworth's purchase of the place he named Glen Iris, combined with his understanding of land preservation as inherently connected to historical preservation, saved both himself and the White Woman of the Genesee from the destructive powers of the city of Buffalo. He used the Jemison statue dedication to make this connection clear and to reiterate in a public display his

THE INDIAN AND THE ACTIVIST   85

control over the fate of the land and the statue he had given to the state. Although nearly dead on September 19, 1910 (seventy-seven years to the day from the day Jemison died), Letchworth spoke his point through Charles Dow's voice:

> It is my intention and desire that this bronze statue of Mary Jemison shall always remain where it now is placed, and that it shall remain as much a part of these lands and grounds as the grave itself. It has become in law a part of the real estate and passes under your control and management at the same time and upon the same condition as the rest of the property.[73]

Thus did William Letchworth make his last public statement that would ensure that the state of New York was legally responsible for the protection of the river, the forest, the statue, and the Indian artifacts held there. He would be dead in fewer than three months. But before he went, he assured that the Genesee River could not be dammed anywhere because a dam even far upstream would disrupt its flow through Glen Iris, now Letchworth State Park, and violate Letchworth's will. Nowhere in the letter read at the dedication ceremony did he discuss Dehgewanus's personal characteristics, what originally drew his interest to her, nor his connection to her beyond his "long-cherished" intention to erect her statue. By then, it seems, in his old age and from his revered position, he did not care to reveal motivations that had begun so long ago in the youth of a sickly man. Those topics he left to the other speakers of the day; for him, the most important point to be made at the ceremony, perhaps the main point of having the ceremony in the first place, was to inform the public that the state was legally bound to protect both the park and all its contents.

William Letchworth published five different editions of the Jemison narrative first published in 1824 by James Everett Seaver.

To Seaver's version he added appendices that included newspaper accounts of Jemison's reburial, and illustrations and ethnographic footnotes provided by Ely S. Parker and Lewis Henry Morgan. Interestingly, the cover of Letchworth's 1898 edition shows a portrait not of Dehgewanus but of the Seneca war chief Cornplanter. In addition to Jemison's narrative, her bones, and her cabin, Letchworth saved the artifacts of her adopted people, as well as her daughter Nancy's cabin, which he bought and relocated so that it overlooked her mother's grave and statue. Letchworth used Dehgewanus as a way to tie himself to the glen that saved his life. Others saw the two as connected because he told them they were.

But Letchworth also used Mary Jemison's historical bond to the place to help justify his conservation of it. Had it just been a pretty place, what worth would it have had to anyone besides him? He looked for several ways to connect human lives to the land he loved. First, he created the Wyoming Benevolent Society in order that hope for the future of urban indigent boys would serve as a buffer between Glen Iris and the Genesee River Company. When that didn't seem to work, he discovered that his personal interest in the Seneca Indians and Dehgewanus could draw people to his cause. Many places, however, across the state and the country had historical Indian connections. That fact would have made the beloved glen only as unique as many people's back yards where they could pick arrowheads out of the grass. But Jemison, this white woman found so far from where she logically belonged, made Letchworth's glen and the Indians who once lived there distinctly more important, and therefore more worth saving, and, quite possibly, more worth visiting.

Moreover, unlike Cynthia Ann Parker, whose story, as discussed in chapter one, was eclipsed in the late nineteenth and early twentieth centuries by the national importance of her Indian son Quanah, Jemison had no living relative to upstage her. She did have Indian relatives still living in New York State, and quite a few came to and participated in the unveiling of her statue, but they were not celebrities or people of national or even regional importance. Both Jemison's whiteness, then, and her connection to historical Indians that Letchworth and many others wanted to remember, as well as her lack of well-known modern Indian descendants, made her the most logical historical figure to link to the park.

L. H. Bailey ended his speech at the Jemison statue dedication by outlining the connection both Mary Jemison and William Letchworth had to the wilderness in and around Glen Iris, stating, "We come here, therefore, under these trees, feeling the wind in our faces, looking into the blue sky above us, for the purpose of dedicating one more landmark to the memory of those who have made this region eventful."[74] Bailey believed that the eternal presence of both William Letchworth and Mary Jemison could draw people away from the cities and back to the countryside, not just for a recuperative vacation or to shoot deer, elk or bear (as the Boone and Crockett Club would have it), but as a place to make a full and complete life. Letchworth, after all, had done just that, and the country life had served him well.

It appears that Letchworth and his Progressive friends were right: Letchworth State Park still exists, is considered one of the jewels of the New York state parks, and is often referred to rather extravagantly as the "Grand Canyon of the East." Letchworth *did* save Glen Iris, and it has expanded from his original gift of 1,000 acres to 14,350 acres. It has 270 campsites, 82 cabins, swimming pools, playgrounds, a museum, athletic fields, trails for hiking, biking, and horseback riding, snow sports, and hot air ballooning, and it attracts possibly one million visitors a year. It is therefore large enough to accommodate both active recreation and solitary spiritual renewal.[75] Likewise, Mary Jemison's grave and her statue remain at their place along the Genesee, protected as Letchworth planned by the state of New York. She continues to be an object of attention for scholars and history buffs alike. In 1995 historian June Namias edited a new version of Jemison's narrative, and a year later Jemison became the subject of a novel.[76] Americans remember her, as Letchworth had hoped they would, in large part because he remembered her and worked so consciously to protect her memory. Like so many Progressives (the Boone and Crockett Club, John Muir, the Park and Outdoor Art Association, and so many others), Letchworth linked history and land, and did what he set out to do: preserve both the cultural heritage and the natural heritage into one unified vision of the United States in which each is vital and neither can exist without the other.

CHAPTER 3

On Creating Americans

To Vanish or Not to Vanish?

Americans in the early twentieth century remained convinced that Indians were doomed to disappear, and cities and towns across the United States began to memorialize their past connections to the vanishing people. On the national scale, Americans could read about the ongoing photography project of Edward S. Curtis as well as Rodman Wanamaker's ill-fated attempt to erect a monumental Indian memorial in New York Harbor. On the local scale, they could, if they happened to be lucky enough to live in the right place, attend a ceremony for a local Indian captive hero. Indian captives became local heroes because of the contact they instigated between white and Indian America. Memorializers sought to prove that Indian captives served as the quintessential Americans. They revered the historical connection to, and knowledge of, historical Indians, and promised continuing government and public support for the process of "Americanizing" living Indians. They also often emphasized that the captive (or at least the captive's family) went through several phases (from European immigrant to captive to redeemed—or rediscovered—white American) in order to become a true American. Captivity narratives and memorials reinforced a national belief that Indian history and ethnography was vital to the American identity, and supported the federal project to civilize and Americanize the "first" and "vanishing" Americans.

Captivity narratives published between 1880 and 1916 did not seek to resolve the "Indian problem" that faced both scientists and policymakers of the day. Instead, these narratives linked a seemingly chaotic contemporary daily life and an often contradictory modern understanding of race to a national past that reminded readers and audiences that "going Indian" had been a necessary step in the frontier experience of their ancestors—a step that had made their ancestors Americans. Miscegenation with Indians (as much as they were destined to die out) had not degraded whites psychologically or physically, but in fact had helped to create the positive traits that made Americans unique in all the world. In order to continue and expand what many viewed as America's special and favorable place in the world, those of European background would need to continue to recreate themselves as Americans through contact with Indian history. Tales of captivity allowed for a continued connection between "savagery" and civilization in a modern, post-frontier country. Captivity tales became important to individual readers and to the story locals told of their history because these tales did not vilify the ancestors who "went" all or partially Indian. Rather, those ancestors became heroes precisely because of the contact they instigated and the connection they maintained between races.

In the first decades of the twentieth century, the future of the country seemed to depend on its ability to take distinct groups—Jews, Catholics, Italians, Russians, or Indians—and turn them into a single, definable "people, not a polyglot boarding-house," as Roosevelt wrote in 1918.[1] This nationalist vision left no room for ethnic diversity from any source. Immigrants and Indians, in order to become "Americans," needed to distance themselves from their aboriginal or European roots. In any case, Euro-Americans had long believed that Indians were vanishing, so helping them to do so via Bible reading and land ownership seemed kinder than accomplishing this inevitable end through the gun. But Indians did not seem to be vanishing at all. Even when they could read and write English, even when they cut their hair and got off the horse and into the Model T, they did not cease to be Indian. As early as 1887, the *New York Times* periodically reported that, although numbers were incomplete and probably "made up largely from conjecture," Indian populations did not appear to be dying out but rather were "multiplying, improving in numbers as well as condition."[2] Just a few months later the *New York Time* noted that "little by little [Indians] are learning to appreciate the comforts [civilization] brings."[3]

But neither the Indians' appreciation of civilization nor their increasing population came with a corresponding rejection of Indian culture. In 1911, even as eulogizers at the Mary Jemison statue dedication declared that the memorial would "remind us of the vanished people among whom she lived," the *Times* again wrote about the false assumption held by most Americans of decline of American Indians. "It is a remarkable fact," the article noted, "that there should be such a universal impression among even the well-informed of the country that the Indians are dying out," for, despite that impression, "It is very doubtful, experts say, whether there ever existed within the North American Continent an Indian population greater than that existing at the present day."[4]

Maconaquah's and Dehgewanus's (Slocum's and Jemison's) stories supported the census conclusion that Indians were not dying out. Maconaquah's relatives certainly flourished, and by 1900, at least one hundred Indians with connections to Maconaquah showed up at the unveiling of the Francis Slocum memorial in Peru, Indiana. Dehgewanus's Indian relations, too, remained both connected to, and yet distinct from, the white Americans celebrating her story. They certainly had increased in number, and perhaps some of them really did appreciate "civilized" comforts and manners, but they did not disappear, and they did not cease to be Indian. The 1910 census reported 305,000 Indians within U.S. borders, with steady increases seen in all Indian groups across the country. Even in those tribes with the largest numbers of white–Indian marriages, numbers continued to increase, and the offspring of white–Indian marriages, though perhaps more "civilized," were recognizably Indian. As the Indian sides of the Slocum and Jemison families demonstrated by their mere presence at the memorials, many, probably most, of these Indians, despite greater "civilization," seemed unlikely to abandon their Indian identities. Indians at Mary Jemison's statue dedication reminded the audience of their distinctive culture by excluding every white person not directly connected with the family (except a representative of William Letchworth's) from their separate ceremony held the morning after the main dedication.

It was not just those captives who had assimilated into Indian societies whose stories supported the 1910 census conclusion that Indian populations were growing. In fact, one of the most anti-Indian narratives of the late nineteenth century, that of Abbie Gardner-Sharp, dedicated a great deal of time in the appendixes of its later editions to detailed discussions of Indians and their progress towards "civilization." The first edition of her narrative ends with chapter 26, "A Visit to the Old Home." By the 1889 and 1910 editions, she had added a sixty-one-page final chapter entitled "An Epoch of Advancement," with subheadings like "Visit Indian Reservations in the Dakotas" and "Wondrous Change in Condition of Sioux." In this chapter, Gardner-Sharp claimed "even the difficult Indian problem has to a great extent been solved in the present generation." "I must confess," she stated, "that my confidence in the capacity of the Indian race for elevation has increased a hundred fold," primarily because of the "large expenditures" made "by the government each year for the past ten years."⁵ Like Gardner-Sharp, many authorities on Indian policy saw the increase in Indian population as proof of the success of federal Indian policy. F. W. Broughton, head of the Bureau of Indian Affairs (BIA) statistical division, explained it thus:

> Why should they not increase. . . . A large part of the work of this bureau is the protection of him against his own improvidence. . . . There is no class of people anywhere on the face of the earth who has so much done for them.⁶

Dr. Jacob Breid, head of the BIA medical division, added,

> The prevalent idea that the Indian, as a race, is dying out, that the race-vitality, so to speak, is waning and growing old, just as an individual grows old, is all erroneous. Whether such a thing can exist or not in a race, I do not care to answer, but I am sure that it does not exist among the Indians. As for individual vitality, that is as great among them as among any other people.⁷

Despite knowledge of Indian population increase in the BIA, the assumption remained within both popular and expert opinion that Indians would die away, if not physically then at least culturally. In 1925, the *New York Times* would again report, with no little astonishment, on the population growth of these dying people, this time giving the topic front-page billing.⁸

Only four months before its 1910 report declaring that Indian populations were on the rise, the *New York Times* wrote that Edward Curtis had reached the halfway point in his project "to secure a permanent ethnological and pictorial record of the fast-vanishing race, which shall preserve it for the student hundreds of years after it has been lost from the face of the earth."⁹ Later in the same year, just two months after the *Times* declared that Indians populations were increasing, Congress set aside land on Staten Island for "a suitable memorial to the memory of the North American Indian."[10] Although the memorial was to be dedicated to the *memory* of the vanishing people, Rodman Wanamaker, son of retail tycoon John Wanamaker, rather ironically traveled twenty-two thousand miles to gain support for the plan from the tribes themselves, who, apparently, were alive and well.[11] Photographer Joseph Kossuth Dixon, a former Baptist minister and Indian enthusiast, paired with Wanamaker for the expedition. Like so many other "friends of the Indians," Dixon found no contradiction in simultaneously classing Indians as terrible and as noble.

At the Jemison memorial ceremony at Letchworth State Park in September of 1910, we also find that same juxtaposition of the two images—noble and savage Indian. Historian Edward Hagaman Hall told the crowd at Letchworth State Park that Mary Jemison, the "White Woman of the Genesee," had never *become* Indian. Regardless of the fact that even the engraving on her statue stated that her "home during more than seventy years of a life of strange vicissitude was among the Senecas," Hall made it clear to his audience that "although living the life of an Indian, her innate humanity never left her." The implication, of course, and not a very subtle one, was that the Indians among whom she lived were, on some level, not human. Jemison remained white in some very important ways (morally and psychologically at least, commentators generally agreed) throughout her forced, and then chosen, life as the Seneca woman Dehgewanus.

Yet according to another speaker of the day, Dehgewanus's identity was not such a given. Arthur C. Parker, the part-Seneca historian, archeologist, and brother of Ely S. Parker (the first native Commissioner of Indian Affairs), took pains in his address to inform the audience that Dehgewanus's life as a Seneca woman would not have been one of misery. In doing so, he connected her lot to that of the typical Seneca woman, thus connecting her being, her fundamental self, to that of the typical Seneca woman.

Contrary to popular images of Indian women as neglected, abused, and overworked, Parker argued, "those sterling qualities that under stress bring out the wonderful moral courage of women never received greater appreciation than that given by the Iroquois Indian." Moreover, Iroquois women held considerable political influence, and their opinions on the governing of their society received credit as the "foundation of Iroquois society." Parker stopped short of saying outright that white society should emulate Iroquois gender relations, but his implication was clear: the women of modern American society had at least some reasons to envy their Indian sisters.[12]

Dr. Hall presented Indians as completely undesirable, and Arthur Parker described them as enviable. Although the two descriptions of Mary Jemison—Parker's happy Indian woman and Hall's unsullied white ancestor—seemed to contradict each other, the Euro-American understanding of, and relationship with, the continent's first inhabitants has since first contact been beset with peculiar contradictions that have made that relationship difficult and, at times, unmanageable. The duality of Hall's untarnished white woman and Parker's esteemed and happy Indian woman, in fact, captures well the idea about Indians that many white Americans held at the turn of the century. Significantly, after all, the two most reprinted captivity narratives during the Progressive Era (Frances Slocum's and Mary Jemison's) told tales of women who refused to return to white society even when given the chance. Yet the tales did not focus on their "Indianness," or their degradation, but on their retained "whiteness" and the "white" qualities of their offspring, specifically thrift, a love of hard work, Protestant religious devotion, and respect for private property.

In a similar fashion, Wanamaker and Dixon held contradictory attitudes about Indians. They lamented the abuses Indians had suffered at the hands of the American government and military, all the while declaring that the mission of the American government (to remove Indians physically from the landscape and culturally from American society) was inevitable and desirable. In order to invest American Indians themselves in this contradictory process, the Wanamaker ceremony at each reservation presented a three-part message. It classed the audience (Indians) as fundamentally unable to survive in modern America, while simultaneously encouraging both assimilation and the preservation of artifacts of a previous "savage" culture, thus suggesting, just as William Letchworth's park implied, that modern America had no room for Indians living in traditional ways but needed historical Indians in order to gain legitimacy. Finally, the ceremony, with no actual governmental authority, promised that the federal government would protect and treat fairly any Indian who promised devotion to the United States and who agreed to become hardworking individualistic farmers.

Wanamaker's memorial project, then—unaffiliated as it was with the federal government, and yet claiming to speak for the nation and for government policy—must, to Indians who heard it, have seemed ridiculously contradictory. In Iowa, after all, Abbie Gardner-Sharp had, in the Progressive Era versions of her narrative, added the final chapter that defended federal policy, and promised more federal aid for Indian "uplift" to come, given the growing evidence that Indians were capable of adopting and embracing civilization. But Gardner-Sharp's support for the "civilizing" of Indians did not alter her belief that Indians in their "natural state" were savage and better eliminated.

From Victim to Advocate

Abbie Gardner-Sharp's change of heart in the later versions of her narrative was surprising to her, and must also have been surprising to anyone who had read her first 1857 narrative. However, the fact that she openly supported policies designed to make Indians less hostile should not be a great surprise. Upon returning to Iowa in 1883 after a number of years drifting about the Midwest, she triumphantly declared that civilization had won the Midwest. "The groves and hills," she wrote, "which once echoed with the war whoop of the savages now reverberates with the shrill whistle of the locomotive," and "the whole face of this once wild region has been transformed into a fashionable summer resort."[13] Later she marveled that "the difficult Indian problem has to a great extent been solved in the present generation."[14] Gardner-Sharp's captivity narrative, notably one of the only Progressive Era narratives written by the captive herself, took great pleasure in the gore and misery inflicted upon her and her ill-fated family, horrors that she revisited throughout her life. Her narrative described the flashbacks she experienced upon returning to the scenes of her torture with as much luxurious language as she described the actual event:

> No language can express the thrilling emotions that I experienced on my return to this place. . . . As the shadows darkened I could almost see the dusky forms of the savages filing up to the doorway, rifles in hand, crowd into the house, shoot my father when his back was turned, drive my mother and sister out of the house, killing them with their guns, tearing the children from my arms, and beating them to death with stovewood. All this, and much more, came involuntarily before me, not as a picture in memory, but as a present reality.[15]

Yet while standing in the same place where this gruesome slaughter took place twenty-seven years later, she declared the "Indian problem" "solved." She claimed "the wise will no longer apply the word 'impossible' to the proposed civilization of Indians."[16] She travelled among the Dakotas, visiting reservations, schools, and churches, and became convinced, for all that they had done to her and her family, "the same law of development that has been illustrated in the progress of all nations can also be traced . . . among the Indian tribes."[17] She noted the number of Indian schools and their successes, and took great joy in seeing white and Indian ministers together in one church. "The change that had come to pass" in the Sioux who had brutalized her to near insanity "seemed truly marvelous." She worked for the Indian right to be admitted to the civilized cultures of the world, defining what it meant to be "civilized" and applying those qualities to Indians. "Nearly all," she said, "can read in their own language, and many can read and write in English also. They live in houses, which contain many articles used by white people . . . [and] the more progressive [Indian] families have as well furnished houses as you often find in the average home of the white man."[18] Moreover, they voted, and by a "freak of Cupid's arrow," some white women preferred Indian men; interracial marriages near reservations were "considered no marvel."[19] Indians, then, according to Abbie Gardner-Sharp, could and would assimilate, Christianize, and generally become a civilized literate people with short hair, shoes, and houses full of material goods, but only if white America gave them the credit they deserved. Government policy must support civilizing forces (schools, churches, and the like) in order for Indians to reach white levels of civilization. They were *capable* but could not do it alone. Their "nature," by which she meant culture, was savage and barbarous, but through education and God, they could become as white men.

Not so for white captives. Their "nature" was civilized, and so they remained. Charles Elihu Slocum read a paper at the 1900 meeting of the American Association for the Advancement of Science entitled "A Civilized Heredity Stronger Than a Savage Environment," which argued that Frances Slocum's life as an Indian proved nature over nurture. She was industrious, clean, unadorned by trinkets (all "savages" love shiny things, after all), practical, intelligent, and responsible. All these, according to Slocum, were decidedly non-Indian characteristics, a list fundamentally in opposition to Gardner-Sharp's list of civilized qualities that Indians were adopting. No matter how well or poorly captivity narrative authors thought of Indians individually or collectively, they hoped that Indians were intelligent enough to advance culturally, but few were completely convinced of the Boasian theory of cultural relatively. Rather, they argued, because Indians were destined to vanish, and because they were capable of cultural progress, the Christianization and the intentional civilization of Indians could and should be undertaken. The result would be a happily assimilated Indian population, rather than one that died out in misery and alienation.[20]

Franz Boas versus Madison Grant

The two main conflicting views of race can be summarized in the opinions of Franz Boas and Madison Grant. By the late nineteenth century, the concepts of race and culture had become thoroughly confused by notions of "scientific racism" and ethnic psychology. If evolution ruled human development, could humankind influence its own evolutionary direction? Social Darwinism, an idea that combined the work of Charles Darwin with that of Herbert Spencer and eugenicist Francis Galton, led some to propose controlling human breeding to remove undesirable characteristics, a movement referred to as eugenics. Meanwhile, the work of anthropologist Franz Boas and his students led others to argue for an understanding of each human culture in terms of itself rather than in terms of other cultures. These conflicting theories highlighted two vastly different ways of viewing human development and the relationship of different groups of people to one another.

In his 1916 *The Passing of the Great Race*, Madison Grant, "the prophet of scientific racism," argued against immigration from Southern and Eastern Europe and for eugenics.[21] Based on the popular notions of Social Darwinism, *The Passing of the Great Race* defended eugenics thus:

> Where two distinct species are located side by side, history and biology teach that but one of two things can happen; either one race drives the other out, as the [Euro-]Americans exterminated the Indians, or as the negroes are now replacing the whites in various parts of the South; or else they amalgamate and form a population of race bastards in which the lower type ultimately preponderates.[22]

Grant's calls for racial segregation and eugenics competed with the views of Franz Boas who, in the early twentieth century, placed as much faith in "science and reason to benefit humankind and transform the world" as did Grant. Boas admitted that many proponents of eugenics desired to advance humanity, but stated that their ideas remained unrealistic, primarily because biologists promoted them, and they did not understand the connection between biological truth and the human soul; only anthropologists could have that insight.[23]

Generations of the same family may exhibit the same traits, but that does not prove that those traits are genetic. Those qualities might be learned in infancy and childhood and thus if the child were raised elsewhere. Familial or racial tendencies, then, might spring from social, cultural, familial, and structural causes rather than from genetics. "'Nature not nurture,'" Boas complained, "has been raised to the rank of a dogma and the environmental conditions that make and unmake man, physically and mentally, have been relegated to the background."[24] Boas never implied that genetics played no role in human behavior, only that genetics could not be assumed to play the dominant role without scientific evidence supporting that assumption. "The first duty of the eugenist," he stated, "should be to determine empirically and without bias what features are hereditary and what not."[25]

Compare Boas's statements with the defense of eugenics found in *The Passing of the Great Race*, and we find two very different visions of white and non-white America, their relationship to one another, and the nation's position in relation to other cultures. And that tension, so present in the debate between Boas and Grant and their followers, was also present in tales of Indian captivity told at the time. This is demonstrated by the juxtaposing of images of the captives' "civilized" Indian descendants—for example, Slocum's and Jemison's descendants—with the reassuring incorruptibility of the captives themselves (i.e., Slocum and Jemison).

Allotment

Progressive Era captivity narratives also supported the government process of allotment and active "civilization" of Indians. Indian families who had not been moved to reservations or western "Indian territory" in the mid-nineteenth century were significantly more civilized than those "wild" western Indians, in part because of their proximity to "civilized" neighbors, and in part because of the land granted to those with white mothers or grandmothers. Owning land individually and not as part of a collective tribal holding had apparently helped to "civilize" Maconaquah's descendants. Hence, the story of her land grant by Congress appeared repeatedly in every retelling of her tale. Martha Bennet Phelps and John Meginness both dedicated a full chapter to the story of Maconaquah's grief over the removal of most of the Miami Indians from Indiana in the 1840's. They praised Maconaquah's white relatives, though, for seeing that Congress granted her full ownership of her land, allowing her to stay in her home. Dehgewanus (Mary Jemison), however, chose to sell her individually held land on the banks of the Genesee River and went to live on a reservation near Buffalo, New York. And, although one of her sons murdered two of his half-brothers, authors celebrated Dehgewanus's surviving children as "respected" and her grandsons as "esteemed" and generally highly respected by Indians and non-Indians alike.[26]

None of the stories published in the early twentieth century—from Maconaquah's, which told of a woman who stubbornly refused to leave Indian culture, to Mary Jemison's, which presented the tale of a woman who found the choice to stay with her captors complicated and difficult yet nevertheless made that choice, to Abbie Gardner-Sharp's, which told of a woman who longed only to leave Indian society—presented any evidence that isolation on reservations would successfully achieve Indian Americanization. These women's stories could be interpreted to suggest that eugenicists might have been correct in the assumption that a personal tendency towards virtue or vice could be inherited, but terribly wrong in their hypothesis that racial integration would corrupt all peoples. The story of Maconaquah's Indian–white family reiterated the notion that characteristics could be bred, but, contrary to worries posited by eugenicists (who were as confused about the link between genetics and culture as everyone else), "white virtues" did not become degraded or overwhelmed by the insertion of Indian blood into the family gene pool. The sustained contact between the Indian and white sides of the family lead (according to this interpretation) to the greater civilization of the Indian side; the white side did not decay. Acculturation through allotment and education was designed to transform Indian cultures and thus save Indians from extinction. Whites, meanwhile, could absorb enough "Indianness" through the occasional ceremony, memorial, or book to feel a connection to a continental history.

The theoretical underpinnings that placed cultural anthropology on one side and eugenics on the other held very real practical consequences as the federal government tried to decide what to "do" about its Indian "wards." In 1871, Congress had passed the Indian Appropriation Act, changing the status of the tribes from what Chief Justice John Marshall had formerly defined as "domestic dependent nations" to "wards of the state." Indian peoples throughout the United States were, then, although not citizens, politically a part of the nation of the United States, both as a group and individually, and thus no longer able to sign treaties with the country on their own behalf or (at least theoretically) defend themselves against U.S. armies. No longer politically separate, they nonetheless disrupted the homogeneous vision Americans then had of themselves by insisting on conceiving of themselves as separate. Twenty years after the Appropriation Act, the census had announced the frontier closed, and Indian resistance effectively died at the battle of Wounded Knee, ending the military conflict between the United States and its "wards." Although white America lamented the loss of the frontier and feared that there would now be no way to turn the flood of new immigrants into capitalist, Protestant Americans, it could now explore the nonthreatening, contained Indian as a welcome source of national renewal. Tales of Indian captivity presented the perfect opportunity to investigate the "tamed" Indian's connection to Americanism, since captivity stories told both of a white American ancestry *and* of an Indian national past. As historian Brian Dippie has explained, "Yesterday's warriors [turned] into immigrants in their own land, [and] the white man had discovered that they possessed something precious, something basic to the nation's identity." Indian captivity narratives allowed Progressive Era Americans to explore just what that "something" was and where it belonged in a post-frontier world.[27]

Although Indian captivity stories printed in the Progressive Era reiterated the terrors of kidnap by "savages," they did so almost exclusively in the passages reprinted directly from earlier periods, those unchanged older sections of the tale. The newly written parts of these narratives, which generally consisted of introductions, appendices, and transcripts of memorial services, almost uniformly ignored the horrors wrought on the pioneers by their

Indian foes. Almost all the modern additions to the tale of Mary Jemison's life, for example, left out any mention of her second husband's barbarity and bloodthirsty nature. Those who did mention that her youngest son murdered two other children often attributed this fact to ongoing land struggles exacerbated by bad management on the part of federal agents, rather than to a genetic predisposition to violence inherited from his father. Likewise, although Maconaquah (Frances Slocum) lived as an Indian for more than sixty years, at least fifty years of which she chose without overt compulsion by her captives (except that created by affection), her white relatives who told her story fixated on her retention of characteristics they attributed to "white blood."

The evolutionary model of social development that came to prominence in the 1880s, after the publication of Lewis Henry Morgan's *Ancient Society*, asserted that "the principle institutions of mankind originated in savagery, were developed in barbarism, and are now maturing in civilization." All races, then, reached toward the same goal of liberal democracy and economic capitalism. Those races (or societies) that had already achieved the final political and economic stages should care for and guide those races that had yet to move forward. The American continent was particularly lucky, Morgan argued, as it was "rich in" Indians, whose "human record" taught us not just of their history but of all human history. "The ethnic life of the Indian," Morgan wrote, "is declining under the influence of American civilization." Indians, then, were dying culturally and anthropologists needed to study them now, before they wholly disappeared. Moreover, while Morgan reminded his readers that "we owe our present condition [of civilization] to the struggles, the suffering, the heroic exertions and the patient toil of our barbarous, and more remotely, of our savage ancestors," he did not suggest that those dying Indian societies should be saved. Rather, he looked forward to an even greater stage of civilization that valued not just the accumulation of property but "democracy in government, brotherhood in society, equality in rights and privileges, and universal education." This process, he argued, from "the arrow head . . . to the smelting of iron ore . . . to the railway train" and then into a more equal future "may be called the triumph of civilization."[28]

In this theoretical context, politicians, Indians themselves, and the self-named "friends" of the Indians all struggled with the question of the place Indians would have in a modern America. In 1887, with Indians now contained on reservations and no longer a military threat, a new policy surfaced with the intention of full Americanization that would be complete only with the "total detribalization" of Indian individuals.[29] Indians would be rushed through the stages of social evolution, a procedure that meant both white-style education, cultural detribalization, and, when the individual was deemed capable, allotment of tribal lands into individual plots. At the end of this road lay full citizenship. The upshot of the whole process was twofold: first, when the process was completed, the federal government would be relieved of the tedious responsibility of caring for its Indian "wards." Second, once Indian land was allotted, all remaining tribal lands would open to white settlement. In practice, many white settlers, unwilling to wait the twenty-five year period that the Dawes Act envisioned, and impatient when 1912 rolled around and fewer than half of all Indians had been allotted, began settling on reservation land long before the completion of the process.[30]

The dual goals of land acquisition by whites and civilization of Indians did not fundamentally contradict one another, although sometimes they were at odds. By the time they became truly Americanized yeoman farmers, the reasoning went, Indians would also be so culturally indistinguishable from their white neighbors that the old land battle would cease to rage because the now ex-Indians would cease to care about their tribal rights. Because Indians' best interest lay in uprooting them from their land and culture, and because the country's best interest lay in creating "useful" land (i.e., individually held farms) out of perceived wilderness, Progressives sought to promote Indian prosperity and welfare by taking Indian land.[31] Removing Indians from their cultures and so altering them that they not only put on pants and hard-soled shoes but actually forgot that there existed an alternative, forgot that they had once commonly held the land they now lived on as individual proprietors—forgot, that is, that they were Indians at all—would benefit not only Indians, but also the whole country by providing the land necessary to turn new immigrants into Americans. Indians, immigrants, and native-born white Americans all, it seemed, required the seizure of Indian land and the Americanization of Indian peoples.

Maconaquah had already achieved the landholding phase of this process and so, by implication, her descendants had absorbed that part of the lesson of civilization. In 1845, in response to the 1840 removal of the Miami tribe to Kansas, Maconaquah appealed to her white brothers to save her family from the same fate. The appeal to Congress asked that Maconaquah and twenty-one Indian "children and grandchildren . . . and such children as they may hereafter have" be allowed to stay in Peru, Indiana, and "hereafter receive their annuities at Fort Wayne, or at Peru Indiana," whichever was most convenient. The petition gave several good reasons why the now-old woman should be allowed to stay in her current home. First, of course, she was white and, after having been taken captive at six years of age, she "heard nothing of her white relatives and friends" until about 1838. This statement was actually not true, as several times in the narrative of her story Martha Phelps, and Maconaquah herself, stated that she knew her brothers were searching for her and that she actively hid from them. However, given her reunion with her white relatives, she "would deplore the necessity of being placed beyond the reach of" them. Moreover, her children "reside upon and cultivate" her land. Alphonso A. Cole, Maconaquah's lawyer, sent the petition to Samuel C. Sample, her representative in Congress, and included a letter with the petition arguing that her Indian relatives were "respectable, honest, and, for Indians, uncommonly industrious people, and, in every sense of the word, good, orderly citizens." Cole also reiterated Maconaquah's precarious double-identity, stating "I have no doubt she would more willingly meet death, than either to be obliged to remove . . . beyond the reach of her white relatives, or to be left here alone by her Indian relatives." She herself would rather die, then, than be parted with either side of her family; moreover, her Indian children and grandchildren would not be a bother to any whites who moved into the area because they were, "for Indians," so far along the social evolutionary scale. Congress adopted the resolution with little discussion but added to it the stipulation "that if any of the aforesaid Indians shall hereafter remove to the reservation of the Miamis west of the Mississippi, no portion or share of such annuities shall be paid." These highly "civilized" Indians, then, because of their relationship to the white woman, could live as individual landholders among the white population, but if they preferred to be among Indians, they would lose the money the government paid to them for being Indian. Embracing their Indianness would cost them the one privilege it afforded them in American society. By including a full chapter explaining the land grant as well as the Congressional documents in her editions of Maconaquah's story, Martha Bennet Phelps, granddaughter of one of Maconaquah's white brothers, reminded both the white and Indian side of the family that the Slocum Miamis belonged to modern America and not to their barbarous Indian friends. The allotment process, then, beginning in this case in as early as 1845, was the best course the government could take in regard to their Indian wards.[32]

In addition to speaking for government policy, most captivity narratives also emphasized the development by which the captive became the archetypal American. Both Meginness and Phelps asked readers to remember Maconaquah as a symbol of a glorious national struggle, as a person whose life was torn asunder and recreated by circumstances of national history (the America Revolution), but whose natural values of hard work, love of land, connection to family, and dependence upon oneself sustained her through hardship and led her Indian captors to admire and revere her. Furthermore, she passed those traits on to her children and grandchildren, and the family grew increasingly more acculturated, proving that Madison Grant's fears of race degeneration from inbreeding were unfounded, and verifying the legitimacy of the federal government's project to Americanize and absorb native peoples and new immigrants alike.

In the early twentieth century, Maconaquah's white and Indian relatives continued to live in both Indiana and Pennsylvania, and at least one hundred people claiming kinship arrived at her memorial celebration. The narratives by both Phelps and John Meginness, the memorial celebration, and the memorial itself all presented her story as that of the Great American Past. "Frances was of English descent," Martha Phelps wrote, "an American by birth, and her fate was a result of the Revolution. For this cause she is sacred to its Sons and Daughters."[33] Like Mary Jemison, who was born on the boat between the "old" (Irish) world and the "new," and the 1862 Dakota captive Minnie Buce Carrigan, who was born in Germany yet had siblings born in the United States, Frances Slocum "became" American by "becoming" Indian.

Race Contact in Captivity

In the 1891 version of the Slocum family saga, author John Meginness repeated Maconaquah's stated reason for not returning to white society, even when begged by the Slocums: "It is very easy," the old woman said, "to make an Indian out of a white man, but you cannot make a white man out of an Indian." Maconaquah's suggestion, of course, was that she, by her chosen life with her captives, had become Indian and that the transition to that identity had been relatively easy. In other words, culture was something you chose, not something handed to you by blood, at least if that process occurs in youth.[34]

Maconaquah's remark, of course, presents a particular problem that Americans faced in the early twentieth century, and that Americans continue to confront today. The attempts of the allotment policy, boarding schools, and missionaries to "kill the Indian and save the man" implied that all Indian characteristics could be unlearned through education and close contact with white Americans, an idea that also was supported by the repetition of the good, "civilized" qualities of the Indian offspring of Jemison and Slocum. Americans then, as now, confused race, ethnicity, and culture, often using "white" and "civilized" interchangeably to mean "good" and "red," "Indian" and "barbarous" interchangeably to mean "bad." Even those scientists most able to understand the issues of race and culture confused the two, and Franz Boas at one time suggested that intermarriage between whites and Indians would solve the "Indian problem." What Maconaquah suggested was that Indians were genetically predisposed to reject "white" cultural characteristics such as the Protestant work ethic, thrift, and private property ownership. If this were the case, then, perhaps Indians *were* inferior, with smaller brains less capable than whites of complex theory and morality. It might also suggest, however, that Indians simply required a longer period of contact to become culturally "white." It would make perfect sense, in that context, that the captive Jemison or Slocum would prefer Indian life, but that their children and, even more so, their grandchildren would prefer "white" culture.[35]

Which collective or individual qualities and tendencies might be passed on through blood (genetics) and which were acquired as learned behaviors? This question was the fundamental question in the study of race and culture in the early twentieth century, and most Americans remained content to pretend the problem did not exist. Women like Jemison and Slocum did not, of course, become physically Indian, but they did become culturally Indian. As historian Tom Holm has stated, because Americans in the early twentieth century "could no longer justify" past treatment of Indians yet also could not "bring [themselves] to fully admire them," they "[held] completely conflicting views" about race and culture. In the case of Indian captives who had assimilated into Indian society, authors of captivity narratives and speakers at ceremonies honoring the captives presented a conflicting and confusing image of a woman who chose Indian culture, retained the "white" characteristics that marked her as fundamentally more "civilized," and produced children and grandchildren who took up white ways and characteristics but who still chose to identify themselves as Indian and tribal. It is an unwieldy representation, one that suggests that those characteristics deemed "good" are genetic. Therefore, they do not decay in the face of white acculturation into Indian societies and are able to be passed on to offspring through "blood." Those "bad" characteristics, captivity tales suggest, are learned and therefore temporary. "Red," then, is a surface level identity, a cultural varnish painted over the real "white" person inside the captive.[36]

Maconaquah's statement about the ease with which she turned into an Indian, however, did not appear in any of her stories after 1898, although others of less dramatic, though similar, sentiments did. More often, twentieth century versions of the tale presented the story of a gradually "whitened" and "civilized" Indian family, one that should not be feared as a source of barbarity but that could stand as an example of successful racial uplifting. Again, the implication was that cultural characteristics or tendencies (at least the "bad" Indian ones) could be altered. The Frances Slocum narrative examines not only this individual choice but also the generational modification within one family. All versions of the narrative tell of Colonel Ewing, who first discovered Maconaquah's white identity. Ewing reminded the Slocum family several times that she was, although "by long habit" an Indian, at least a "better sort," by which he meant respectable, hardworking, honorable.[37] Her "white blood" had won out, preventing her from moral degradation even as she "went" and remained culturally native. What is more, the insertion of her "white blood" into the Indian family, authors of her story claimed, contributed to, even caused, the wealth, morality, Christianization and overall integrity of her Indian offspring.

This tale substantiated beliefs that whites would not be degraded by contact with other races, and that the project of actively "Americanizing" Indians could prove effective. The story did not suggest that Indians, at least those of mixed blood, were poised to physically die out, as generations of Euro-Americans had posited, but rather that they would naturally assimilate into mainstream American culture if they maintained close and consistent contact with white America. Although Osawshequah (sometimes spelled Ozahshinquah), Maconaquah's youngest daughter, "was always a thorough Indian and never learned to speak the English language," nonetheless, "Indian habits and superstitions were largely banished from her mind" once she accepted Christianity.[38] Indeed, all of Maconaquah's offspring became Protestant. The Slocum and Jemison tales and memorials did not hint that cultural assimilation would result in cultural death for Indians or the degradation of whites, but rather that Indians could both become "American" and remain "Indian," while whites would become better Americans by remembering and valuing their ancestors who "went Indian." Ceremonies and the printed narratives reminded audiences and readers of the connection between Indians and white Americans. Here was the national story on a local scale. At the Mary Jemison memorial ceremony, after all, Arthur C. Parker, a highly educated and "civilized" yet culturally intact Indian, addressed the crowd on the admirable aspects of Seneca society. The best qualities of each race, in a family like the Slocums, united to create a unique and strong "American," and any alterations that individuals had to go through to become American, while sometimes painful, were for the best.[39]

Playing Indian

The turn of the twentieth century saw a shift in the cultural presentation of Indians from hostile savages to benign, even beneficial, national ancestors. This change came about in response to both the "taming" of violent Indians with the end of the Indian Wars on the now closed frontier, and the "perceived crisis in national identity triggered by 'new' immigrants."[40] As proto-Americans, Indians found themselves in a curious place in twentieth century mainstream culture as both disqualified from, and essential to, the sustainability of that culture. Excluded from citizenship unless they could prove themselves appropriately "American" in behavior, Indians found themselves at once *of* the land but not *of* the nation—American in the most fundamental sense and yet completely foreign. In this role, although generally agreed (by non-Indians, at least) doomed to die away, they deserved credit for their part in nation-building, for being gracious enough to be the ones who helped make Europeans into Americans.

"Playing Indian," as the colonists who in 1773 dressed as Indians to protest British rule in the Boston harbor had proved, became a way of "playing American" and distinguishing oneself from one's European origins.[41] "American" was something native-born Euro-Americans, Indians, and immigrants alike chose by behaving in prescribed ways, and the ultimate proof of that choice came in displaying it to others. Indian captives, whether they lived with their captors for a day or for their whole lives, "played" Indian, and thus American, better than perhaps anyone else in the country. By exhibiting that role in the form of ceremonies and memorials, their descendants could prove their transformation from Europeans to Americans through "Indianness."

Americans exhibited their historic sensibilities in a number of ways, including historic pageantry, Civil War memorials, and Indian memorials. David Glassberg has noted that "amid a burgeoning multiplicity of external connections and internal divisions" that grew in small towns in the Progressive Era, "the town's unique identity and role as a social unit . . . required redefinition."[42] Civic and social leaders used connection to frontier America, and the memory of contact with historical Indians, to effect that redefinition, both in stone and in print. Indian captivity memorial ceremonies, and the narratives that were reprinted with the transcripts of those ceremonies, claimed historical importance for the town or area they were connected to, but perhaps more importantly, they claimed future importance as well. At the memorial celebration of the Spirit Lake Massacre memorial, enacted by and printed by former captive Abbie Garner-Sharp, on July 26, 1895, nearly 5,000 people gathered in Arnold's Park, Iowa. R. A. Smith told this crowd that while the memorial stood mainly to remember "the unfortunate victims" of the massacre, it also, "expresses the hopes and aspirations of untold generations yet to come."[43]

But neither Maconaquah nor Dehgewanus cared to exhibit herself at all, nor had either allowed herself to be "redeemed" by her white relatives during her lifetime. Their stories were taken and written by others, and both actively resisted redemption. Dehgewanus went so far as to hide in the woods from her own Indian family (some of whom considered ransoming her to white "redeemers") rather than return to white society, and Maconaquah did not reveal herself to the white world until she believed she was dying. Both women simply *were*, in their own minds at least, Indian. Dehgewanus apparently struggled with her own identity more than Maconaquah did, and even named her children after her lost white relatives. In the end, though, she chose her Indian identity, and even went so far as to abandon her 2-mile plot and cabin and follow her adopted people onto the reservation.

The job of redemption, then, fell to descendants of the white side of each family many years later. It must have seemed important, indeed vital, to those descendants to hold such a display on behalf of their "Indianized" relative for the same reason that many redeemed white captives wrote their own stories in the first place. By taking Dehgewanus's body away from her reservation grave and burying it at the site of her privately held plot on the Genesee River, William Letchworth publically demonstrated that she was American, not Indian—that her body belonged on her land, not on the Seneca's communal land. Years after her captivity, and even after her death, Letchworth redeemed the White Woman of the Genesee. She was, after all, referred to as the "White Woman of the Genesee," not the "White Woman of the Seneca."

Throughout American history, some non-Indians had found Indian societies more satisfying than white society. Those genuinely Indianized whites, the so-called "White Indians," created problems for the American national story of conquest and superiority. In 1753, Benjamin Franklin commented on the difficulty of redeeming white captives, complaining that they were always "escaping again into the woods."[44] Those successfully redeemed white captives remained under suspicion for the rest of their lives, and many went to great pains in their narratives to prove that they had not "gone native," or, if they had, it had been a "rational ruse" to lessen their own suffering.

Charles Dennis Rusoe d'Eres, for example, captured by Canadian Indians at the age of fourteen, noted in his 1800 narrative that he watched in horror as his captives slaughtered enemies in battle and drank their blood. When pressed to join them in the rite, he "scoop[ed] up blood into my hands and daubed it over my mouth and face, to make them believe I drank it; they then said I was a good man."[45] Likewise, John Dunn Hunter, who had been captured by the Kickapoo as a toddler and adopted wholly and willingly into the tribe, still felt it necessary to remind his readers that, although he had taken one scalp during his near-twenty-year captivity, he did so only "with great repugnance."[46] Mary Rowlandson also noted that during the first week of her captivity, she could barely eat anything, since she found Indian fare revolting, calling it "revolting trash," but by "the third week [the food was] pleasant and savory to my taste." Later, she actually snatched food from a child's hand, "and it was savory to my taste."[47] The adoption of some Indian characteristics, these captives had argued, occurred out of desperation, such as developing a taste for Indian food after a period of starvation, and the experience had often been so foreign and unnatural that the captive never psychologically recovered from the trauma. Some redeemed captives, such as Abbie Gardner-Sharp, played that damaged role for the rest of their lives. Genuinely unapologetic "White Indians" such as Maconaquah went "against the 'natural' flow in the triumphant telling of the history" of the United States in particular and European races in general. As a result they were often "portrayed as idiosyncratic individuals and historical oddities, or, alternatively, as despicable and immoral renegades."[48]

The white Indians that Progressive Era audiences celebrated certainly did not present captives like Maconaquah and Dehgewanus who "went Indian" as oddities, as immoral, or as "becoming Indian" to lessen their suffering. Rather, exactly the opposite vision was portrayed: authors and eulogizers reminded audiences of the dignity involved in the captives' choice, and the morality of their lives and the lives of their children. A short retelling of Frances Slocum's story, published in 1900, stated that "her life was not one of hardship or suffering," in terms similar to those Arthur Parker had used to defend the dignity of Dehgewanus's life at the statue dedication. Both narratives suggested that Miami life was not as bad, perhaps, as many believed it to be, and that a white girl would have good reasons for choosing it.[49]

Likewise, in 1891 John Meginness claimed "there is nothing in the annals of Indian history more pathetic and impressive than the story of the captivity, life, wanderings, and death of Frances

Slocum," but this statement did not make it into later versions. Meginness had, in 1891, stated that Maconaquah's "hesitancy and . . . extreme caution" when telling her story for the first time "shows how she had been taught by the Indians to keep her secret, and made to believe that if her friends among the white people came to know of her existence, they would come and tear her away from her *true* friends."[50] Such teaching was, he said, quite "pathetic." Martha Bennet Phelps, writing her version of the story twenty years later, came to a very different conclusion. Although she also deemed it "pathetic" that Maconaquah had carried her secret all her life, and although Phelps's version was mostly a copy of Meginness's, she did argue that Maconaquah was disinclined to reveal herself to her white relatives because of the "fear that she might be taken from her children."[51] So, whereas in 1890 Meginness was blaming Indian trickery and deceit for Maconaquah's choice to "go Indian," by 1906 Phelps was attributing Maconaquah's choice to her motherly instincts and her genuine affection for her Indian family. This shift reflected the growing belief in the legitimacy of the choice to "go Indian." Phelps did not suggest that it was always a happy choice, of course, but that when forced, Maconaquah made the choice herself and was content with it.

We can see this shift even more clearly when we compare George Peck's 1858 version of Maconaquah's story with Meginness's and Phelps's stories. Both Meginness and Phelps cited Peck, to the effect that in 1851 "she looked like an Indian, lived like an Indian, seated herself like an Indian, ate like an Indian, lay down to sleep like an Indian; she had no longings for her original home." The Slocum family could rejoice, Peck said, that "they had found their long-lost sister," but they lamented that "they had found and left her Indian, with almost every trace of Christian civilization erased, both from her soul, body and being." She had, then, through her life with the Miami, ceased to be culturally "white" and became culturally "Indian." Somewhat problematically, Peck went on to say that "Anglo-Saxon blood had not been tainted . . . but bore itself gloriously amid the long trials through which it passed." Obviously, Phelps and Meginness remained as confused in the Progressive Era as Peck had been in 1858 about the link between personal character, learned cultural traits, and "blood."[52]

John Meginness quoted Peck almost word-for-word, in both the declaration that Maconaquah had not been "degraded," and in the lamentation that she had "gone Indian," adding a brief explanation for her Indianness: "And yet," he said, "after her long captivity, what other condition could we have expected?" After all, "association, influence, and daily teaching mould the mind, warp the judgment, and, if bad, destroy moral sentiment."[53] Peck, then, had failed to explain how her "blood" kept her in some ways culturally white, but Meginness, writing 32 years later, explained that her descent into Indian identity was a cultural, rather than a biological, movement from one society to another. In this way, her moral center, dictated by "blood" or genetics, could remain untainted and unchanged, while her cultural self changed quite dramatically. This vision of Maconaquah's Indianness and whiteness reveals a complex and highly contradictory set of images, both in 1858 and in 1890. Meginness told his readers that Maconaquah was an Indian but that she "had not been tainted"; her judgment and morals had been "warp[ed]," yet she had not "degraded."[54] These contradictions revealed Meginness's attempt to come to terms with what race, genetics, and culture meant in 1890, and exposed quite a bit of wishful thinking. Written immediately after the Dawes Allotment Act, and published in the same year as the Wounded Knee Massacre that marks the end of the Indian Wars, Meginness's narrative represents the extended moment when Indians ceased to be a threat but had not yet become benign. The government policy of acculturation was also clouded by these confusions.

By the 1906 publication of the narrative, Phelps felt much more comfortable arguing that her great-aunt had not been tricked or coerced into becoming Indian, but rather that she had chosen her lot (with all its accompanying disadvantages) as a willing adult. Phelps also quoted Peck that Maconaquah "thought, felt and reasoned like an Indian" and that she "could only breathe freely in the great unfenced out-of-doors which God gave to the Red Man." Phelps did not attempt to hide the extent to which her ancestor had been assimilated into Miami culture, or the affection she held for her Indian friends; Phelps also did not place blame for that assimilation on Indian coercion. Although Phelps had copied much of Meginness's narrative verbatim or in simple rearrangements of his paragraphs, she did delete his statement that Maconaquah could not help becoming something of an Indian because of the "association, influence, and daily teaching" of her captors. It is interesting, then, that while Phelps continued to credit Maconaquah's "white blood" with keeping her moral and to some extent civilized, she also did not take the decision to "go Indian" fully out of Maconaquah's own hands. Phelps's implication was clear: having superior racial "blood" meant that she also would have had the ability to choose a different way of life and not be totally "degraded" by the choice. Phelps also left out Meginness's very clear statement that she had been *forced* to stay with her captors well into adulthood. After recounting the numerous times Maconaquah herself stated her satisfaction with her Indian life, Meginness had gone on to say that "the statements of Frances seem to convey the impression that she was not always satisfied with her captivity, notwithstanding her declarations to the contrary."[55] Phelps did not imply that Maconaquah's own words were not to be trusted. By 1906, Phelps was quite satisfied with Maconaquah's defense of her own happiness and deleted Meginness's clumsy analysis of the "impressions" created by Maconaquah's statements.

The case of the" Indianization" of Mary Jemison was a bit more complex and problematic. While the Miamis took Frances Slocum when she was only five years old, Mary Jemison, later Dehgewanus, was fifteen at the time that the Senecas took her, and she never quite made peace with the two competing cultures in her life. While she refused several times to return to white society, she did name her children after her lost white family members. In 1759, four years after her captivity and a year or so after her first Indian husband died, a Dutchman tried to carry her off by force to get the bounty offered for the return of white captives. When she refused to go, her Seneca brother defended her by stating that he would rather kill her than have her forced into a life she did not submit to. No author of the Jemison narrative commented on the irony of this statement, given how she came to live with the Seneca in the first place, but Dehgewanus apparently believed he meant it. She fled with her young son, then just over a year old, and hid in the long grass by a river until the Dutchman gave up and she no longer faced the danger of a forced redemption or her brother's defense against it. The possibility of redemption for Mary Jemison came again at the end of the Revolutionary War when the same Seneca brother offered her another chance to leave voluntarily. She, however, would not leave without her grown son Thomas, and she would not take her younger children into the white world to be despised for their racial makeup. Hence, after considering the matter, "I told my brother that it was my choice to stay and spend the remainder of my days with my Indian friends."[56]

Far worse in the eyes of some Progressive Era authors than her choice to remain Indian, though, was Jemison's defense of second husband Hiokatoo. Although June Namias believes the information on Hiokatoo and the long chapter on him was mostly made up, readers of the Jemison narrative would have had little reason to question her honesty in calling him a great warrior.[57] She repeated often that he was excessively kind to her, and "never offered" her "an insult." Kind as he was to her, though, he was a warrior, and "his cruelties to his enemies perhaps were unparalleled, and will not admit a word of palliation."[58] His cruelty in and obsession with war began early in his childhood and became more pronounced as he got older. In spending his life focused on the art of war, he "blunted all those fine feelings and tender sympathies that are naturally excited by hearing or seeing a fellow being in distress."[59] Dehgewanus did not attempt to apologize for or explain away her husband's barbarities, and she told them readily. They included dashing out the brains of infants, burning women and children alive, and cannibalism. Indeed, she seemed to take some pleasure in recounting his violent acts. Her son Thomas, the son of her first husband, was by nature good and kind, but Hiokatoo's boys, especially John, turned out quite wild and just as violent as their father. John, in fact, in a series of violent, alcoholic rages, murdered both his brother Jesse and his half-brother Thomas.[60]

Those in the late nineteenth and early twentieth centuries who memorialized Mary Jemison, or included her story in anthologies of Indian histories or histories of New York State, hardly mentioned Hiokatoo at all. William Pryor Letchworth's editions of Seaver's original 1824 narrative are the exception, primarily because Letchworth published the narrative word-for-word, adding relevant appendices, but not changing Seaver's text. But others left Hiokatoo out or significantly minimized his importance. He was simply too wild, too barbaric. Jemison's marriage to him, and particularly her apparent pride in his violence, was simply too problematic. John Meginness (one author of the Frances Slocum narrative), who must have been familiar with Hiokatoo's character, gave him one brief mention in *Otzinachson: A History of the Western Branch Valley of the Susquehanna*, stating only that Mary Jemison married him in 1763 and they lived "in happy wed-lock for forty-eight years." In the 1880 *History of Wyoming County* he is mentioned as being cruel, but all the details of his atrocities, to which the Seaver narrative (originally of 1824) dedicated the better part of fourteen pages, were missing. Neither of these histories mention son John's character or the murders that took place within the family. A short article in *The American Monthly Review of Reviews*, 1907, said only that Dehgewanus "became the wife of ... the most blood-thirsty of all the Indians." Nonetheless, "she spent forty years with Hiokatoo" and "declared ... [that] he had uniformly treated her with tenderness." In 1913, *The American Antiquarian and Oriental Journal* declared "although [Hiokatoo was] a man of jealous and disagreeable disposition, he became her efficient protector for forty-eight years." In marrying Hiokatoo, Grace Taft suggested, Dehgewanus gained protection rather than genuine affection.[61]

The only author to explore Dehgewanus's affection for Hiokatoo in any real depth drew a quite harsh conclusion about her character, deciding, as others had, that her "blood" was the key to her personality. In his 1907 *Historical Sketches of Western New York*, Elisha Vanderhoof wrote that because of Jemison's love for a savage husband, "the attempts that have been made to treat her as a heroine and model worthy of imitation are not well advised." After all, he argued, "she was ... a generous, plucky, little Irish peasant woman who loved a fight as dearly as any of her countrymen." As such, she "extolled the good qualities of the red-handed fiend," and even her conversion to Christianity, which occurred when she was 91, "may be taken at any valuation the reader chooses to put upon it." It is clear what value Vanderhoof put on it.[62] Vanderhoof, then, a founding member of the Holland Society of New York, a society of the descendants of Dutch settlers of New York, focused his blame for Jemison's Indianization not just on the Indians who captured her, but on her own objectionable Irish tendencies.

The desire not to have Euro-Americans "go Indian," and a wish to redeem lost relatives posthumously, did not mean that there was no place in the Euro-American story for "Indianness." Rather, there was a very important place in post-frontier America for Indian stories. "It was hoped," historian Alan Tracthenberg has explained, that Indians, "would leave something of themselves behind, not merely their bones but also their spirit and their virtues."[63] Modern American society could learn a great deal from Indians, and that post-frontier society would be made stronger, indeed made more "American," by retaining contact with Indians through the study of history, the publication of pioneer accounts—including captivity narratives—and the erection of monuments that reminded viewers of their national bond to the continent's aboriginal inhabitants. Anthropologist Lewis Henry Morgan argued as early as 1851 that Americans could learn something valuable from Indian virtues and particular social arrangements, and that they could serve as a critique of the "unmanageable power" of the "outgrowth of property" brought by modern society that was later echoed by Frederick Engels.[64] Americans in the Progressive Era discovered, in large part through the works of thinkers like Frederick Jackson Turner and Theodore Roosevelt, that its national characteristics came from the wilderness experience and from, as the Mary Jemison memorial ceremony reminded its audience, "that great historical period in which the Caucasian met the aboriginal American and struggled for control of a continent."[65] In order to retain the unique and special "Americanness" developed through that meeting and struggle, the echo of it would need to reverberate in the national mind, not just to emphasize who won "control of the continent," but to refresh the qualities they had adopted from those peoples they had defeated.

Harnessing Indian Qualities

The perceived value of contact between whites and Indians shifted after the closure of the frontier. If, as Frederick Jackson Turner posited, European immigrants needed contact with the wilderness and natives in order to become Americans, so Indians in the twentieth century required, many believed, contact with the white world in order to become Americans. Memorials to captives and reprints of captivity tales thus served a dual purpose: to make Americans out of Europeans by allowing them to "go Indian," and to make Americans out of Indians by assimilating them into Euro-American culture. White captives provided a vital link to a traditional American heritage lost with the end of the frontier but still deemed necessary to the American mind.

Americans got something besides a few good qualities from the historical presence of Indians. Both the wilderness itself and the native inhabitants of that wilderness signaled to Americans that their country had an ancient history as impressive and important as that of Europe, so Indians could be seen as both "savages" in need of "civilizing" and "first Americans" to be incorporated into a national identity. During early contact and settlement of North American, Europeans "became" Indian because, as Frederick Jackson Turner put it, the harsh wilderness forced them to "accept the conditions" they found or "perish." Wilderness first took the European and "strip[ed] off the garments of civilization . . . array[ing] him in the hunting shirt and the moccasin." Later those same settlers (or their offspring) began to "little by little . . . transform the wilderness" and produce what Turner called "not the old Europe . . . [but] a new product that is American."[66]

Captain Richard H. Pratt, founder of the Carlisle Indian School, saw the fate of America's Indians in the twentieth century as reflective of the fate of the nation's immigrants. According to Pratt, Indians, like immigrants, required consistent contact with "real" America. It was, Pratt stated, universally acknowledged that immigrants only "gave trouble" to the country when they isolated themselves in neighborhoods populated by their own kind; only intentional and sustained integration could create Americans out of either group.[67]

White Indian captives, especially those redeemed to, or posthumously redeemed *by*, white society, embodied the Turner-Pratt process (Europeans becoming Indian followed by Indians becoming American) more completely than any other American. Mary Jemison, after all, was born in the transition from one country to another, and so was *of* neither Ireland nor the United States. Likewise, the German Buce family, whose daughter Minnie Buce Carrigan had been captured and held by the Dakotas for six months in 1862, had children born both in Germany and the United States. Her family was *of* both countries, or perhaps of neither. Frances Slocum's parents were English, their children were American, and their youngest daughter, of course, became Miami Indian. But, at least according to those who remembered them in the early twentieth century, these captives became completely and uniquely American by "going Indian." Certainly none of these women remained European.

The historical captives that Progressive Era Americans celebrated brought two distinctly "American" racial groups together as Turner's "new product," but of course neither Frances Slocum nor Mary Jemison were themselves this new product. Try as they might, their eulogizers could not erase the fact that both women believed themselves to be, and behaved altogether as, Indians. Maconaquah's objections to the prospect of becoming white again included, "Why should I go, and be like a fish out of the water," and "The Indians are my people."[68] And although Dehgewanus missed her white family enough to name all her children after them, she had at least two major chances to return to the white world, and she refused. And last, she refused to subject her mixed-blood children to what it would mean to be Indian in white America. In order to bring these captives back to white society, to "detribalize" them just as biological Indians were being "detribalized" through allotment and acculturation, many narrative authors and memorials emphasized their return to Christianity and, in particular, their Christian burials.

The Importance of Burials

Indianized captives' religious position at death became a central feature in white memories of them, as if the burial told more about the captive's real character than any of her behaviors in life. Maconaquah herself wrote no version of her tale, and, in fact, became highly suspicious when her long-lost relatives began to take notes on her story as she talked with them during their first meetings. Most of her narrative, written by John Meginness and Martha Bennett Phelps, consisted of the tale of her devastated mother, her endlessly searching brothers, and the letters of the white men, and occasionally women, who had contact with or knowledge of her. Maconaquah held her tongue. As soon as her white relatives found her, they tried to persuade her to return "home" with them. When she repeatedly refused, a nephew, the Reverend George Slocum, took his wife and two daughters to live with his Indianized aunt; he was so "impressed with the family's heathenism" that he lived with them for fifteen years, until his death in 1860, in order to Christianize them.[69] These white relatives became so entrenched in her Miami family's life, in fact, that Maconaquah passed her own name onto her George's daughter. And George Slocum did accomplish his goal. "Indian habits and superstitions [were] largely banished" from many of her Indian relatives. After George Slocum had been with the family for a number of years, her children and grandchildren came to live as active Christians (two sons-in-law even became reverends), but they did remain Indian "in [their] habits and manners." Yet the Frances Slocum memorial bragged that, although she "became a stranger to her mother tongue . . . [and] a stranger to her brethren, and an alien to her mother's children," nonetheless she "was given a Christian burial."[70]

Captivity narratives published in the Progressive Era wanted to remind readers and audiences that degeneration, either because of acculturation in the case of the captive, or because of "mixed blood" in the case any mixed-blood offspring, had not occurred. Even those tales that told of captives who produced no (known) children focused on the Christianization of the captives. In the 1904 introduction to Nehemiah How's narrative, Victor Hugo Paltsits, the State Historian for New York, reminded his readers that his colonial subject "belonged to a worthy family of Massachusetts Puritans" and that he "had behav'd himself as a Christian from his youth."[71] Likewise, in the 1903 introduction to the narrative of John Leeth, Reuben Gold Thwaites argued that the story of Leeth's 1793 conversion to Methodism held as much "historical interest" as his captivity did, and for similar ethnographical reasons: it revealed the "phraseology, psychological conditions and methods" of conversion. Conversion, Thwaites stated, was, after all, just as much a frontier experience as Indian captivity, and thus just as important to the American national identity.[72] The Christian burial served as evidence for Progressive Era Americans that captives had not "gone" completely Indian, and it also seemed to signal hope for their children. Mary Jemison's biographer, James Seaver, noted in great detail in the edition edited by William Letchworth in 1880, that Dehgewanus sought out missionaries just months before her death in September 1833 and "seceded from the pagan party of her nation and joined the Christian party," although Elisha Vanderhoof, of course, did not give her conversion much credit.[73]

The Perfect American

The whole point of the Jemison and Slocum memorials and the appendices of the Gardner-Sharp narrative was that the Indians were not dying out, and that, with the proper guidance, they would happily "yield" to mainstream American culture. Yet Rodman Wanamaker declared in his book *The Vanishing Race* that the memorial, which would stand in the New York harbor "where the red men first gave welcome to the white man," would celebrate the "memory of a noble, though vanishing race," and serve as "a token to all the world of the one and indivisible citizenship of these United States." Joseph Dixon was even more explicit: "The door of the Indian's yesterdays opens to a new world," he believed, "a world unpeopled with red men, but whose population fills the sky, the plains, with sad and spectre-like memories."[74]

After 1914, a combination of factors, including increasing press derision of the Wanamaker project and the distraction created by the Great War in Europe, made the national Indian memorial less appealing than it had been during its planning stages from 1909 to 1913. Rodman Wanamaker eventually abandoned the project, choosing instead to sponsor the full education of two Indian boys through high school and Princeton. Evidence that Indians had not, in fact, vanished apparently did not contribute to the decision to ditch the scheme, and it seems that the irony of abandoning a project to celebrate the vanished Indian in order to support living ones was lost on Wanamaker.

Although the national Indian memorial never materialized, a number of communities had by then created regional memorials of their own. In 1899, James F. Stutesman, a member of the Indiana State House of Representatives and future U.S. Minister to Bolivia, and at least eleven members of the Slocum family formed the committee to erect a monument not only to the family's "lost sister," but also to her Indian descendants. Gabriel Godfroy, son of Miami Chief Francis Godfroy and husband of Maconaquah's Indian great-granddaughter, appeared among the many speakers at the Slocum ceremony. Although discussion of his speech was absent in newspaper reporting on the event, he did speak to the crowd in both English and Miami.

The main event brought "more Indians together than have been assembled in this section at any one time since the Miamis held their powwows half a century ago," including about four hundred people "with a drop of Indian blood."[75] The *Peru Evening Journal* estimated attendance at between three and four thousand people, with more than one hundred direct relatives from Pennsylvania and Indiana; the *Wabash Times* claimed five thousand in attendance, and two hundred Indian and white relatives, and included with its article short biographies, paintings, and photographs of the

Indian side of the family.[76] Regardless of the actual number, the influx of people caused parking chaos, and Judson Bundy, who lived across the road from the cemetery where the ceremony took place, found his yard, barnyard, and orchard filled with horses and "his pockets . . . lined with silver."[77] Likewise, the morning following the official dedication of the Jemison statue, "an Indian dedicatory was held" that excluded white audiences.[78] Appendices to each subsequent edition or retelling of Frances Slocum's story revealed an increasing interest in the Indian side of the family, with growing lists of descendants and short biographies of living family members.

By pairing the stories (in print or in monument form) of white Indian captives with those of Indian descendants or participants, captivity tales indicated that racial contact and even mixing had been, and remained, an important part of what made Americans unique and strong. Most of the Miami Indians remaining in Indiana could trace their family connections to Maconaquah, and these Indian relatives of the "White Rose of the Miamis" found the white Slocum family fairly open, and taking not a little pride in the connection between Indian and white. The south face of Frances Slocum's monument reads, "She-po-con-ah, a Miami Indian Chief, husband of Frances Slocum—'Ma-con-a-quah,' died here in 1833 at an advanced age. Their adult children were: 'Ke-ke-nok-esh-wah,' wife of Rev. Jean Baptiste Brouillette, died March 13th, 1847, aged 47 years, leaving no children. "'O-zah-shin-quah,' or Jane, wife of the Rev. Peter Bonda, died January 25th, 1877, aged 62 years, leaving a husband and nine children." The other inscriptions on the monument point out Maconaquah's Christian burial and English descent. Together they complete a picture of the near-perfect American whose identity lay somewhere between the Indianized European and the civilized Indian.

CHAPTER 4

Character Building and the Manly Mother

The Spirit of President Roosevelt

"They stood for principle," the Reverend William Skinner Hazen told the crowd gathered on the green at Royalton, Vermont, on May 23, 1906. He spoke of the first 300 or so settlers of the town who together had suffered the burning of their town by a group of Kahnawake Indians and Englishmen in October 1780.[1] "With the courage of their convictions they were true to the highest type of manhood," Hazen went on, "they had the spirit of President Roosevelt."[2] Hazen's speech, along with the entire program from the unveiling of the Royalton memorial, appeared in print in the 1906 reprint of Zadock Steele's narrative. Captured during the burning of the town, the young New Englander Steele, then in his early twenties, remained with his captors for about a year, first as a prisoner and later as an adopted member of the tribe. He then spent another, much more horrific year (he claimed) as a hostage of the English before escaping with a group of other prisoners back to Vermont. Prior to the 1906 memorial celebration,

Steele's narrative had been published twice, once in 1818 and once in 1854; after 1906 it appeared in print two more times, making it one of the most republished male captivity narratives in the first twenty years of the twentieth century.

While speakers at the Royalton ceremony celebrated Zadock Steele, a man, and discussed issues of national manhood, those towns and people in the Progressive Era that celebrated local captives overwhelmingly chose *female* captives. Given that this kind of terminology and discussion of "manhood" and "manliness" appeared in all areas of American life at the turn of the century, we might expect to find numerous retellings of male captivity narratives. But, in fact, women's narratives appeared more often, and social commentators seemed to have had significantly more interest in the women themselves than they did in individual male captives of Indians.

While 1904, 1913, and 1915 all saw more than one male narrative come out in print, none, save that of Zadock Steele, was printed or published in more than one edition. By contrast, multiple editions of at least six female narratives appeared between 1885 and 1916. Moreover, no single male captive had a monument erected to him during this period, while at least two female captives (Maconaquah and Dehgewanus) did. While the stories of male captivity appealed to readers enough to justify their continued publication, it was the tales of particular female characters that caught and retained the interests of readers and publishers alike. In 1904, the Burrows Brothers Company, a Cleveland publisher, produced a series of "Narratives of Captivity." All four of the works in this series were male narratives, and make up almost a third of all male narratives published in the thirty years prior to U.S. entrance into World War I. What would account for the greater popularity of female captivity narratives?[3]

Some scholars have suggested that female narratives attracted a larger audience primarily because of the issue of sex.[4] According to this argument, women's narratives were fundamentally more appealing because the possibility of white female sexual encounters with native men was more titillating than the suggestion of white men having sex with Indian women. I do not want to downplay the ability of sexually proscribed subjects to attract an audience—indeed, they always have. However, given that most captivity narratives printed in the early twentieth century did not mention sex at all, and that all held up their protagonists as examples of virtue and moral judgment, something more complicated and probably less exciting than simply sex explains the greater prevalence of publication of captivity narratives featuring females. Francis Slocum (Maconaquah), after all, had two Indian husbands, marrying the second after the first left, and she voluntarily refused to go with her first husband. This made her technically guilty of polygamy—a fact that is not mentioned in any of the retellings of her tale. Rather, authors and eulogizers repeatedly portrayed Maconaquah as an ideal wife and mother.

The gendered message of Progressive Era captivity stories was that *women*, not men, were the most perfect embodiment of traditional American character because they were more naturally focused on the needs of the community. Progressive Era commentators fixated upon those captivity narratives which reminded readers that the moral virtue of the United States came from "manly" behavior (in the form of bravery and individualistic ambition) *and* from women (in the form of dedication to community).[5] "Manhood," in this context, became something that came not from one's *sex* but from one's *character*. Women could, of course, be turned away from that "highest type of manhood" by extreme individualism (i.e., untempered by community-mindedness) just as men could, and they, like men, needed guidance in developing the best character possible in order to steer them in the right direction in modern times. Reprints or new editions of, and memorials to, Indian captives served to remind audiences of the importance of character, and that the American character demanded individualism and community-mindedness. But in a modern world without a frontier to provide such experiences, female captivity narratives also presented a kind of voyeuristic character-building opportunity for post-frontier readers. Tales of captivity could accomplish this dual task because they included new material (appendices, introductions, full chapters, and texts of monument unveiling ceremonies) that directly linked those old stories to modern life, ensuring that readers properly interpreted the past and correctly applied its lessons to their modern lives.

The Manly Mother

Monuments took the process of developing American character one step further, guaranteeing that the message would endure for future generations. "Bronze or marble," Dr. George Kunz stated at the unveiling of the Mary Jemison monument, had value precisely because it "outlast[ed] the creature of flesh and blood."[6] He went on to explain why monuments had greater importance even than printed documents:

> Long after most of our political leaders and wealthy men have passed out of mind, this statue of Mary Jemison will stand here as a commemoration of an humble but striking figure of the past . . . [creating an] ever-present reality, as enduring as the bronze of which the statue is made.[7]

Historian June Namias has outlined three main types of white female captives that corresponded with stages in American history. The "Survivor," Namias writes of the Colonial archetype, is "the woman who experiences and feels a wide range of stress in, but ultimately adapts to, tries to make sense of, and comes to terms with her situation." The "Amazon" figure, who arose in the Revolutionary period, was "overtly racist and bloodthirsty . . . [and] not only defend[ed] [her] dwellings but often enjoy[ed] the gore and violence." The "Frail Flower" archetype that appeared in the 1830s and 40s, with the rise of sentimental fiction and notions of True Womanhood, was a "poor, hapless woman who [was] taken unawares . . . she rarely emerges from her shock, distress, and misery."[8] The narratives of this last type "include[d] brutality, sadomasochistic and titillating elements, strong racist language, pleas for sympathy and commiseration with the author's suffering, special appeals to her sad lot as a distressed mother."[9]

Early twentieth century narratives combined these three types—the Survivor, the Amazon, and the Frail Flower—into one more-cohesive vision of American womanhood, one that I am calling the "Manly Mother." The Manly Mother depended upon husbands, fathers, sons, and the military when she could, but willingly took the defense of her home and children upon herself when a male defender was absent, although her actions were often ineffectual or only partially effective. Frances Slocum's mother, for example, successfully appealed for the release of her twelve-year-old son; she apparently singled him out for release because she believed his lame foot would make him less useful as a captive, and therefore that her chance of making a successful plea for him was higher than with healthy Frances. She then had to watch helplessly while the Indians carried her shrieking five-year-old daughter into the woods. Frances Slocum's mother always lamented that she had let Frances go, and spent the rest of her life worrying that the child had been taken while wearing no shoes.[10] The Manly Mother was both horror-struck and strong, often damaged by her experiences, often wallowing in self-pity while being remembered for, and indeed often possessing, a rare strength or bravery in times of stress. The Manly Mother had more in common with the colonial "Survivor" than with the bloodthirsty nationalist who appeared during the Revolution or the Victorian "Frail Flower," but in a single story she might exhibit elements of all three. Abbie Gardner-Sharp, for example, suffered physically and mentally during her captivity, and the suffering crippled her for much of her life. But she later came to defend and actively campaign for Indian rights. She used the combined role of damaged victim and Progressive reformer to get the money she needed to support herself and her son, and to bring about the creation of a memorial that she needed to satisfy her damaged soul.

Most importantly, though, the Manly Mother—always slightly shocked by her own actions and usually tortured by them in retrospect—ultimately "did right" because of an internal morality that guided her actions. The true character of the Manly Mother was not always obvious until years after publication of her story. Abbie Gardner-Sharp, as we shall see, presented herself as the quintessential "Frail Flower," but her actions in adulthood portrayed a strong, resilient woman who, in fact, learned to use her "Frail Flower" persona to sell herself and her causes to the public. Progressive Era commentators saw that the example of the Manly Mother could be useful in their mission to foster internal morality in modern people. To accomplish this mission, Progressive Era captivity tales focused as much on the surrounding community and on events after the captivity itself as they did on any single captive.

On a national level, the Daughters of the American Revolution (DAR) set about commissioning a series of 12 commemorative statues which they first called the Madonna of the Prairie, and eventually renamed The Madonna of the Trail. In 1911, the DAR established the National Old Trails Road Association and worked "to carry forward its purpose of making the National Old Trails Road the National Highway." The National Old Trails Road Committee, composed completely of men and headed by future U.S. president Harry S. Truman, had "over 7,000 members and handles the business and practical side of the question while the Daughters of the American Revolution handle the historic and sentimental side." Eventually, the DAR would succeed in establishing the National Old Trails Road from Maryland to California. In each state along the route they would eventually place a statue of the Madonna of the Trail.[11] Elizabeth Butler Gentry, longtime president of the Women's National Old Trails Road Association, argued in 1913 that the statues were necessary because "history has failed to record the pioneer woman who braved the unknown wilderness; who reared her children, inspired her man, and planted the fruits of civilization on the frontier; the pioneer woman, the Madonna of the Trail, will take her place in history."[12]

The statue eventually chosen to depict the Madonna of the Trail showed a mother in mid-stride, wearing bonnet and boots, with an infant in her left arm, a young son clinging to her skirts, and a rifle clutched by the barrel in her right hand. Although not sculpted and erected until 1928 and 1929, this Madonna personifies the Manly Mother, but in the Progressive Era, when the Madonna of the Trail was conceived, she would find her most obvious representation in tales of women taken captive by Indians.

Abbie Gardner-Sharp

Dehgewanus (Mary Jemison), Maconaquah (Frances Slocum), and Abbie Gardner-Sharp, whose experiences provided three of the most often retold stories of female captivity between 1890 and 1916, all acted, either in tribal or white life, as businesswomen or respected community leaders. Yet, to be clear, none of these stories told the simple tale of a "strong" woman; rather, their stories paid close attention to their roles as beloved and devoted mother, rediscovered sister, damaged victim, and memorialized ancestor rather than those of a "lost" or fallen woman. In Frances Slocum's story, for example, Martha Bennett Phelps emphasized that separation from her tribe led to a depression that actually killed the old woman. In other words, even though she had become an Indian, she was still a woman so attached to her family that she was unable to handle the loss of them. One of Slocum's daughters, moreover, died of grief quickly after Slocum did. Tragic female emotion killed off two generations.

Perhaps the best example of this paradox between a traditional female role and the complex community leader is the story of Abbie Gardner-Sharp (Abbie Gardner at the time of her captivity, but Gardner-Sharp when she first published her narrative). As one of the few Progressive Era captivity narratives written by the captive and not a third party, Gardner-Sharp's book used her self-assigned role as a physically and psychologically damaged girl-victim to campaign for a memorial to the Spirit Lake Massacre victims, to lobby for the reform of Indian policy, to witness for Christian Science, and to sell her story and make money.

Abbie Gardner's story had its origin in the tale of the Spirit Lake Massacre of 1857, which was truly horrifying, and we can be sure that the experience did genuinely scar the girl, who was only 13 years at the time. The severe winter of 1856–57 had left both the white settlers of northwestern Iowa and the Dakota people also living there half-starved. In early March, the Indians, following Inkpaduta, leader of the Santee Sioux, arrived in the Okoboji Lake region, which lies just over 100 miles directly east of modern-day Sioux Falls, South Dakota. Anger quickly boiled into violence when the settlers refused to give the Indians food; in the ensuing carnage, the Dakota killed 33 white settlers and kidnapped four women and girls. They would kill two of their captives later that spring. One of the remaining captive girls was ransomed in April, as was Gardner-Sharp at the end of May, after a three-month captivity.[13]

Gardner-Sharp's narrative concentrated primarily on the stories of others, and in lamenting her miserable lot, and provided relatively few details about her own experiences, although she clearly outlined the moments when she suffered most, including every item in the pack she was forced to carry.[14] Although her account is short on some essential details, it is clear that Inkpaduta's group took Gardner-Sharp with them as they fled north and then west into the Dakota Territory. The bulk of Gardner-Sharp's narrative dealt more with what others did for her (how the Army discovered the massacre, and what actions they took to redeem her, and how her fellow captives died) than her own story. Most of her story, in fact, focused on what happened after her captivity ended. She added new chapters with each edition, updating readers on her life. By the 1910 edition, her post-captivity life had become the central story in her narrative.

More than almost anything else, her story bewailed her sad and lonely lot, making it a kind of literary self-flagellation as she dredged up every painful memory and relished reliving it (except, of course, when she took time out to explain how Christian Science healed the physical damage caused by the privation she suffered during captivity). "Misfortune," she wrote in the 1910 edition, "seemed to follow on my track." Gardner-Sharp recalled reuniting with her sister (who had escaped captivity or death because she was not at home at the time of the attack) for the first time after her redemption: "We met here as two torn, bleeding lambs, all that had escaped the wolf's devouring jaws. . . . We then realized that a dark shadow had fallen upon us."[15] In 1883, upon returning to the family cabin for the first time since the massacre, she experienced a frightening flashback that "came involuntarily before me, not as a picture in memory, but as a present reality. . . . The swarthy creatures seemed all about me, murdering, plundering, and ravishing."[16] Surely, this woman who, twenty-seven years after the event, recalled it so involuntarily and so vividly, was little more than the quintessential "Frail Flower"—or so she would have had her readers believe.

Understandably, the massacre became the defining moment of her life, and she became rather obsessed with the site of her family's slaughter and her own misery. Her fixation may have sprung from a legitimate attempt to understand her experiences and the loss of all her family and friends, but it may also have developed, at least in part, from a very pragmatic understanding that in the public fascination with her experience lay the only possibility for a divorced mother to support herself and her child.

Samuel Pillsbury purchased the Gardner family cabin and the land surrounding it in 1863. Upon the discovery that there were surviving Gardner family members, Pillsbury paid Gardner-Sharp and her sister a small restitution. Still, after a failed (probably abusive) marriage, the now-single mother struggled to support herself. She returned to the site in 1883 and set up shop beside what was now the Pillsbury cabin, selling copies of her self-published 1857 narrative to tourists. With the proceeds of the 1885 edition of her narrative, she purchased the cabin in 1891, and set about the project of commodifying the most horrific experience of her life, which had occurred 34 years earlier.

Gardner-Sharp and her son Allen turned the family cabin into a tourist attraction, selling copies of her narrative, Indian artifacts, postcards, her own paintings of the incident, and other remembrances of her captivity and her family's demise. She constructed an elaborate lattice around the building so that only paying customers could see the site; on the outside, a sign that spanned the whole length of the cabin read, "Within this lattice you see the sights of a *lifetime!!* The ONLY log cabin and historical relics of the Indian massacre of 1857." Gardner-Sharp told visitors that she had put up the lattice to protect the building, as relic hunters and vandals would have destroyed it. "But for that protection," she told Theodore Sutton Parvin during his visit, "The old log cabin would in a short time have been carried away." Inside, the paying customer would find "a sacred, shrine-like atmosphere" that presented the interior of the cabin exactly as it was on the eve of Inkpaduta's arrival. The only changes were the addition of a display case for the various knickknacks for sale and Gardner-Sharp's paintings of the incident on the walls.[17]

Despite being plagued by a series of mysterious ailments that she blamed on the exposure to cold, hunger, and hard labor suffered during her captivity, some of which made it periodically impossible even to sit up unaided, Gardner-Sharp gave lectures (sometimes from a chair), and wrote (with "a great deal of embarrassment") new versions of her book. Even before Christian Science cured her of these illnesses in 1889, she had begun to travel to reservations in the Dakota Territory, learning about present-day Indian life, supporting policies to Americanize and "civilize" natives, and lobbying the Iowa State government to appropriate funds for a memorial to the Spirit Lake Massacre victims. She successfully convinced the Iowa legislature to appropriate $5000 for a monument to the victims of the massacre. She served on the commission that oversaw the erection of the 55-foot obelisk beside the cabin.[18] During her travels, she was frequently asked to speak about her experiences, and she reminded readers that she was never prepared for such a request. At one point, she claimed to be so nervous that she "could scarcely utter a word," but

> with a faltering voice I related the story of the massacre, the fearful fate of the two captives put to death, and the subsequent rescue of Mrs. Marble and myself by friendly Indians. While I stood before them I exhibited the illustrations of the scenes that appear in this volume, together with the eagle-feather war cap.[19]

She sold two copies of her narrative that day. So, this woman, who described herself as demure, terrified, and periodically terribly ill, and claimed she sought no public attention, would proceed to whip out her paintings (which she apparently kept at the ready), tell the whole story, and make some money while she was at it. She became so accustomed to public speaking, in fact, that she spoke twice at the Woman's Building and once at the Children's Building during the 1893 World's Columbian Exposition in Chicago. Throughout all of this, only once in her narrative did she break her "Frail Flower" persona, when she stated that "this is woman's age," implying that women like her would exert even greater influence in the new century.[20]

Abbie Gardner-Sharp well understood the appeal she held for audiences, and she figured out that it depended upon her presentation of herself as the "Frail Flower." She used her position as a psychologically and physically damaged victim of massacre and captivity to campaign for causes she considered righteous, especially for "civilizing" Indian policies and a Spirit Lake Massacre memorial. As Greg Olson has noted, the image of Abbie Gardner-Sharp as the quintessential "Frail Flower" persisted despite the fact that she "was an extremely strong figure who crusaded not only to memorialize the Spirit Lake Massacre but also to 'reform' the Indian population through Christianity." Her victim image endured, not because of anything inherent in her story itself, but because Gardner-Sharp chose to advance herself as such. Maconaquah, who chose to stay with her Indian captors and never promoted or wrote her story for public consumption, would, of course, never have envisioned herself as a victim in this way (although she did seem to have some concern about becoming a victim of white anti-Indian policy). Gardner-Sharp, though, positioned herself as a Progressive reformer and as a national (or at least regional) moral guide, by marketing an embellished victim image of her own experiences.

From Gardner-Sharp's promotion of the memory of her tragic life, readers of the narrative and visitors to the cabin memorial would learn how to address their problems using the renewed characteristics Americans developed on the frontier. Gardner-Sharp discovered that her draw as a tourist attraction and her power to influence reformers and lawmakers came from her girl-victim persona, which allowed for her nontraditional behavior as a businesswoman, entrepreneur, and divorced mother. The very space in which she conducted her business—the pioneer cabin where her suffering began—confirmed that she was the living embodiment of antimodernism, her statement that the new century would become "the woman's age" notwithstanding. She surrounded herself with proof of her link to frontier tradition; even the lattice that enclosed her cabin served not just to keep out nonpaying visitors, but also to keep her inside a non-modern world. The visitor to her home could well imagine that the mother and son were left without a patriarch not through divorce (as was the actual case), but because he had been dragged off by the Indians still waiting outside the cabin to ferret out and carry away the rest of the family. It must have been rather spooky.

If captivity narratives and monuments allowed the public to experience something of frontier life, Abbie Gardner-Sharp's cabin must have been the most perfect place to gain an authentic frontier experience after the official end of the frontier. *The Midland Monthly Magazine* described a visit to her cabin in 1895. The "only survivor" of the Spirit Lake Massacre "lives in the cabin and relates incidents of the spectacle witnessed by her own eyes. Visitors to the cabin shudder at the narrative and for a moment realize the dangers encountered by the first settlers." Outside the cabin, though, visitors found "pretty woods" and "a resort for rest, health and pleasure . . . [that] cannot be excelled."[21] Twenty-four years later, in 1919, the monthly magazine of the Order of Railway Conductors included a letter describing a trip to the cabin. The author found Gardner-Sharp "76 years of age, rather feeble, but very spirited at times when relating her experiences with the Indians." The author and his traveling companions each paid 25 cents to enter the cabin and listen to the redeemed captive speak, and the author later bought "one of her linen-bound books at $1.50 relating the great Indian days of her career." He declared it "the greatest book value I've ever received—so different from most books of this nature, as it is gotten up with truthful intent."[22]

In about 1908, W. H. Steele and his wife Alice traveled to Spirit Lake and found Abbie Gardner-Sharp less willing to recount the massacre than the above visitors suggest. Steele and his wife described Gardner-Sharp as "a sweet-faced, gray-haired little lady, whose every feature tells the tale of sorrow and suffering through which she has passed." She displayed "a fine collection of Indian relics," and Steele managed to "gradually dr[aw] out her story," although other visitors to the cabin found her ready and willing to talk. The tenderness Steele had to employ, and the difficulty with which he convinced her to talk, implies that either she really did have days when the memories were too painful to talk about or she sometimes played the role of a reluctant narrator in order to draw her visitors into her story. Whatever the reason, Steele was highly impressed by the "quiet, sad-faced lady" as she "described the scenes of that March day," and "pointed out the place where each scene in the tragedy was enacted." While her demeanor hinted to Sharp that she was reluctant to discuss the event, she clearly had a standard speech and a practiced delivery of which that hesitant bearing might well have been a part.[23]

Her image as a living casualty of the clash between "civilization and savagery" allowed Gardner-Sharp to position herself as a bridge between traditional virtues and modern causes.[24] Gardner-Sharp consciously used her traditional persona as wounded daughter of America to justify her actions as a businesswoman and social campaigner; she also promoted herself as the living embodiment of the frontier traits that the country needed to preserve. Like the rhetoric that surrounded the monument at Royalton and the Zadock Steele narrative, the Gardner Cabin and Spirit Lake Massacre monument that Gardner-Sharp presented to the public served as a source of national renewal in the face of confusingly contradictory ideas about gender in the new century.

The Benefits of Individualism

The Progressive Era understanding of gender connected a tradition of individualism with what it meant to be a "real" man, and those who commented on tales of Indian captivity at this time found that they could use the tales to apply conservative masculine ideals to modern life. In particular, captivity tales as presented to early twentieth century audiences valued a pre-modern, sometimes even a colonial, tradition of masculinity that called for commitment to community needs rather than individual desires. Individualism in the industrial world had become threatening because it injured so many people, and many socially concerned Progressives began to look back to a pre-industrial definition of masculinity to find guidance about how to respond to the perceived present crisis and direct the future.[25] The memorials erected to captives between 1890 and 1916 told viewers that there was a different, more virtuous way of responding to modern conditions, that greed and too much ambition were un-American, and that virtue could be found by looking backwards.

Yet dedication ceremonies for captive monuments, and the impulse to erect monuments in the first place, reflected the modern sense that Americans could understand, address, and solve their modern problems. The "highest type of manhood" that William Hazen advocated made use of the modern faith in progress and science to understand and define the problems of a modern world and the ability of Americans to solve those problems by applying traditional behaviors and values to them.

Women, so captivity stories claimed, could embody that "spirit of President Roosevelt," as well as—perhaps even better than—men could. For one thing, the men in captivity stories were often immobilized fairly quickly, either killed or ferried away immediately. The women left alive, who later told the story, had taken on "male" characteristics of bravery, strength, and ambition in order to survive. They found they were rather good at adapting these characteristics. Women were also included in this Progressive Era definition of "manly" behavior because, by the turn of the century, most Americans saw gender as an incredibly complex entity where both sexes had male and female traits, instincts, and tendencies. The trick was to attain a proper balance. The runaway ambition and individualism that developed from a focus on money, business, and industry had ruined many men by enabling them to deny their "feminine side." Women also suffered from too much individualism, but theirs sprang from isolation in the home.[26]

Historically, American political individualism has stressed liberty and individual freedom, while economic individualism has meant a lack of government control on the national scale, and being "masterless" (i.e., self-employed) on the personal level. Manhood, as defined in America, has, for all the changes it has gone through, always struggled to find a balance between dedication to the needs of the community and to the wants of the individual, and some scholars have seen "individualism" as a euphemism for masculinity. Prior to the Revolution, social individualism conflicted with the obligations men were understood to have as the religious, economic, and social heads of their families, although individualism in spiritual conversion remained important. With the Revolution, the link between individualism and manhood became explicit, as individual liberty and personal freedom became the cornerstone of the new Republic's political vision—but, of course, only white men could participate politically, and so only white men could be whole individuals.[27]

In the nineteenth century, economic rather than political or spiritual individualism came to dominate the American. In this sense of individualism, "real men" found adventure on the frontier as they searched for riches, or at least some personal economic prospect. Thus, while Colonial and Early National notions of individualism condemned the search for wealth as a personal failing that threatened the unity of the community, during the nineteenth century this idea gradually reversed, as did concepts of masculinity. "Making it on one's own," "pulling oneself up by the bootstraps," and other such Horatio Alger-isms came to dominate ideas of manliness, and were especially connected to the frontier, and to "going west" to see what one could make of oneself alone. Likewise, during the nineteenth century, the individual, not the community, gradually began to be seen as the base unit for society; thus, individual greed and ambition, springing from a competitive spirit believed to be a fundamentally male characteristic, could actually be good for society. Women continued, in this perspective, to serve society by helping men find a balance between their own greed and the needs of society. A nineteenth century man, properly morally guided by a mother or wife, could use his natural instinct of competition to support the nation, indeed to make it a world economic power.[28]

And men did just that. Economically the United States thrived. Industrial output rose 500 percent in the last thirty years of the nineteenth century; in the same years, the nation's population doubled to 76 million. Miles of railroad during the same years jumped from 53,000 to nearly 212,000; the production of steel rose 145 percent; more than 500,000 new products received patents. Ambitious (white) men got rich in the years after the Civil War, and they had also changed the world around them.[29] Many saw this as proof that "manly" individualism worked; others saw that the benefits created since the Civil War had come at a great cost. These ambitious men had created a world that looked like them: "restless, insecure, striving, competitive, and extraordinarily prosperous."[30] By the turn of the twentieth century, even the most devotedly "manly" men (such as, of course, Theodore Roosevelt) began to see cracks in the notion of a "self-made" and selfish man. For one thing, few men, if any, had ever been "self-made," and even those who tried to claim the title began to lose their economic independence as more of them went to work for other men. Those self-made men of the nineteenth century had become the "robber barons" of the twentieth century who kept thousands of other men in wage-slavery and dependence.

Theodore Parvin, former secretary of the Iowa Territorial Council, lawyer, and active Freemason, spoke at the "Pioneer and Old Settlers' Day" in Burlington, Iowa, on October 2, 1896. In describing his first act of voting in the Iowa territory, Parvin became distracted from his historical topic and commented on the election of the day. "I will not cast my vote," he said, "for any man who . . . repudiates the national honor . . . by . . . seeking personal aggrandizement at the expense of the Nation." Apparently Parvin aimed his criticism at William McKinley and supported William Jennings Bryan. He concluded his speech by suggesting that McKinley was a "fierce demagogue" and that the "national honor" (a phrase he repeated several times) depended upon "payment of honest debts in sound currency." He compared the free coinage of silver fight to the Civil War, "another crisis, not of blood, but of fierce contention of the right against the seemingly wrong." His suggestion, of course, was that McKinley represented the selfish individual interests of what Theodore Roosevelt called "those artificial individuals called corporations," while Bryan defended the needs of the nation and of the "toiling millions in the fields, the work-shops, and upon the public highway."[31]

Middle-class Progressive Era men were becoming fearful of their place in a changing society because they felt their position threatened by the decline of that very same individualism that they had been using to define themselves. At work, apprenticeship declined and standardization of shifts, tasks, and tools increased, taking independence and control out of the hands of individual men and giving that control over to ballooning companies. Writers such as Horace Greeley lamented that wage labor degraded (middle-class white) men and left them emasculated, since it made them dependent upon another, just as women and children were dependent. Moreover, men in the twentieth century competed with the "New Woman," educated, independent, and spirited, for new white-collar jobs. Nationwide, in 1870, women numbered only 5 percent of stenographers and typists and a shabby 2.5 percent of all white-collar clerical workers. But by 1930, women made up a whopping 96 percent of typists and 52.5 percent of clerical personnel. The number of female workers in all industries rose less dramatically, but rose nonetheless. In 1870, 1.8 million women worked (or about 16 percent of the total workforce); thirty years later, the number totaled 5.3 million (20 percent of the workforce), and by 1930 women would make up some 50 percent of the total workforce. Some men, of course, applauded that "New Woman," believing that no society could be whole without true equality between the sexes, while other men rejected them outright and called for the complete return to a traditional domesticity.[32]

Because more men worked outside of the home, the vast majority of married women (who, despite popular fears, did not work) were left to raise children virtually on their own. The reality of sons living in predominately women-directed environments frightened many American middle-class men as much as the prospect of independent women working in large numbers; many men longed for the return to a traditional family arrangement that revolved around a homestead where both parents worked in partnership, rather than the situation of a male provider in perpetual, middle-management wage-dependency.[33]

The American understanding of gender connected with a tradition of individualism that has defined what it means to be "authentically" American. Gender historian Linda K. Kerber explains that "the 'authentic' American narrative" has always consisted of tales of individual experience against the world, against, often, the wilderness. "The classic statements of American individualism," Kerber writes, "are best understood as guides to masculine identity."[34] Historian Kevin P. Murphy has argued "by the turn of the twentieth century, a 'red-blooded' Rooseveltian model of masculinity proved ascendant and functioned as a prescriptive ideal for American men."[35] In the same month that Reverend Hazen gave his address at Royalton, the first part of Jack London's *White Fang* appeared serialized in *Outing Magazine*. The next month, June 1906, *Outing* ran a short article by author Ralph D. Paine entitled "The Author of 'White Fang.'" Admittedly, this magazine had an investment in making the book sound good, and Paine did his job well. "There are men in the story," he wrote, "and they are red-blooded, elemental types." London handled the themes well, Paine wrote, having "dealt much with cruelty and lust of blood and the raw and naked brute in man."[36] Toward the end of the year, the journal of literary criticism *The Dial* used, by way of an example of London's "understanding of animal psychology which seems almost uncanny" the fact that White Fang first entered a relationship with a human because, as London had written, "'he recognized in man the animal that had fought itself to primacy over other animals of the Wild."[37] The novel reflected a national obsession with wilderness, strength, and primal instincts, and the clash that occurred when they met civilization. In the case of *White Fang*, civilization won in the end; in his previous work, *The Call of the Wild*, wilderness won. It seemed that Jack London, like so much of the country, was experimenting with the question of which elements most controlled a being: wild brutishness or love and civilization.

The Dangers of Individualism

Yet individualism had a dark side as well, and men worried that it would take them down a slippery slope into selfishness. By the turn of the century, "men no longer worried about controlling their own passions," sociologist Michael Kimmel has explained, "now they were fretting that the new crowds surrounding them would put them in a straitjacket."[38] Crowds, in fact, seemed to define modern life. Without a frontier to run to when the urban world became overwhelming, without a place to go to start or restart life, many men worried that they would have no escape from the overcivilization and hyperfeminization of their homes and communities. Men found themselves crowded at work as factories and businesses grew at alarming rates. (Edison Electric, which would become General Electric, had only 1,000 employees in 1880, but had more than 10,000 by 1892.) Crowds surrounded them on the streets of their neighborhoods, and by 1890, one in three Americans lived in a city with a population larger than 8,000; in 1830, only about one in fifteen had.[39]

In response, American men began to look to their biology to explain their personalities. By the turn of the century, discussions of masculinity began to "self-consciously use Darwinian biology to classify 'brutishness' as an essential natural male trait."[40] This sense of men as animals permeated cultural discussion and action. Violent competitive sports, especially collegiate football and prize-fighting, became highly popular. Literary naturalism, which in the United States included such authors as Frank Norris (*McTeague*, 1899; *The Octopus*, 1901) and Theodore Dreiser (*Sister Carrie*, 1900), highlighted instinct and animalistic manliness, and the horrors brought on others because of the unchecked release of such instincts. Weekend camping and casual outdoor recreation increased. Muscular Christianity, epitomized by such figures as Billy Sunday, showed up in the United States from its foundations in Victorian England in the form of the YMCA and other men's and boys' Christian organizations.[41] New York clergyman Carl Delos Case pointed out that a focus on "feminine" Christianity arose quite naturally in reaction to the "domination of the religious life in the Middle Ages by men" that held women outside the important functioning of the church.[42] Case, however, lamented that the overfeminization of organized religion resulted in a deficiency of logic, ruggedness, and militarism in Christianity, and a focus on forgiveness and emotionality. This resulted in a religion that valued dependence over independence and meekness over assertiveness, and this drove boys away because "obedience to Christ [was] made synonymous with the loss of manhood."[43]

At the beginning of the nineteenth century, four-fifths of all men worked for themselves; seventy years later, just one in three did, and the trend continued into the twentieth century.[44] Roosevelt warned several times in his autobiography of the dangers of out-of-control individualism. He spoke of the idiocy of the "old *laissez faire* economists [who] believ[ed] in unlimited competition, unlimited individualism." He reminded readers that "a simple and poor society," that is, a pre-industrial one, could "exist as a democracy on a basis of sheer individualism" because everyone in such a society is "of about the same size." But in the "rich and complex industrial society" that Americans now found themselves in,

> some individuals, and especially those artificial individuals called corporations, become so very big that the ordinary individual is utterly dwarfed beside them, and cannot deal with them on terms of equality. It therefore becomes necessary for these ordinary individuals to combine in their turn, first . . . through that biggest of all combinations called the Government, and second, to act, also in their own self-defense, through private combinations, such as farmer's associations and trade unions.[45]

Real men, according to Roosevelt, did not use their strength to "wrong the weak," be they children, women, employees, or other weaker people.[46] Just three months before *The Midland Monthly* describe a visit to the Gardner-Sharp cabin, it carried a short article by R. W. Johnson—presumably this author was Robert Wood Johnson, co-founder of Johnson & Johnson—entitled "A Home Talk with the Boys." In this February 1895 essay, Johnson argued "what the world needs today is *men*" (original italics). Those men were not modern "supple-kneed sycophants [or] human nonentities" but "men of iron mould and dauntless purpose." They should not shrink from hard work or sacrifice, as "the age has had enough of tinsel." He reminded readers that "proficiency . . . at whist, fondness for music and the frivolities of fashionable life, will not qualify you for position when men such as I have described are called for." As masculine and hard as men needed to be, however, they must guard against becoming "intoxicated by shallow droughts from the beaker of success."[47] In order to be manly in the best way, a man needed to temper his individualistic tendencies with his good character, his "internal gyroscope" that gave him moral direction.

Manliness in Captivity

For all these reasons, the commentators at the Royalton celebration, especially Reverend Hazen—whose speech must have seemed interminable (it filled 11 pages in the reissue of Ivah Dunklee's *Burning of Royalton* and narrative of the captivity of Zadock Steele that accompanied the event)—looked wistfully back to a preindustrial vision of manhood that valued the needs of the community over the wants of the individual. Hazen did not, however, suggest that modernism should be abandoned completely, for he, like most Progressives, sought the practical solution rather than an idealized impractical one. Rather, he wished to encourage a blending of the modern and premodern into a definition of masculinity in which ambition was rewarded but selfishness disparaged.

Many Progressive Era captivity narratives demonstrated in their very titles that they were about the group rather than the individual. Steele's narrative, for example, never appeared as just "the captivity of Zadock Steele," but rather was published in both 1818 and 1908 as *The Indian Captive . . . to Which is Prefixed an Account of the Burning of Royalton* and the 1906 version, printed just after the memorial celebration, was entitled *The Burning of Royalton, Vermont . . . Including a Reprint of Zadock Steele's Narrative*. Steele, then, was never presented as a freestanding individual; rather, he was always associated with the fate of Royalton, despite the fact that he did not even live in Royalton, but in Randolph, nearly fourteen miles north of Royalton. Other captivity narratives also expressly linked their captives to the story of the community.[48] Frances Slocum's story, for example, defined her in the title of both the 1891 and 1906 versions as *The Lost Sister of Wyoming*. The first chapter of the 1891 version gave a "description of the valley," while the first chapter of the 1906 narrative told how the Slocums came into the Wyoming Valley many years before the captivity. The publisher, The Burrows Brothers of Cleveland, attached a new "Genealogy" to its 1904 reissue of Nehemiah How's 1748 narrative.

Once readers opened the cover, they also found evidence that the story of the group took precedence over that of the individual. Rather than leaping right into the story of individual experience, authors generally spent significant time tracing the whereabouts of family and community members and the way each met his or her fate. During the attack on Royalton, almost all of the men were killed, captured, or otherwise prevented from reaching their families, for, although it was early morning, many husbands and fathers had already gone into their fields while their wives and children slept. Hence, the first several pages of Steele's narrative were little more than a list of prominent local men and what happened to them. Before the narrative got to the stories of the women and children, and even before it provided any real information about Steele himself, it first disposed of almost all the townsmen. Indians killed Elias Button, John Hutchinson, and Hutchinson's brother Abijah; they took Simeon Belknap, Giles Gibb, Jonathan Brown, Joseph Kneeland (and his elderly father), Elias Curtis, John Kent, and Peter Mason captive; Mr. Havens hid under a log and listened as his family was butchered; Daniel Havens, son of the log-man, Thomas Pember, General Elias Stevens and Captain Joseph Parkhurst, and Deacon Rix ran into the woods.

In their defense, some of those men who fled reappeared at various points in the narrative, trying and failing to warn or save some group of women and children. At one point, Captain

Parkhurst actually tripped over a dog and thus watched helplessly from the ground as several women and children were captured. "Conjugal and paternal affection alone," Ivah Dunklee said, "can suggest to the imagination what were the feelings of Gen. Stevens, when compelled for his own safety, to leave the wife of his bosom, and their little ones, to the mercy of a savage foe!"[49]

This pattern appeared in other captivity narratives of the Progressive Era as well. The Dakotas who attacked settlers in Iowa in the 1856 Spirit Lake Massacre killed many more of their victims than those who attacked Royalton did. (The goal of the Dakotas at Spirit Lake, unlike that of the Mohawk at Royalton during the Revolution, was mainly revenge and the expression of long-repressed anger rather than participation in an organized, European-centered war.) Abbie Gardner-Sharp recounted the fate of all the neighboring men: Mr. Mattock, Dr. Harriot, Mr. Snyder, Carl Granger, Mr. Luce, Mr. Clark, and Mr. Marble all met their doom before their wives and children did.[50] In the story of Frances Slocum's captivity in 1778, the Miami Indians, apparently intent mostly on capturing children to adopt, attacked a single home by stealth when the men were away working in the fields; thus, those men were also removed from the event in this case, not by death but by absence.[51]

Perhaps the absence of men explains why the memorial ceremony at Royalton—which, after all, had been linked in all its versions to the story of a male captive—had the women at its center. What eulogizer, after all, would want to repeat the heroic tales of men hiding under fallen trees and tripping over dogs? The Royalton Woman's Club set up and largely ran the Royalton Historical Society in order to plan and erect the monument to the victims of the raid. They selected the first members of the Historical Committee (which later became the Historical Society) in 1896; of the eleven members of the Committee, four were also members of the Woman's Club. The women of Royalton clearly felt a connection to their colonial ancestors.[52] Likewise, despite the fact that Steele's narrative spent its early pages recounting the fate of the townsmen, the tale contained in the narrative of the burning of Royalton really finds its heart in the story of its women.

The Moral Gyroscope

If the Manly Mother of the turn-of-the-century captivity narrative had some internal moral guidance system that taught her how to behave in each new situation, how could readers of new captivity narratives develop that same moral center? Surely it was a sign that frontier individuals had some moral knowledge that post-frontier people did not. Americans began early in the nineteenth century to search for the source of this moral center. In the antebellum period, youth counselors began to focus their advice to boys on what Baptist minister John Foster called the "decision of character." People had behaved properly in the Puritan world because of the fear of public reprimand, but in the nineteenth century, social commentators began to tout "character," that internal guidance system that caused people to do right not out of guilt, obligation, or fear of humiliation, but because that was their genuine preference. Character could be taught, and, what is more, an individual could choose to develop it; therefore, the internal qualities you developed in any given situation were more important than what you actually did, except that in doing "right" and making good decisions you demonstrated to the world that you had a "good" character.[53]

Historian Joseph Kett points out that antebellum youth counselors, most of whom were clergymen, presented religious conversion or commitment as an important experience for a boy, not because of the religion itself but because the process—generally spiritually painful—would teach him "resolution," "moral obligation," the "force of character," and the "inward power," "executive force," and "propelling power" of his own will.[54] He would then learn to be his own censor, and to use his own good judgment to direct his behavior. He would develop, then, a morality that depended not on pressure from without but on guidance from within. "Character," Kett explained, "was not a set of doctrines or even a code of behavior, but an internal gyroscope, a self-activating, self-regulating, all-purpose inner control."[55] Horace Greeley addressed the issue of the formation of character in 1850, and concluded that there were many ways parents inadvertently taught their children bad character. One "monstrous error" was the tendency of parents to reward with "some dainty confection or glittering toy" an act of virtue, integrity, or duty. This habit "doubly corrupted" children, who were taught "not to do right without payment," while at the same time having their childish tendency toward greed and gluttony inflated.[56] Because it came from the inner person rather than from an external force such as a family member or a community leader, "character" would be particularly useful in navigating times of great change. After all, if the United States consisted of citizens of good character, then no matter what the modern problem, they would face it with their internal moral direction intact and therefore make the "right" decision.

The notion of "men of character" persisted throughout the nineteenth century, and Theodore Roosevelt wrote of its importance in his 1913 autobiography. The country depended upon its men building and maintaining good characters, for, he said, "no man can lead ... no man can act with rugged independence in serious crises, nor strike at great abuses ... if he is himself vulnerable in his private character." Boys, moreover—and girls, too—needed adults not just to *tell* them how to behave but to *show* them the methods by which they could develop a good character. Roosevelt praised such magazines as *Our Young Folks* that "instilled the individual virtues, and [showed] the necessity of character as the chief factor in any man's success." "A vote is like a rifle," he went on, uniting his twin loves of hunting and statesmanship, "its usefulness depends upon the character of the user."[57] In January 1895, the same year that it reported on the Gardner-Sharp cabin and carried R. W. Johnson's advice to boys, *The Midland Monthly* included "Sketches of Prominent Members of" the Society of the Army of the Tennessee. The author of this article, W. S. Moore, stated that "students of history and of character will find in the portraits an interesting study," because "the achievements of these men are both an example and an inspiration," because the "chief glory of America is . . . that we are a nation of self-made men." According to Moore, then, one could study character as one studied history, and learn from it how to add to the national glory by becoming a "self-made man."[58]

Issues of character appeared in early twentieth century captivity narratives and even more so in the dedication of captivity monuments. Although Roosevelt and others worried about the state of men's characters, captivity tales in this period found their internal gyroscope most often in the actions of women. Martha Bennett Phelps assured her readers that her great-aunt Maconaquah (Frances Slocum), despite her life as an Indian, "was not degraded in her habits or character." She exhibited "moral dignity," and "all that abundance and respectability could do for a woman in savage life was hers."[59] Reverend Hazen's address at the monument dedication at Royalton used the term "character" some eight times in the single speech. He assured his audience that "these early settlers in the face of fearful odds, even at the risk of life . . . [acted] never with loss of self-respect, or character." They had, he went on, a "devotion to principle and integrity of character . . . they produced strong characters, developed men and women of power and commanding influence"; they "developed men and women of more sterling integrity of character" than existed in the modern world.[60]

Men or Women?

When discussing character, Hazen spoke often of "men and women," but he also talked of "manhood." He worried that "commercialism and modern thought" would result in "lowering the standard of manhood and the plane of action of men in their dealings with one another" that the "noblest character, the strictest integrity" would not be able to overcome. Hazen did not exclude women from his analysis of the importance of good character; he used terms like "settler" and "people," and made it clear that he was talking of both "men and women" when he spoke of good character and its importance to the community. Theodore Roosevelt likewise included women explicitly in his discussions of character. He thought that the country was in danger from weak women just as much as it was in danger from weak men. Roosevelt did not want a nation of "Frail Flowers," but neither did he want a country of "Amazons." He outlined his definition of men and women of good character in *The Strenuous Life:*

> A healthy state can exist only when men and women who make it up lead clean, vigorous, healthy lives . . . the man must be glad to do a man's work, to dare and endure and to labor; to keep himself, and to keep those dependent upon him. The woman must be the housewife, the helpmeet of the homemaker, the wise and fearless mother of many healthy children. . . . When men fear work or fear righteous war, when women fear motherhood, they tremble on the brink of doom. . . . As it is with the individual, so it is with the nation.[61]

The fundamental characteristic of the captivity narrative featuring the Manly Mother is that her "manly" behavior (strength and bravery certainly, and possibly aggression, anger, ambition, and individualism) came from her good character, which was offended at having her sacred role as a mother threatened. She often acted aggressively, angrily, and with great indignation, but she did so almost exclusively when men were absent. The Manly Mother *wanted* to be the "housewife," "helpmeet," and "mother," and when her natural desire to fulfill those roles was interrupted, her womanly "internal gyroscope" led her to defend her sphere with aggression and violence if necessary.

The Manly Mother can be seen perfectly in the anecdote of Mrs. Hendee, whose story found its way into every repetition of the history of the attack on Royalton. During the 1780 attack on Royalton, Mrs. Hendee, then age twenty-seven, fled with her two children toward the hoped-for safety of a neighbor's house. A group of Indians took the seven-year-old boy and left Mrs. Hendee and her younger daughter weeping, "defenceless [sic] and exposed." In what appears to have been an almost hysterical fit, Mrs. Hendee followed her son and his captors along a riverbank, screaming along the way, dragging her daughter with her. She met with several Indians and Englishmen, who all told her that her son would be killed. As she slogged through the wilderness, she seems to have regained some of her rationality. Her strength and determination so impressed the Indians she met that, when she needed to cross the river to follow her son, an "old Indian" offered to carry her and her daughter across. "Braving every danger and hazarding the most dreadful consequences," Mrs. Hendee walked up to the young British commanding officer, Lieutenant "Horton," (who was clearly a Lieutenant Richard Houghton, then about 21 years old) and demanded to know what would become of her son.[62] He answered that he would be trained as a soldier but not hurt; Mrs. Hendee accused the officer, however much he might have believed in following orders, of "yield-[ing] [the younger captive boys] into the arms of death," as, she argued, the younger boys would not stand the march to Canada nor the military training. They would be killed, she said, when they became burdens. Houghton, after Mrs. Hendee threatened him with, among other things, punishment in the afterlife for having offended her status as a mother, extracted her son from his Indian accomplices. Houghton told her to stay with the Indians until "all the scouting parties had returned, lest they should again take her boy from her."[63]

While waiting there, she took several other boy captives back and sat them on the ground about her. Nonetheless, an "old Indian" (apparently not the same one who had ferried her across the river) took back her son by force, threatening her with a knife, and Houghton had to interfere on her behalf a second time. She ultimately secured the release of nine boys. Ivah Dunklee wrote of her, "the boldest hero of the other sex could never have effected what she accomplished." Simultaneously praising Mrs. Hendee and justifying those men who fled or hid, Dunklee went on to say that, had a man attempted to free the boys, he "most surely would have brought upon himself a long and wretched captivity, and perhaps even death itself." A woman, though, because of her position as a mother, could accomplish what a man could not.[64] The tale of Mrs. Hendee might well have inspired the DAR's depiction of the Madonna of the Trail, although there is no record that Mrs. Hendee carried a rifle as the Madonna of the Trail did. Indeed, she rescued her son and the other boys barehanded.

Other women become Manly Mothers during the raid on Royalton. One woman walked up to a group of warriors plundering her house and asked why they were "distressing helpless women and children . . . [for] if they had the courage of warriors, they would cross the river and fight men at the fort." The Indians only answered that "Squaw shouldn't say too much," but took no action against her. Another woman, thoroughly offended that her best gown had been thrown into a pile of plundered goods, attempted to take the dress back. At first "one of the Indians knocked her down with his gun," but after waiting for him to become distracted in ransacking another house, she "seized the gown, and walked off, having one child in her arms and leading another by the hand."[65]

Mrs. Hendee and her companions displayed "masculine" individualistic qualities of aggression (in the case of the "squaw" who accused her attackers of being unmanly), bravery, and competition (in the case of the unnamed defender of the dress) and combined them with a concern for and defense of the community. With a decidedly female mindset, they focused all those "manly" qualities on the needs of children, on pointing out the moral failings of others, and on clothes. In a rather bizarre fusion of images that reveals just this combination of gendered traits in Mrs. Hendee, Mary Lovejoy's *History of Royalton* stated, "Young Lieut. Houghton could not withstand the charm of the agonized mother, beautiful in the strength and courage of her mother-love." Forgotten by those who wrote mainstream histories, she "sleeps today in an unknown grave," although Lovejoy asks her readers to "picture the joy of each household . . . as she restored to the sorrowing parents their children." The "noble woman," then, in the readers' imagination, strode back into town the victor, not unlike a general returning from a glorious and just war, leading her wards by the hand. Lovejoy immediately followed this description with an illustration entitled "Mrs. Hannah Handy's Spool Holder." Could a more domesticated illustration have been chosen?[66]

Manliness and the State

The Manly Mother, then, as seen in the early twentieth century, united a traditional femininity with what the publisher's introduction to the 1908 edition of Steele's Narrative called "the genuineness of character, the sturdy faith, and the superb physical endurance which, with the love of liberty, form the choicest portion of the inheritance which these early settlers have passed on to their descendants, to their country, and to the world."[67] She, as much as her husband, was responsible for the preservation and development of the United States. In his address to the crowd gathered at the dedication of the Royalton memorial, Reverend Hazen declared that, despite "their sternness and so-called narrow-mindedness," the colonists of Royalton, and by extension New England and the nation as a whole, "produced strong characters, developed men and women of power" unlike modern ones who insist on "drifting away from the ideals of the fathers . . . lowering the standard of manhood and the plane of action of men in their dealings with one another and management of the affairs of state." Hazen explicitly united individual "manliness" and the proper functioning of the government. His message was clear: if individuals did not remember and renew the values of their forefathers though the intentional masculinization of themselves and their children, the government and national culture of the United States would suffer and perhaps decay. Hazen then announced that the Royalton monument would uphold those values "long after the poet and the orator had been silenced," and future generations would "learn to commit themselves anew to the principles for which [the Colonists] stood" simply by visiting the site.[68]

Reverend Hazen was not alone in believing in, and actively promoting, a connection between "manly" behavior, the development of good character, and national moral health. Theodore Roosevelt, western author Owen Wister, and the entire membership of the Boone and Crockett Club had intentionally developed a manly ideal in themselves through such activities as dude ranching, hunting, military service, and the near-worship of "wild" outdoor space. Roosevelt also coupled manliness in individual behavior with active good citizenship in much of his own writing.[69] In his autobiography, for example, he argued that "all the laws that the wit of man can devise will never make a man a worthy citizen unless he has within himself the right stuff, unless he has self-reliance, energy, courage, the power of insisting on his own rights and the sympathy that makes him regardful of the rights of others."[70]

With this definition of manhood *and* the ideal American so outlined, Roosevelt claimed, "the future greatness of America in no small degree depends upon the possession by the average American citizen of the qualities which my men showed when they served under me at Santiago," the loss of which, he claimed, was "as dangerous as it [was] ignoble." Without it, the United States would crumble.[71] Those who published captivity narratives and erected captivity monuments in the early twentieth century did so with the assumption that their actions would defend against the loss of the "virile virtues" and aid in creating a nation of Theodore Roosevelts. The citizens of such a country would have sympathy for the weak and concern for others, and would use the power of their government to enforce the protection of the weak against the strong. Therefore, the manliness and character that captivity narratives of this era wished to promote was not reserved only for men, and it required a careful balance of both community-mindedness and self-interest.[72]

Feminization

Manliness-preachers and character-builders like Hazen and Roosevelt saw an "overfeminization" in the home as well as in public life, and it was in the home where it scared them the most. Many men in the early twentieth century embraced a new male domesticity made possible by increasing leisure time and disposable income for the middle- or upper-class father and husband. As historian Margaret Marsh points out, a growing regard for "masculine domesticity" led men to spend more time at home participating in childrearing and recreating with wives and children.[73] As these "domestic men" embraced greater time and involvement in the home, part of that increased responsibility for the raising of children must have included ensuring that their sons did not grow up emasculated by modern culture. On the other hand, if fathers worked for wages and children spent all their time with their mothers and female teachers (teaching was, after all, quickly shifting from a mostly male to an almost exclusively female vocation), who would teach them to develop a properly male yet "good" character?

Of course, extreme views existed on both sides. Many argued that a man who participated in domestic duties at all, or who spent his leisure time with his wife, would become what clergyman James M. Buckley called the "womanish man." Others made the case that a woman who participated in any public life outside the home would become the dreaded "mannish woman."[74] Most men, however, seemed to feel that a middle ground would be best for themselves and for their families. They both celebrated their wives and mothers as the natural caretakers and moral guides of the family (and the nation), and sought to mitigate their wives' feminizing influence by creating nature-oriented male-only spaces for their sons, such as the Boy Scouts and the YMCA.[75]

While Progressive Era sexologists began to develop a complex understanding of sex and gender in which no one person was completely "male" or "female" in behavior or instinct, they also believed that gender behaviors would define sexuality. Sexologists believed that gendered behavior created, rather than reflected, sexual preference. A "mannish woman," then, would by necessity be a lesbian, just as a "womanish man" would be a "sexual invert." Too much time in the exclusive company of women would teach boys feminine behaviors and hence push them towards homosexuality, which sexologists termed "sexual inversion." The best defense against raising a homosexual son was concentrated time spent away from women, alone with men where boys would learn masculine, and thus heterosexual, behaviors.[76]

Although this understanding of the causes of homosexuality contradicts modern understandings of the connection between gender and sexuality, in 1908 Indiana Senator and historian Albert

J. Beveridge demonstrated that, to minds at the time, there may have been no incongruity whatsoever. Beveridge encouraged young men to commune with nature in concentrated doses to restore manliness and combat the feminizing quality of everyday modern urban life, while at the same time arguing that "home . . . constitutes the motive for all manly effort." "Nothing," Beveridge went on, "means so much to the Republic as the influence of the American home upon the young manhood of the nation."[77] That home, however, needed to include an engaged father who showed his son how to access "manly" character-building activities like camping, hunting, and competitive sports.

Beveridge, like so many of his time, linked an intentional masculinization of boys with the virtues instilled by home and mother as a combination necessary to both individual and national strength and vitality.[78] Ernest Thompson Seton, founder of the Boy Scouts of America and an "Indian fanatic," had, as early as 1902, conceived of an organization that taught Indian woodcraft. Seton named himself "Black Wolf" and taught boys "'woodlore activities such as archery, tracking, and handicrafts" for which boys were rewarded "coup." He concluded that "the highest aim of education is not scholarship but manhood."[79] The *Handbook for Scout Masters*, published in 1913, stated that one of the main purposes of the Boy Scouts of America was to "weld manly principles into [the boy's] character," but only as a complement to the home. The shy boy, the handbook states, generally became so because he had "been brought up with his mother and sisters." Not to worry: the handbook assured scouters that with enough time spent with other boys, shyness would "wear away." The Boy Scouts of America sought to instill "efficient manhood" consisting of "faith, unbending rectitude, self-control, a brave, buoyant, religious manliness, and social service." Scout-craft then, would serve "to conserve, to concentrate, and to put into character-shaping application all the corrective training and moral ideals" taught, in the abstract, by mothers and teachers.[80]

A lack of manly training and proper character-building activities with their fathers or other male leaders could lead to the development of a soft, feminine character, to a runaway individualism, and to significant health problems. As early as 1881, neurologist George M. Beard outlined what the results of an overcivilized, overfeminized society would be on individual men. Medical nervousness, defined as a "deficiency or lack of nerveforce," could lead to everything from headaches and baldness to drug addiction, insanity, and diabetes. Not only were effeminate men (generally the small, the weak, usually upper-class, and those engaged in "brain" rather than physical work) more likely to exhibit nervousness, American *women* suffered from the ailments caused by a slothful life as well. According to Beard, American women were unable to tolerate hard work and had become accustomed to a life lived almost entirely indoors; the result was increased inability to deliver full-term babies or to nurse them sufficiently.[81]

How Physical Education Will Save the Country

Since women were not excluded from the perceived ailment of "nervousness," many Progressive Era observers believed that girls needed to develop physically just as boys did, and physical education classes for both sexes became an essential part of the curriculum of the growing number of high schools. Interestingly, physical education proponent Dr. Luther H. Gulick, president of the Playground Association of America and husband of Charlotte Gulick, founder of the Camp Fire Girls, argued that individualism had gotten out of control with women, just as it had with men, and the only cure was cooperative sports and physical education. His logic went like this: because women's work and place had historically been in the home rather than in the community, "those qualities which depended upon such individualistic action" had been overdeveloped, leaving the modern woman unable to cooperate well with others. Boys learned to cooperate, though in a "rough way," through participation in team sports and "gangs." Girls, Dr. Gulick argued, needed to develop teamwork skills through team sports, although intense competition should be avoided; athletics, gymnastics, and folk dancing were the best team sports for girls because they did not put any one person in control over the others, and developed both the whole body and the "all-around character" of the girl, including "qualities of skill, quickness of perception, readiness to meet emergencies, and the like." For the boy, the purpose of team sports was to give an outlet to his brutish and competitive instincts while teaching adherence to rules and teamwork; for girls, team sports taught cooperation while developing communal, cooperative tendencies. In both cases, developing physically and melding individualism and the needs of the group perfected one's "character."[82]

Juliette Gordon Low, inspired by Robert Baden-Powell's British Boy Scouts and Girl Guides, started the American Girl Scouts in Savannah, Georgia, in 1912. According to Low, girls needed, among other things, to prepare to do their duty as the moral guides for men by enjoying "exercise of vigorous outdoor games." Not necessarily important just for physical fitness, outdoor activity developed, again, the strong moral character. "A girl who develops a strong agile body," Low wrote, "at the same time improves her brain. A girl with weak flabby muscles cannot have the strength of character that goes with normal physical power."[83] Indeed, it is hard to imagine a Mrs. Hendee, had she spent her life indoors doing nothing physical, slogging along a riverbank after her son, daughter on her hip, and then camping in the open air the following night with nine rescued boys. It is also difficult to imagine a Mrs. Hendee suffering from "nervousness."

The qualities of these captivity narrative heroes and heroines were the very ones twentieth century social engineers sought to perpetuate. Physical education, then, could prevent over-individualization, and it could help combat the growing concern that too much civilization would result in what Roosevelt called "a life of slothful ease."[84] Even Franz Boas, that champion of relativism, believed a lack of suffering, on either an individual or a collective level, would "lead to an effeminacy that must be disastrous to the race."[85] Both men referred to the dangers of too much individual comfort, as well as the damage that would come to society as a whole without collective "hard and dangerous endeavor."[86] Again, we find the advice that the desires of the individual (to lie around and relax) must be overcome for the good of the collective, since lazy, soft people did not develop good characters. One developed good character through vigorous action, and vigorous action demonstrated that one had good character.

Captivity narratives of every period of American history have been fundamentally about the frontier experience and have told the story of individuals consciously embracing hardship for the betterment of the country, or so commentators liked to say. The point was not that captives wanted to be carried off into a hostile, unknown wilderness, but that they had consciously risked that possibility to expand and improve the nation (not only to find a home or economic opportunity, the message went) because they had good characters. Abbie Gardner-Sharp, for example, told her readers that the government "should manifest its gratitude to its early settlers for the dangers and hardships they underwent in bearing its banner of civilization to the front, by appropriately marking the scenes that attest their bravery and sacrifices in the cause of their progress."[87] Martha Bennett Phelps asked her readers, "does not history prove [Frances Slocum] to have been a veritable suffering Daughter of the American Revolution?"[88] The 1904 edition of the narrative of Nehemiah How (who was captured in October, 1745, from Fort Drummer, Vermont, about 80 miles northeast of Albany, New York, and taken to Quebec where he died in captivity) contained a new introduction that called the colonial settlers "intrepid pioneers," who conquered the wilderness and Indian threat "by the dint of assiduity."[89]

These narratives reflected the views of the main cultural and intellectual commentators of the day who wished their readers to believe that American pioneers would not allow such a little thing as the risk of slaughter or captivity by Indians to prevent them from carrying their civilizing mission into the wilderness. Theodore Roosevelt's *The Winning of the West* declared that only "a single generation, passed under the hard conditions of life in the wilderness, was enough to weld together into one people" immigrants from many European countries, and "the children of the next generation became indistinguishable from one another." The "settler-folk whose destiny it was to make ready the continent for civilization," thus had become, in one generation, a single people out of many.[90] In that generation, "the settler-folk" developed characteristics that, if not distinctly American, when taken as a whole, define the American national personality: independent, democratic, materialistic, anti-intellectual, and inartistic but quick and inventive.[91] Once again, these stories of individual action served the cause of the collective. And it had all happened because of a good national character imparted by the experience of the wilderness.

In the post-frontier new century, how would Americans continue to develop that good character? Partly, they would learn it from the Manly Mothers celebrated in captivity narratives and monuments. Abbie Gardner-Sharp and Mrs. Hendee, although their experiences and their reactions to those experiences differed dramatically from one another, both fit into the Manly Mother type. They each exhibited "manly" individual action, as in the story of Mrs. Hendee confronting both Indians and British army officers to liberate nine boys, or Gardner-Sharp promoting her business enterprise through her tale of suffering. Yet they combined that action with a fixation on the needs of the community, as in the case of Mrs. Hendee's refusal to leave her neighbor's children behind—although she might well have left once she had freed her own son. Likewise, Gardner-Sharp used her damaged persona to promote Christian Science and the civilization of Indians. This combination made these women the ideal personification of the "spirit of President Roosevelt" so revered by Reverend Hazen, and the best method through which to pass that spirit on to future audiences.

Epilogue
The Captive as Conduit

William Munson declared that he would marry one of the redeemed Sauk Indian captives, Rachel or Sylvia Hall, before he had even met them. He was "an admirer of the brave." Surviving the 1832 Indian Creek Massacre that killed fifteen people and the eleven-day captivity that followed certainly qualified the sisters as "brave." Although his acquaintances laughed at him, Munson was apparently serious. He moved from Indiana to Illinois in 1833 and took a land claim near the sight of the May 21, 1832, Indian Creek Massacre during which the two girls had been captured and held by the Sauk Indian leader Black Hawk for eleven days. Munson did meet and marry Rachel Hall, and the couple "becam[e] one of the foremost families of La Salle County."[1] Whatever affection Rachel Hall and William Munson might have developed for each other, his interest in her first came from a desire to unite himself with a woman whose life epitomized the frontier experience and whose character personified the Manly Mother.

In his 1916 edition of the story of the massacre and captivity of the Halls, Charles Scanlan explained that Rachel first considered marrying Munson because "every good woman is not satisfied until she has a home of her own." In Rachel's case, according to Scanlan, the destruction of her family and home at Indian Creek by Black Hawk and his band exaggerated her essential female need for a home. The couple settled only "a mile and a half east of the scene of the massacre" and went on to produce children who "became very prominent." Scanlan's narrative followed the Hall–Munson genealogy into the twentieth century, describing one grandson as a "well-known lawyer in South Dakota," and another as "a prominent lawyer in Ottawa, Illinois." Scanlan also explained that Rachel, sixteen at the time of her captivity, had been so shocked by the experience that the "unusual vigor" of her youth was "impaired" and she "thereafter suffered from nervousness." Rachel died in 1870, and she was buried "about one and one-half miles east of Shabona (sic) Park, on the original Hall homestead."[2] In 1877, William Munson erected a monument costing seven hundred dollars to the memory of his wife's murdered family and the sisters' captivity. In 1905 the state of Illinois appropriated five thousand dollars for a monument to be placed on the same spot. On August 29, 1906 a crowd of five thousand people came to Shabbona Park to see that monument unveiled and to dedicate the park.[3]

In a single ten-page preface, Scanlan managed to exemplify the Progressive Era uses of captivity narratives: dedication to ancestry, genealogy, and place; the association of frontier history with park creation (in this case, Shabbona Park in Earlville, Illinois); a confusing conflict between the behaviors of "good" women (who kept house and were damaged by trauma) and admiration for their bravery and survival; repeated declarations that the captive and her descendants were the "right" kind of people; women as the carriers of national characteristics; justification of the "Americanizing" of Indians; and individual action to memorialize the captives and the dead followed by state-sanctioned action. As in the case of Mary Jemison, Frances Slocum, Zadock Steele, and

Abbie Gardner-Sharp, these themes, jumbled as they seem when crammed together in the short space Scanlan allocated for them, converged with the erection of a monument.

Like the extended Slocum family of Indiana and Pennsylvania, who worked from 1890 to 1910 to erect a monument to Frances Slocum, speakers at the 1906 Indian Creek Massacre monument ceremony made it clear that the monument honoring the event was perhaps more important than the actual event itself. M. N. Armstrong, who gave the monument's Dedicatory Address, announced that "we have met here today on this historic spot to do something, or rather shall I say to applaud what has been done to commemorate the virtues of those hardy pioneers." Although Armstrong went on to describe those pioneers, he emphasized that the memorial—not the massacre, not the pioneers, not the captives, not the Indians, not the survivors—was the center of celebration. In the post-frontier country, pioneers were not important so much because they had "endured the greatest hardships . . . in order that we, their descendants, might enjoy the comforts and blessings of civilization," but because "their descendants" chose to remember them and thus used their frontier qualities to address the problems of the present and the future.[4]

The descendants who remembered their captive ancestors used that memory to prove a frontier pedigree but also to demonstrate that, by family longevity in a particular place, they belonged to what Roosevelt called the "gentry" of frontier settlers. Scanlan's declarations that Rachel Hall Munson and William Munson became one of the "foremost families of La Salle County" and that their grandchildren were socially prominent and professionally successful, then, were not just offhand comments, but concrete reminders of the family's importance to national development and present achievement. Likewise, the celebration around the unveiling of the Mary Jemison monument focused more on the actions of William Letchworth than on Mary Jemison herself. It would have been hard to stand in the audience at Glen Iris on

EPILOGUE

September 19, 1910, and miss the implication that Letchworth's efforts to preserve her memory were more valuable to the country in the twentieth century than was the actual fact of her captivity. A monument would, then, serve the dual purpose of remembering the historical figure and proving to future visitors that the men and women who erected it had acted to develop and defend American frontier characteristics in the post-frontier world.

As proof of the importance of the people who made the monument a reality, the Indian Creek Massacre monument included on its plinth not just the names of those who had been slaughtered and captured, but also the "names of the board of directors of the association who were in office at the time the monument became a reality."[5] Likewise, the Frances Slocum memorial included the inscription, "this monument was erected by the Slocums and others who deemed it a pleasure to contribute," and one side of the monument to the Burning of Royalton reads, "erected by Royalton Woman's Club, Oct. 16, 1905."[6] When commentators hoped their statues would "stand for many generations" to remind visitors of the role "now vanished" Indians and pioneers played in the national creation, and when they extolled the virtues of the pioneer character, they might also have been hoping that the future would remember them in the same terms.[7]

Evidence of the similarity in character between past Americans and current ones can also be found in the positioning of new monuments next to old ones. The Jemison memorial went up next to the site of the 1872 "Last Indian Council on the Genesee" that reburied Jemison's remains; similarly, the Indian Creek Massacre monument was placed beside the monument erected in 1877 by William Munson. In 1895, the Spirit Lake Massacre Commission constructed its monument next to the one "spontaneously" created by visitors to the place. If Progressive Era commentators wanted to suggest that they, like their pioneer ancestors, were the creators and defenders of American character, they could hardly have found a more obvious or more concrete way to do so.

In 1902, the county of La Salle, Illinois, allocated just over seven acres in Earlville for Shabbona Park (not to be confused with Shabbona State Park, also in Illinois, or Shabbona Municipal Park in Chicago). It was, after all, the scene of the Indian Creek Massacre, and the setting aside of land as a memorial park was one step in the process of memorializing the event. On a far smaller scale, this action to apportion land as a government-protected park, and then erect a monument on it, echoed the actions of William Letchworth as he bought and conserved Glen Iris, and linked its existence to the monument and memory of Mary Jemison. In case his audience should miss the importance of the connection between the sacred ground on which a captive lived and the continuation of frontier characteristics in the future, N. M. Armstrong ended his speech at Shabbona Park by proclaiming, "For this, your property is given, devised and bequeathed to you and to your heirs as a heritage forever."[8] Armstrong's "you" was apparently the people of Illinois and—by extension—the United States.

Land was important for another reason as well, for on it witnesses could point to the exact places where Indian attackers dashed out children's brains or dragged mothers from their screaming children. Indeed, Abbie Gardner-Sharp made her living displaying the location of her family's demise, and visitors to the Gardner family cabin found an aging woman eager to walk them through the events in the exact places where they happened. In a similar fashion, another speaker at the Indian Creek Massacre memorial ceremony, John W. Henderson, took the crowd of some five thousand people through just such a tour of the massacre site. Those who promoted tales of captivity around the turn of the century reminded visitors of the connection to the frontier experience that a particular place had, and protected that place as well as the memory of the captives who lived there.

If place was important to the captives' stories, gendered behaviors were as well. The way Scanlan presented the roles of women encapsulated the combination of qualities embodied in the Manly Mother. Munson became fixated on the Hall sisters because of their bravery, but apparently Rachel chose to marry Munson because she, as a "good woman," could not be happy until she "had a home of her own." Yet although Munson was fascinated to the point of love by the tale of the Halls' bravery, Rachel "suffered from nervousness" for the rest of her life after her captivity. Scanlan emphasized that prior to her captivity she had "manifested unusual vigor." Apparently she used that vigor to survive the captivity and, like Abbie Gardner-Sharp, her experience had left her damaged and had sapped her vigor. Courage and independence of spirit and action—so appealing that it drew a man to the sisters before he had even met them—combined with a traditional constitutional weakness, fixation on domesticity, and dependence that proved the sisters to be "good women."[9]

Women served another purpose. Scanlan emphasized in his preface that he acquired his version of the Hall sisters' captivity from their daughters and granddaughters.[10] Scanlan also used his own nieces to aid him in his research. In this case, then, women had been the main actors in the historical drama, but they also acted as the carriers of that story in the twentieth century. By doing both, then, women were the fundamental heart of the creation of the American character and its protectors in the modern age.

Scanlan did leave Indians out of his preface, suggesting at first glance that, with the Indian threat solved, Indian presence ceased in the twentieth century. Yet the echo of Indians did find its way into Scanlan's story in the form of Shabbona, a Potawatomi chief who had warned the settlers of the coming attack. Shabbona later became Christian, and depended upon the settlers he had saved for financial support. In the conflict with settler William Davis (who dammed the creek upriver of a Potawatomi village, thus eliminating their supply of fish), Shabbona had encouraged his people to respond with restraint. When Shabbona could not avert the attack, he sent his son and nephew to warn white settlers at

Bureau Creek while he went to the settlement at Indian Creek. The Bureau Creek residents fled to safety in the town of Ottawa, but some of those at Indian Creek refused to leave. These people became the victims of the Indian Creek Massacre.[11] Shabbona was acknowledged early on as the hero of the story. He later used that reputation to secure favor from white settlers, and he converted to Christianity and gave himself and his family English names. His name connected to the park suggests the belief that "civilizing" Indians would lead them to temperate behavior and would convince them of white superiority.

Shabbona was present in more than just name at the unveiling of the Indian Creek monument. The story of Shabbona's warning to the settlers, which indeed saved many lives, eclipsed the story of the massacre itself and the Halls' captivity. What had in reality been a complex response to convoluted circumstances was presented at the ceremony as Shabbona's acknowledgement of white superiority and the inevitability of white Americans taking over the country. Armstrong recounted that, in response to Black Hawk's appeal to join in the raid, Shabbona only said "the palefaces will soon bring an army like the leaves on the trees and sweep you into the ocean beneath the setting sun." As Armstrong described it, then, Shabbona, a "friend of the whites," made his choice from a pragmatic acknowledgement of what most white Americans took to be historical and evolutionary fact: that Indians would disappear in the face of white advancement.[12] They could opt to be swept away by white military might, or they could submit to natural forces over which they had no control and live out their lives in peace. If they picked the former, they would be remembered as savages; if they chose the latter, they could enter national folklore in the role of primitive, heroic "first Americans" who had made the country safe for white Americans. Shabbona picked the latter because, Armstrong suggested, he had become "civilized" to some extent and so understood the supremacy of whites.

Unlike many other ceremonies of this type, no Indians participated in the Indian Creek monument dedication. Shabbona had his own monument by now, "a huge boulder" erected in 1903 before a gathering of "about fifty people." Apparently what remained of his family had "moved west" after his wife died in 1864.[13] But despite the fact that actual Indians did not take part in the unveiling, Shabbona's presence seemed very real. Armstrong dedicated almost his entire speech to explaining Shabbona's choice to warn the settlers. At the 1902 monument and park dedication, Armstrong briefly mentioned that the settlers existed and that they were good people, and that Munson had erected the 1887 monument. If not for those few passing comments, the audience might well have left the 1902 ceremony under the impression that the monument was for Shabbona rather than the victims or captives of the massacre. Like so many tales of captivity and monuments at this time, then, this one emphasized that Indian virtue remained vital to the story of Indian brutality. As Armstrong put it, "the history of the trials of the pioneer settlers of this country could not be written without also writing of the virtues of the great chief, Shabbona."[14]

The fact that Shabbona had become "a traitor to his own people" when he decided to "save the lives of the frontier settlers from the terrible torture of the tomahawk and scalping knife" proved to many that he had chosen to align himself with white "civilization" over Indian "savagery." Furthering that viewpoint, sometime in the 1850s Shabbona "gave all his family Christian names" and selected the name Benjamin for himself.[15] Like the Indian descendants of Mary Jemison and Frances Slocum, Shabbona and his family shifted their loyalty from hostile Indians to white settlers—although in the process they did not abandon their Indian identities. That shift was embodied by Shabbona's warning to settlers of the coming attack in 1832, and was symbolized by his family's taking up of Christian names in the 1850s.

Shabbona died in 1859, and his wife died five years later when her wagon overturned while crossing a river. She drowned and apparently crushed her young granddaughter to death in the fall.[16] Perhaps this affected how his story was told in later years. None of Shabbona's relatives remained in Illinois to represent the views of living Indians, and his story entered white Illinois history as the account of a great "friend of the whites" who made the territory safe for "civilization."

Those whites who remembered Shabbona took center stage at the monument unveiling, and their knowledge of the dead chief seems to have given them a more legitimate right to speak for the frontier past than did a personal connection to the actual pioneers. Armstrong remarked several times that he remembered Shabbona's "frequent calls at my father's house," and that his father had labored beside Shabbona to build a house for another settler.[17] Indian contact, then, was a fundamental part of the frontier "first period" of American history, and one could prove one's frontier pedigree by recounting family stories of such contact. Historical Indians, vital to the national history, became the subject of anecdotes by which twentieth-century Americans could place their families in the national frontier heritage. Other captivity stories made this link even more clear. After all, the Hall sisters had only been held for eleven days, hardly long enough to make lasting relationships with their captors as had Frances Slocum, Mary Jemison, and even Abbie Gardner-Sharp. These captivity stories that carried the Indian connection into the twentieth century used that link to support directly the federal process of Americanizing the remaining, living Indians.

Tales of Indian captivity have had considerable longevity in American history, and their complexity can appear to a twenty-first century reader as a shallow illusion precisely because these tales belong to such an old genre. Revolutionary War Era captivity stories had often linked Indian attack and Americans' captivity by a hostile force to collective captivity by the British crown, and had used that allegory to examine the faults in British society. Serving alternately pro- and anti-nationalist purposes—and sometimes both at once—captivity narratives have always been with us.

In the Progressive Era, the symbolism contained in narratives of captivity required little imagination, and the authors and eulogizers who interpreted these stories for the public left little to doubt about their meaning. Indian captives were not frightening or confusing because they had "played" or even "gone" Indian. Rather, they held a special place in the national soul: they were the "missing link" in the national evolution. They, and especially their offspring, became the heart of the national identity that privileged the frontier experience over all others. As twentieth century Americans looked to the frontier period to find the source of their national soul, perhaps no one could be trusted more than the Indian captive—especially one who had descendants alive in the twentieth century—to lead the way into a unique and dominant American century. The "strange vicissitudes," as Mary Jemison's statue stated, through which they had gone, from European to immigrant to captive to Indian to American, embodied the Turnerian process by which all those confused identities became "single-minded[ly]and wholehearted[ly]" American. The complexities of the frontier experience that produced captives were not necessarily forgotten, but they were retold with a single, unifying message: the past could send its national characteristics to the future through the conduit that was the Progressive Era commemoration of those events.

APPENDIX

Progressive Era Indian Captivity Narratives

These narratives are listed in chronological order in order to demonstrate the continued popularity of the narratives and to emphasize the repetition of certain stories throughout the period.

1890–1899

Walton, William. *A Narrative of the Captivity and Suffering of Benjamin Gilbert and his Family: Who were Surprised by the Indians and taken from their Farm, on Mahoning Creek, in Penn Township.* Lancaster, Pa.: Privately Printed, 1890.

Kelly, Fanny. *Narrative of My Captivity among the Sioux Indians.* Chicago: R. R. Donnelley & Sons, 1891.

Meginness, John F. *Biography of Frances Slocum, the Lost Sister of Wyoming: A Complete Narrative of her Captivity and Wanderings Among the Indians.* Williamsport, Pa.: Heller Bros. Printing House, 1891.

Fuller, Emeline L. *Left by the Indians: Story of My Life.* Mt. Vernon, Iowa: Hawkeye Steam Print, 1892.

Baker, Charlotte Alice. *The Sayward Family of York, Maine. Experiences of Mrs. Mary and Her Two Daughters, May and Esther, as Captives in Canada.* Greenfield, Mass,: 1896.

Bookstayer, James N. *Indian Massacres and Tales of the Red Skins: An Authentic History of the American Indian from 1492 to the Present Time.* Augusta, Maine: P. O. Vickery, 1896.

Brayton, Matthew. *The Indian Captive: A Narrative of the Adventures and Sufferings of Matthew Brayton in His Thirty-four Years of Captivity Among the Indians of North Western America.* Fostoria, Ohio: Gray Printing Co., 1896.

Baker, Charlotte Alice. *True Stories of New England Captives Carried to Canada during the Old French and Indian Wars, by C. Alice Baker.* Cambridge, Mass.: Press of E. A. Hall & Co., 1897.

Johnson, Clifton. *An Unredeemed Captive: Being the Story of Eunice Williams, Who at the Age of Seven Years, was Carried Away from Deerfield by the Indians in the Year 1704, and Who Lived Among the Indians in Canada as One of Them the Rest of Her Life.* Holyoke, Mass.: Griffith, Axtell & Cady Co., 1897.

Millet, Pierre. *Captivity Among the Oneidas in 1690–91 of Father Pierre Milet of the Society of Jesus.* Chicago: Blakely Print Co., 1897.

McElroy, John. *Abby Byram, and Her Father: The Indian Captives, with Some Accounts of their Ancestors and a Register of Their Descendants.* Ottumwa, Iowa: Cook & Algire, 1897.

Seaver, James Everett. *A Narrative of the Life of Mary Jemison, De-he-wa-mis, the White Woman of the Genesee.* 6th ed. With notes by Wm. Pryor Letchworth. New York: G. P. Putnam, 1898.

Methvin, J. J. *Andele, or, The Mexican-Kiowa Captive. A Story of Real Life Among the Indians.* Louisville, Ky.: Pentecostal Herald Press, 1899.

Thayer, Henry Otis. "The Indian's Administration of Justice: The Sequel to the Wiscasset Tragedy." In *Collections and Proceedings of the Maine Historical Society,* Vol. 10, 185–211. Portland, Maine: Maine Historical Society, 1899.

1900–1909

Brown, Samuel J. *In Captivity: The Experience, Privations and Dangers of Samuel J. Brown and Others while Prisoners of the Hostile Sioux.* Washington, D.C.: Government Printing Office, 1900.

Janney, Abel. "Narrative of the Capture of Abel Janney by the Indians in 1782." *Ohio Archeological and Historical Quarterly* 8 (1900): 465–72.

Brush, Edward Hale. *Iroquois Past and Present.* Buffalo: Baker, Jones & Co., 1901.

Gardner-Sharp, Abbie. *History of the Spirit Lake Massacre and Captivity of Miss Abbie Gardner,* 5th ed. Des Moines, Iowa: Iowa Print Co., 1902.

Hicks, Elizabeth. *Elizabeth Hicks, A True Romance of the American War of Independence, 1775 to 1783. Abridged from Her Own Manuscript by Her Daughter Fanny Bird, Completed and Edited by Her Granddaughter Louisa J. Marriott.* London: W. Hardwick, 1902.

Brown, James Moore. *The Captives of Abb's Valley.* Philadelphia: Presbyterian Board of Publication, 1903.

Parish, Jasper. "The Story of Captain Jasper Parrish, Captive, Interpreter and United States Sub-Agent to the Six Nations Indians." *Publication of Buffalo Historical Society* 6 (1903): 527–38.

Rowlandson, Mary White. *The Narrative of the Captivity and Restoration of Mrs. Mary Rowlandson.* Lancaster, Mass.: J. Wilson & Son, 1903.

Sophie C. Becker. *Sketches of Early Buffalo and the Niagara Region.* Buffalo, 1904.

Eastburn, Robert. *The Dangers and Sufferings of Robert Eastburn And His Deliverance from Indian Captivity: Reprinted from the Original Edition of 1758 with Introduction and Notes by John R. Spears.* Cleveland: The Burrows Brothers Company, 1904.

How, Nehemiah. *A Narrative of the Captivity of Nehemiah How in 1745–1747: Reprinted from the Original Edition of 1748 with Introduction and Notes by Victor Hugo Paltsits.* Cleveland: The Burrows Brothers Company, 1904.

Leeth, John, and Ewel Jeffries. *A Short Biography of John Leeth, with an Account of His Life Among the Indians: Reprinted from the Original Edition of 1831, with Introduction by Reuben Gold Thwaites.* Cleveland: Burrows Brothers Company, 1904.

Walton, William. *The Captivity and Sufferings of Benjamin Gilbert and his Family, 1780–83: Reprinted from the Original Ed. of 1784, with introduction and Notes by Frank H. Severance.* Cleveland: The Burrows Brothers Company, 1904.

Phelps, Martha Bennett. *Frances Slocum: The Lost Sister of Wyoming. Compiled and Written by Her Grandniece, for Her Children and Grandchildren.* New York: The Knickerbocker Press, 1905.

Johnston, Charles. *Incidents Attending the Capture, Detention, and Ransom of Charles Johnston of Virginia. Reprinted from the Original, with Introduction and Notes by Edwin Erle Sparks.* Cleveland: Burrows Brothers Company, 1905.

Dunklee, Ivah. *The Burning of Royalton, Vermont, by Indians: A Careful Research of All that Pertains to the Subject, including a Reprint of Zadock Steele's Narrative.* Boston: G. H. Ellis Co., 1906.

Phelps, Martha Bennet. *Frances Slocum: The Lost Sister of Wyoming. Compiled and Written by Her Grandniece, for Her Children and Grandchildren.* Wilkes-Barre, Penna.: Published by the Author, 1906.

Severance, Frank H. "The Tale of Captives at Fort Niagara." *Publications of Buffalo Historical Society* 9 (1906): 222–307.

Carrigan, Minnie Buce. *Captured by the Indians: Reminiscences of Pioneer Life in Minnesota.* Forest City, S.Dak.: Forest City Press, 1907.

Brackenridge, H. H. "Narrative of a Late Expedition Against the Indians with an Account of the Barbarous Execution of Col. Crawford and the Wonderful Escape of Dr. Knight & John Sloyer from Captivity in 1782. To which is Added a Narrative of the Captivity and Escape of Mrs. Frances Scott, an Inhabitant of Washington County, Virginia." In *Narrative of the Mission of the United Brethren Among the Delaware and Mohegan Indians from its Commencement in the Year 1740 to the Close of the Year 1808,*

John Gottlieb Ernestus Heckewelder. Edited by William Elsey Connelly. Cleveland: Burrows Brothers Company, 1907.

Johnson, Mrs. Susannah Willard. *A Narrative of the Captivity of Mrs. Johnson. Reprinted from the 3d ed., Published at Windsor, Vermont, 1814, with all Corrections and Additions.* Springfield, Mass.: H. R. Huntting Company, 1907.

Slocum, Charles Elihu. *History of Frances Slocum, the Captive: A Civilized Heredity vs. A Savage, and Later Barbarous, Environment.* Defiance, Ohio: Published by the Author, 1908.

Steele, Zadock. *The Indian Captive, or, A Narrative of the Captivity and Sufferings of Zadock Steele. Related by Himself. To which is Prefixed an Account of the Burning of Royalton.* Springfield, Mass.: H. R. Huntting Co., 1908.

Wakefield, John. *Wakefield's History of the Black Hawk War: A Reprint of the 1st Edition by John A. Wakefield, from the Press of Calvin Goudy, Jacksonville, Illinois, 1834; With Thirteen Photogravure Illustrations, and Preface and Notes by Frank Everett Stevens.* Chicago: Caxton Club, 1908.

Williams, John. *The Redeemed Captive Returning to Zion or the Captivity and Deliverance of Rev. John Williams of Deerfield, Reprinted from the 6th Edition.* Springfield, Mass.: H. R. Huntting Co., 1908.

Dodge, John. *Narrative of Mr. John Dodge during his captivity at Detroit, Reproduced in Facsimile from the 2d. ed. Of 1780, with an Introductory Note by Clarence Monroe Burton.* Cedar Rapids, Iowa: Torch Press, 1909.

Stratton, Royal B. *Captivity of the Oatman Girls: A True Story of the Early Emigration to the West.* Salem, Ore.: Oregon Teachers Monthly, 1909.

1910–1916

Connelley, William Elsey. *The Founding of Harman's Station, with an Account of the Indian Captivity of Mrs. Jennie Wiley and The Exploration and Settlement of the Big Sandy Valley in the Virginias and Kentucky, by William Elsey Connelley to Which is Affixed a Brief Account of the Connelly Family and Some of its Collateral and Related Families in America.* New York: Torch Press, 1910.

Gardner-Sharp, Abbie. *History of the Spirit Lake Massacre and Captivity of Miss Abbie Gardner.* Des Moines: Kenyon Printing Company, 1910.

Seaver, James Everett. *A Narrative of the Life of Mary Jemison, De-he-wa-mis, the White Woman of the Genesee.* 7th ed. With notes by Wm. Pryor Letchworth. New York: The Knickerbocker Press, 1910.

Babb, Theodore Adolphus. *In the Bosom of the Comanches.* Dallas: Press of John F. Worley, 1912.

Carrigan, Minnie Buce. *Captured by the Indians: Reminiscences of Pioneer Life in Minnesota.* Buffalo Lake, Minn.: The News Print, 1912.

Erskin, Margaret. *Old Record of the Captivity of Margaret Erskine, 1779.* Baltimore: Lord Baltimore Press, 1912.

Brown, James Moore. *The Captives of Abb's Valley: A Legend of Frontier Life.* Philadelphia: Presbyterian Board of Publication, 1913.

Lincoln, Charles Henry. *Narratives of the Indian Wars, 1675–1699.* New York: C. Scribner's Sons, 1913.

Seaver, James E. *A Narrative of the Life of Mary Jemison. De-he-wa-mis, The White Woman of the Genesee.* 7th ed. New York: G. P. Putnam's Sons, 1913.

Horace Kephart, ed. *Captives Among the Indians: First-hand Narratives of Indian Wars, Customs, Tortures, and Habits of Life in Colonial Times.* Oyster Bay, N.Y: Nelson Doubleday, 1915.

Merrifield, Edward. *The Story of the Captivity and Rescue from the Indians of Luke Swetland; An Early Settler of the Wyoming Valley and a Soldier of the American Revolution.* Scranton, Pa.: n.p., 1915.

Scanlan, Charles. *Indian Creek Massacre and Captivity of Hall Girls; Complete History of the Massacre of Sixteen Whites on Indian Creek, Near Ottawa, Ill., and Sylvia Hall and Rachel Hall as Captives in*

Illinois and Wisconsin during the Black Hawk War, 1832. Milwaukee, Wis.: Reic Publishing Company, 1915.
Phelps, Martha Bennett. *Frances Slocum: The Lost Sister of Wyoming.* 2nd ed. Wilkes Barre, Penna.: Published by the Author, 1916.
Alexander, Jesse H. *Indian Horrors of the Fifties: Story and Life of the Only Known Living Captive of the Indian Horrors of Sixty Years Ago.* Yakima, Wash.: Yakima Bindery and Printing Co., 1916.

Notes

Introduction

1. Roosevelt, "True Americanism and National Defense," in *Americanism and Preparedness*, 122–23.
2. Renan, "What is a Nation?" 51–60. For a good summary of definitions of nations and its application in the United States, see Scheckel, *The Insistence of the Indian*, 3–14. See also Farmer, *On Zion's Mount*, 12–13.
3. Ebersole, *Captured by Texts*. See especially pages 144–89 and pages 190–237. Unfortunately, Ebersole, like other scholars of captivity, lump Progressive Era narratives together with a broad discussion of twentieth century narratives that usually focuses on juvenile fiction and film. Therefore, while Ebersole's work is highly useful in prompting interpretation, it still fails to recognize a unique Progressive Era use of tales of Indian captivity.
4. Pearce, "The Significances of the Captivity Narrative," 1–20.
5. The Progressive Era did see other captivity narratives published. For example, King's *Three Hundred Days* and Pellow's *The Adventures of Thomas Pellow*.
6. Operé, *Indian Captivity in Spanish America*. Fernando Operé has explained that, in fact, captivity narratives in Spanish America were rare and attracted little attention because the Spanish crown maintained

tight control on which narratives of the colonies reached publishing houses. Because of the religious interest Puritans took in analyzing captivity as a test by God, captivity narratives in the British colonies and the United States took on a cultural popularity that far outlasted the Puritans themselves. In contrast, captivity stories in the Spanish colonies and former Spanish colonies were not nearly as prevalent because they were actively suppressed at the outset.

7. Derounian-Stodola and Levernier, *The Indian Captivity Narrative*, 15–22; Ebersole, *Captured by Texts*, 9–10.

8. Derounian-Stodola and Levernier, *Indian Captivity Narrative*, 26.

9. Burnham, *Captivity and Sentiment*, 42.

10. Derounian-Stodola and Levernier, *Indian Captivity Narrative*, 36–37.

11. Burnham, *Captivity and Sentiment*, 95.

12. Turner-Strong, *Captive Selves, Captivating Others*; Rebecca Blevins Faery, *Cartographies of Desire*. The end result or goal of this exposure, though, has been left unexplored, perhaps because it exists in the narratives in the subtext only, rather than as an overtly stated reason for the narrative's publication.

13. See in particular, for example, Sieminski, "The Puritan Captivity Narrative," 35–57. In this article, Sieminski demonstrates that Puritan narratives served to create a new American cultural identity during the Revolutionary period. The Puritan Indian captivity narrative spoke to the emerging American mind because of known tales of captivity by the British forces during the Revolutionary War and because of a sense of collective captivity by a tyrannical king. Also see Namias, *White Captives*, in which Namias examines what a popular cultural genre revealed about the worries and anxieties of American culture and thus how captivity narratives aided in the creation of a new country that saw itself as unique in the world.

14. Lutz, *Myth and Memory*, 160.

15. Limerick, *The Legacy of Conquest*, 25; Slotkin, *Regeneration Through Violence*, 30.

16. Quoted in Faragher, *Rereading Frederick Jackson Turner*, 5.

17. Limerick, *The Legacy of Conquest*, 24–25.

18. Hoxie, *Talking Back to Civilization*, 4.

19. For a detailed discussion of the creation of the White City, see Larson, *The Devil in the White City*.

20. White, "Frederick Jackson Turner and Buffalo Bill," 7–65.

21. Slotkin, *Regeneration Through Violence*. Also particularly useful are the first two parts of Slotkin's *Gunfighter Nation*, 1–230.

22. Huhndorf, *Going Native*, 5, 8.
23. Deloria, *Playing Indian* (1998), 183. See also Turner-Strong, *Captive Selves, Captivating Others*. Turner-Strong demonstrates the importance of Indians captured and held by Euro-Americans in developing a white tradition of understanding Indians as vital to the wilderness experience, and the benefits (both personal and national) of that experience. In Turner-Strong's understanding of captivity narratives and the way they allowed Euro-Americans to incorporate Indian characteristics into their national identity, captivity was a two-way street, and both captivity *by* Indians and captivity *of* Indians served this nationalistic purpose. In this study, I focus on captivity *by* Indians, although captivity *of* Indians in the Progressive Era would also be ripe for interpretation.
24. The noticeable exceptions are Babb's *In the Bosom of the Comanches*; Brown's *In Captivity*; Kelly's *Narrative of My Captivity*; and Stratton's *Captivity of the Oatman Girls*.
25. Brooks, *Captives and Cousins*, 363.
26. Venebles, "American Indian Influences," 75.
27. Deloria, *Playing Indian*, 98.
28. Seton, *The Book of Woodcraft and Indian Lore*, 8.
29. Quoted in Seton, *The Book of Woodcraft and Indian Lore*, 100.
30. Ibid., 103.
31. Ibid., 103–104.
32. See in particular Wrobel, *The End of American Exceptionalism*, 27–68. In this iconic work, Wrobel moves beyond fixation with Turner's "Frontier Thesis" to argue that as early as the 1870s and as late as the 1930s, preoccupation with the "agrarian heritage" created an anxiety that American political and social institutions would collapse once access to that agrarian ideal was closed (or rather, was believed to be closed) to new settlers.
33. Haberly, "Women and Indians," 431–44.
34. Castiglia, *Bound and Determined*. See also Namias, *White Captives*, and Demos, *The Unredeemed Captive*. John Demos argues that far more women chose to remain with their captors than did men, using the case of Eunice Williams, who was captured in the 1704 Deerfield Massacre, as case-in-point. For a different, somewhat more extreme, take on women in captivity, see Faery, *Cartographies of Desire*. Faery claims that the Euro-American desire for land and the sexual desire for the Indian maiden were, in fact, the same thing. Therefore, the assumption by white males that white women needed protecting from lecherous "dark" men also

represented their desire to defend land already taken from the possible reconquest by those same "dark" men.

35. Leeth and Jeffries, *A Short Biography of John Leeth*, 2.

36. Frances Slocum did eventually dictate a short version of her story, but she never articulated her reasons for doing so. That "as told to" version of her story makes up a very small part of her narrative, most of which is pieced together from the testimonies and documents left by whites who had contact with her. Most of the time, Frances Slocum herself directed outright hostility towards non-Indians who asked her to tell her story, often implying that their ulterior motive was to steal her land.

37. Sieminski, "The Puritan Captivity Narrative," 14–17.

Chapter 1

1. Phelps, *Frances Slocum* (1916), 47. This quotation comes from a letter from Hendrick B. Wright to Mrs. Lord Butler, grandniece of Francis Slocum, December 31, 1877, of which Phelps cites a large section in her narrative. Wright, a U.S. Representative at the time, heard the story from Col. Ewing in approximately 1853. In hopes of tracing the Slocums, Ewing had called upon the politician in order to tell his story to the representative from the region in which Maconaquah believed her white family had lived. Ewing's own letters to the Slocum family were much less detailed than the account Wright provided, perhaps to spare them the details of how little like them their lost sister had become.

2. Ibid.

3. Ibid., 48.

4. Pearce, "Significance," 5; Sieminski, "The Puritan Captivity Narrative," 35–56; Burnham, *Captivity and Sentiment*; Castiglia, *Bound and Determined*; Ebersole, *Captured by Texts*; Namias, *White Captives*.

5. Olster, "Empire and Liberty, 215; Wrobel, *The End of American Exceptionalism*, 54.

6. Brian W. Dippie, ed., *Charlie Russell Roundup*, 2–3.

7. American Scenic and Historic Preservation Society, "Dedication of the Statue of Mary Jemison, 249, 255.

8. James T. DeShields, *Cynthia Ann Parker*; Wellman, "Cynthia Ann Parker," 163–70.

9. Hagan, *Quanah Parker*, 119–27.

10. For a detailed outline of the Parker family, see Exley, *Frontier Blood: The Saga of the Parker Family*; and DeShields, *Cynthia Ann Parker*.
11. Hofsteader, *The Age of Reform*, 5.
12. Ibid., 135.
13. Ibid., 137–39.
14. Carrigan, *Captured by the Indians*, preface.
15. Dunklee, *Burning of Royalton*, 7.
16. Faragher, *Rereading Frederick Jackson Turner*; Roosevelt, *The Strenuous Life*.
17. Shifflett, *Victorian America, 1876–1913*, 78. Whiteness studies such Roediger, *The Wages of Whiteness*, and Guglielmo, *White on Arrival*, trace the way individuals and communities constructed their identities to give themselves access to white privilege, although they come to slightly different conclusions. While Roediger sees a middle stage during which groups that we now think of as "white" were in transition from nonwhite to white, Guglielmo contends that immigrants could be both discriminated against and "white" at the same time.
18. For discussion of the assumption that Indians were "vanishing," see Dippie, *The Vanishing American*; Hoxie, *A Final Promise*; Berkhofer, *White Man's Indian*.
19. Phelps, *Frances Slocum* (1916), 125.
20. Fink, *Major Problems in the Gilded Age*, 118.
21. Glassberg, *American Historical Pageantry*, 15.
22. American Scenic and Historic Preservation Society, "Dedication," 255.
23. Fish, *The Development of American Nationality*, 512.
24. Ibid.
25. See Mattson, *Creating a Democratic Public* for a discussion of debates on how to preserve and expand democracy during the Progressive Era.
26. Roosevelt, *The Strenuous Life*, 265–66. For a detailed discussion of the ways expanded urbanization changed cultural behaviors in the early twentieth century, see Barth, *City People*.
27. Mattson, *Creating a Democratic Public*, 17. Patricia Nelson Limerick has stated that despite the historical reality that open land had not disappeared in the American West or that homesteading did not end either in 1890, "the idea played an enormous role in national behavior" and "the historian is obligated to understand how people saw their own times." Limerick, *The Legacy of Conquest*, 25.
28. Wrobel, *The End of American Exceptionalism*; Slotkin, *Gunfighter Nation*.

29. Knight, *Citizen*; Zipf, *Professional Pursuits*.

30. Nancy S. Dye, "Introduction," in Dye and Frankle, *Gender, Class, Race and Reform*, 1–9.

31. Cooper, *Pivotal Decades*, 1–30.

32. For a broad discussion of the social sciences in practice in New York City in the Progressive Era, see Recchiuti, *Civic Engagement*.

33. American Scenic and Historic Preservation Society, "Dedication," 255.

34. See Roosevelt, *The Strenuous Life*, especially pages 1–9, for his defense of nationalist expansionism and its link to national and individual strength and virtue. For the opposing view, see Bryan, *Speeches*. Bryan uses almost the same arguments—that the democratic and individualist traditions of the United State dictate its course of action—to argue against U.S. occupation of the Philippines.

35. Mattson, *Creating a Democratic Public*, 17.

36. American Scenic and Historic Preservation Society, "Dedication," 256–58.

37. Bailey, *The Country-Life Movement*. Bailey distinguishes the country life movement from the back-to-the-land movement by arguing that the former springs from the actions of those people who live in the country to create a complete and fulfilling culture there, whereas the latter springs from the minds of city dwellers who long to escape urban life.

38. Diner, *A Very Different Age*, 119.

39. *Report of the Country Life Commission*, 14–16.

40. Ibid., 9.

41. Quoted in Diner, *A Very Different Age*, 123.

42. Ibid.

43. Ibid., 119–20.

44. Quoted in Glassberg, *American Historical Pageantry*, 69.

45. Gardner-Sharp, *History of the Spirit Lake Massacre* (1910), 359, 362.

46. Roosevelt, *The Winning of the West*, 183.

47. Ibid., 181–84.

48. Lovejoy, *History of Royalton, Vermont*, 175–78.

49. Ibid., 182.

50. Ibid., 183.

51. Gardner-Sharp, *History* (1910), 353.

52. Pearce, "The Significances of the Captivity Narrative," 1–20.

53. Ibid., 13.

54. VanDerBeets, "The Indian Captivity Narrative as Ritual," 548–62; Allen, "The Double Exposure," 249–61.

55. Dunklee, *Burning of Royalton* (1906).
56. American Scenic and Historic Preservation Society, "Dedication," 234–35.
57. Dunklee, *Burning of Royalton* (1906).
58. Dunklee, *Burning of Royalton* (1906), 70–71. See the narratives of captive Zadock Steele, first published in 1818. (Twentieth century editions by Ivah Dunklee were published 1906, 1908, and 1934.) Andover Theological Seminary, *Necrology, 1911–1914*, 28.
59. Lears, *No Place of Grace*, 5–6. Lears has argued that "Losing cultural authority, the leaders of the American bourgeoisie reasserted their power with rifles and bayonets. The expedient was temporarily successful but ultimately unsatisfying, because more was at stake than mere power. . . . The ruling class required not only more guns but moral regeneration." In order to achieve that moral authority, Americans looked back, but not in a necessarily vapid way. Lears argues, "far from encouraging escapist nostalgia, anti-modern sentiments not only promoted eloquent protest against the limits of liberalism but also helped to shape new modes of cultural authority for the oncoming twentieth century." In this context, anti-modern captivity narratives also helped set the stage for the new century.
60. See, for example, the narrative of Mary Rowlandson, first published in 1682, in which she hopes that her readers will come to know God more completely, as she did, through the reading of her tale.
61. Faery, *Cartographies of Desire*, 12. Turner-Strong, *Captive Selves, Captivating Others*, 3. Pauline Turner-Strong argues that the main feature of captivity was its complexity, and that the suppression of that complexity has given the narratives of captivity their cultural power. Thus, we as scholars, according to Turner-Strong, have to rediscover that complexity.
62. Ebersole, *Captured by Texts*.
63. Turner, "Significance of the Frontier"; Faragher, *Rereading Frederick Jackson Turner*, 60.
64. Phelps, *Frances Slocum* (1916), 147–51.
65. American Scenic and Historic Preservation Society, "Dedication," 257.
66. Ibid.

Chapter 2

1. Seaver, *A Narrative of the Life*, 9; American Scenic and Historic Preservation Society, "Dedication," 251.

2. Letchworth, *Care and Treatment of Epileptics*. Letchworth also published *The Insane in Foreign Countries*. Letchworth signed the prefaces of both works from "Glen Iris, Portage P.O., N.Y."

3. Farmer, *On Zion's Mount*, 4.

4. American Scenic and Historic Preservation Society, "Dedication," 236.

5. Larned, *The Life and Work*, 20–32.

6. Ibid., 42–43.

7. Livingston County Historical Society, "An Address Delivered," 39. Apparently, Dehgewanus carried this wood "on her back, through the unbroken forest from the nearest sawmill."

8. American Scenic and Historic Preservation Society, "Dedication," 236.

9. Densmore, *Red Jacket*, 88.

10. June Namias, introduction to Seaver, *A Narrative of the Life*, 3–48; Smith and Watson, *Before They Could Vote*, 37–123.

11. American Scenic and Historic Preservation Society, "Dedication," 255.

12. Farmer, *On Zion's Mount*, 10–11.

13. Brinkley, *The Wilderness Warrior*, 237.

14. Ibid., 3–5.

15. Dean, "Natural History, Romanticism, and Thoreau," 76.

16. Emerson, *Nature*, 70.

17. Larned, *The Life and Work*, 23.

18. American Scenic and Historic Preservation Society, "Dedication," 240.

19. Larned, *The Life and Work*, 371.

20. Ibid.

21. American Scenic and Historic Preservation Society, "Letchworth Park and Arboretum," 70–75. The social philosophy of many nineteenth century businessmen combined the beliefs of social Darwinism with the tenets of capitalism to argue that their greed benefitted society by adhering to the natural laws of capitalism laid out by Adam Smith. In this case, though, the Genesee River Company seems to have felt the need to prove that their dam would have more concrete benefits by stating that the dam would prevent downriver flooding that caused disease. The Water Supply Commission found not only that the flooding did not cause disease, but in fact that it did not even occur.

22. Ibid., 71–75. Larned, *The Life and Work*, 379. Josephus Larned added italics to emphasize the phrase to the wording of the original

1898 New York law giving that right to the Genesee River Company. The Company, however, failed to meet financial and timeline deadlines. The State Water Supply Commission, studying the viability of the Genesee dam project, decided in 1911 that although the large lake created would be "attractive" and the dam itself "a thing of massive grandeur," building it would interfere with the park and so would "be a violation on the part of the State of the contract made with Mr. Letchworth." If such a violation occurred, the park would "revert to [Mr. Letchworth's] heirs, or be subject to an action by the American Scenic and Historic Preservation Society." The committee concluded that the risk of losing the park (combined with the facts that the dam project would be prohibitively expensive and that no real risk to public health from seasonal flooding had been found) made the dam unviable. The Commission (which was soon abolished and its duties given over to the State Conservation Commission) denied the company's petition to build the dam in a report issued in June, 1911. The company dissolved five months later, just over a year after the Mary Jemison statue went up in Glen Iris. A complete discussion of the proposed dam project, including many of the legal documents relating to the Genesee River Company, can be found in Water Supply Commission, "River Improvement," 21–31.

23. Ibid., 380.
24. Quoted in Randall Mason, *The Once and Future New York*, 2.
25. Seaver, *Life*, 270.
26. Livingston County Historical Society, "An Address Delivered by Mr. J. D. Lewis," 38–40.
27. American Scenic and Historic Preservation Society, "Dedication," 238.
28. Farmer, *On Zion's Mount*, 282–86.
29. Randall Mason, "Historic Preservation," 133–35.
30. American Scenic and Historic Preservation Society, "Dedication," 248–49.
31. "Almost Rivals Niagara: State of Letchworth's Death Will get Beautiful Glen Iris," *New York Times*, January 4, 1907.
32. Webster, "An Ornamental Farm."
33. Olmsted, "The True Purpose of a Large Public Park," 12.
34. Ibid., 12–14.
35. Ibid.
36. Grese, "Jens Jensen," 117.
37. Seaver, *Narrative of the Life of Mary Jemison* (1910), 7.

38. Livingston County Historical Society, "Address Delivered by Mr. J. D. Lewis," 38–40.
39. New York State Museum, "The Mary Jemison Monument," 58.
40. Ranney, "Frederick Law Olmstead, 41.
41. Farmer, *On Zion's Mount*, 6–12.
42. Ranney, "Designing for Democracy in the Midwest," 14.
43. Ibid., 15.
44. Ibid., 19.
45. See Chapter 3 for a detailed discussion of the notion of the "vanishing Indian."
46. The American Numismatic Society, "Henry Kirke Bush-Brown," in *Catalogue of the International Exhibition*, 37.
47. Bush-Brown, "Sculpture in Washington," 70–71.
48. Ibid.
49. American Scenic and Historic Preservation Society, "Dedication," 243.
50. Ibid., 75.
51. Spiro, *Defending the Master Race*, 27.
52. American Scenic and Historic Preservation Society, "Dedication," 241, 243.
53. Livingston County Historical Society, "An Address Delivered by Mr. J. D. Lewis," 40. J. D. Lewis, in his speech to the Livingston County Historical Society, noted that "a friend of mine who was well acquainted with Mr. Letchworth told me that he believed he had more kindness in his breast, and had given more time and money for the good of the public than any other man of his age, and I believe it. May many kind and willing hands strew beautiful wild flowers on his last resting place."
54. Larned, *Life and Work*, 73.
55. "New York State Acquires New Park," *New York Times*, January 27, 1907.
56. Larned, *The Life and Work*, 88–89.
57. Muir, *My First Summer in the Sierra*, 73.
58. Krech, *The Ecological Indian*, 216. 59. Eastman, *From The Deep Woods to Civilization*, 170–74.
60. American Scenic and Historic Preservation Society, "Dedication," 237, 249.
61. Spence, *Dispossessing the Wilderness*, 70.
62. Seaver, *A Narrative of the Life of Mary Jemison* (1910), 197.

63. Ibid., 4.
64. Muir, *My First Summer*, 295.
65. Ibid., 304.
66. See also Spence, *Dispossessing the Wilderness*.
67. Seaver, *A Narrative of the Life of Mary Jemison* (1910), 277.
68. American Scenic and Historic Preservation Society, "Dedication," 257–58.
69. Mary E. Percival, "To William Pryor Letchworth, May 26, 1909," in Howland, *Voices of the Glen*, 84.
70. Amanda T. Jones, "William Pryor Letchworth, LL.D," in Howland, *Voices of the Glen*, 85.
71. Sara Evans Letchworth, "From Inspiration Point, June 8th, 1909," in Howland, *Voices of the Glen*, 82.
72. James N. Johnston, "To Glen Iris," in Howland, *Voices of the Glen*, 97.
73. American Scenic and Historic Preservation Society, "Dedication," 251.
74. Ibid., 258.
75. "Conservationist Left Behind Mini-Grand Canyon," *The Sharon Herald* (Sharon, Pa.), March 27, 2007.
76. Seaver, *A Narrative of the Life*; Gangi, *Mary Jemison*.

Chapter 3

1. Theodore Roosevelt, *The Great Adventure*, 49.
2. "Is the Indian Dying Out: Figures That Seem to Point the Other Way. Statistics from the Days of Jefferson Until Now that are Puzzling in Their Uncertainty," *New York Times*, February 14, 1887, 2.
3. "Indians Not Dying Out: The Chief of the Senecas Before the Anthropologists," *New York Times*, October 31, 1888, 9.
4. American Scenic and Historic Preservation Society, "Dedication," 249; "The Indians are not Dying Out, They are Increasing," *New York Times*, August 13, 1911, Magazine, 2. We now know that vastly more people lived in the Americas prior to European contact than previously thought, with probably 90 percent or more dying in epidemics of small pox, influenza, diphtheria, typhus, and measles. Possibly 90 to 112 million people lived in the Western Hemisphere before 1492. "Another way of saying this," Charles Mann writes, "is that in 1491 more people lived in the Americas than in Europe." Charles C. Mann, "1491," 43.

5. Gardner-Sharp, *History of the Spirit Lake Massacre* (1857); Gardner-Sharp, *History of the Spirit Lake Massacre* (1910), 325.
6. Gardner-Sharp, *History of the Spirit Lake Massacre* (1910), 325.
7. Ibid.
8. "American Indians Increase; Nation's Total Now 349,595," *New York Times*, October 29, 1925, 1.
9. "Lives 22 Years with Indians to Get their Secrets," *New York Times*, April 16, 1911, Magazine Section, 5.
10. Quoted in Franz, "The Colossus of Staten Island."
11. "Wanamaker Party now with Pueblos," *New York Times*, June 29, 1913, 11.
12. American Scenic and Historic Preservation Society, "Dedication," 248, 252.
13. Gardner-Sharp, *History* (1910), 309–10.
14. Ibid., 323.
15. Ibid., 315–16.
16. Ibid., 323.
17. Ibid., 325.
18. Ibid., 328.
19. Ibid., 345.
20. Slocum, *The Slocums, Slocumbs, and Slocombs of America*, 222.
21. Spiro, *Defending the Maser Race*, xii.; Grant, *Passing of the Great Race*.
22. Grant, *Passing of the Great Race*, 69.
23. Boas, "Eugenics," 471–78.
24. Ibid., 472.
25. Ibid.
26. Phelps, *Frances Slocum* (1906), 107–16; John F Meginness, *Biography of Frances Slocum*, 194–97. According to Seaver, in 1825, the Senecas sold their reservation lands along the Genesee River and removed to the Buffalo Creek reservation, "leaving Mrs. Jemison . . . surrounded by whites in every direction." Dehgewanus and her family grew uncomfortable and "discontented and uneasy" on their two square mile plot, and left in 1831.
27. Dippie, *The Vanishing American*, 200.
28. Morgan, *Ancient Society*, vi-viii, 552–54.
29. Berkhofer, *White Man's Indian*, 172.
30. See Barsh, "Progressive Era Bureaucrats," 3; Laderman, " 'It is Cheaper and Better,' " 85–111. For the opposite notion, that advocates of the Dawes Act and assimilation policies were well-meaning but

misguided and naïve, see especially Hoxie, *A Final Promise*, and Prucha, *The Great Father*.

31. Baillargeon, *Legends of Our Times*; Adams, *Education for Extinction*; Laderman, "Cheaper and Better," 89.
32. Phelps, *Frances Slocum* (1906), 107–13, 138–42.
33. Phelps, *Frances Slocum* (1905), 122.
34. John F. Meginness, *Biography of Frances Slocum*, 196.
35. Holm, *The Great Confusion in Indian Affairs*, 114–15.
36. Ibid., 131–35.
37. Phelps, *Frances Slocum* (1905); Phelps, *Frances Slocum* (1906).
38. Phelps, *Frances Slocum* (1905), 128.
39. For a discussion of the impression that Indians were "dying out" and that belief's effect on Indian policy, see Dippie, *The Vanishing American*. See also Hoxie, *Talking Back to Civilization*.
40. Trachtenberg, *Shades of Hiawatha*, xxii.
41. Deloria, *Playing Indian*, 95–126.
42. Glassberg, *American Historical Pageantry*, 281–82.
43. Gardner-Sharp, *History* (1905), 362.
44. Quoted in Dippie, *The Vanishing American*, 259. See also Axtell, "The White Indians of Colonial America," 55–88.
45. Quoted in Ebersole, *Captured by Texts*, 197.
46. Hunter, *Memoirs of a Captivity*, 51.
47. Rowlandson, *The Narrative of the Captivity*, 52.
48. Ebersole, *Captured by Texts*, 240.
49. Bass, *Stories of Pioneer Life*, 77.
50. Meginness, *Biography*, 59–60.
51. Phelps, *Frances Slocum* (1905), 50.
52. Peck, *Wyoming*, 263–64.
53. Meginness, *Biography*, 72–73.
54. Ibid.
55. Meginness, *Biography*, 154.
56. Seaver, *Narrative of the Life of Mary Jemison* (1910), 93.
57. Seaver, *Narrative of the Life of Mrs. Mary Jemison*, Namias, ed. (1992), 36.
58. Seaver, *Narrative of the Life of Mary Jemison* (1910), 104.
59. Ibid.
60. Ibid., 104–105. We can see here another confusing suggestion that "blood" is the cause of personal traits. In this case, the child of a kind man had a kind nature himself, and the son of a violent man was himself

violent. Mary Jemison's "white blood" was, apparently, no match for the savagery contained in Hiokatoo's genes.

61. Meginness, *Otzinachson*, 45; *History of Wyoming County, N.Y.*, 51; Grace Ellis Taft, "The White Woman of Genesee," 238.

62. Vanderhoof, *Historical Sketches*, 104–105.

63. Trachtenberg, *Shades of Hiawatha*, 13. See also Grinde, "Iroquois Political Theory and the Roots of American Democracy," 228–80. In this article Grinde argues that "American democracy is a synthesis of Native American and European political theories."

64. Engels, *The Origin of the Family*, 217.

65. American Scenic and Historic Preservation Society, "Dedication," 249. This statement directly echoes Frederick Jackson Turner's famous declaration that "the frontier is the outer edge of the wave—the meeting point between savagery and civilization" and therefore the defining feature in American history (Turner, "The Significance of the Frontier," 81).

66. Turner, "The Significance of the Frontier," 81–82; Trachtenberg, *Shades of Hiawatha*, 35.

67. Trachtenberg, *Shades of Hiawatha*, 40.

68. Meginness, *Biography of Frances Slocum*, 196; Phelps, *Frances Slocum* (1906), 63.

69. Phelps, *Frances Slocum* (1906), 119.

70. Ibid., 128, 147.

71. Paltsits, *A Narrative of the Captivity of Nehemiah How*, 21.

72. Leeth and Jeffries, *A Short Biography of John Leeth* (1904),18–19.

73. Seaver, 1910, 238.

74. Dixon and Wanamaker, *The Vanishing Race*, xvi, 4–5.

75. "A Notable Meeting," *Peru Evening Journal* (Peru, Ind.), May 18, 1900.

76. Ibid.; "An Impressive Ceremony," *The Wabash Times* (Wabash, Ind.), May 18, 1900.

77. Ibid.

78. Seaver, *Narrative of the Life of Mary Jemison* (1918), 242.

Chapter 4

1. Steele's narrative refers to the Caghnewaga Indians, who were most likely the Kahnawake, one of the eight tribes of the Mohawk Nation, who came into Vermont during the Revolution from nearby Montreal with the apparent intent of burning, looting, and killing as many Americans

as possible. During the American Revolution, the Kahnawake, one of the Iroquois nations that sided with the British during the conflict, ran raids into the United States from Canada. See Snow, *The Iroquois*.

2. Dunklee, *Burning of Royalton* (1906), 68–69.

3. The four male Burrows Brothers captivity narratives are How's *A Narrative of the Captivity of Nehemiah* (1904); *The Dangers and Sufferings of Robert Eastburn And His Deliverance from Indian Captivity* (1904); Walton's *The Captivity and Sufferings of Benjamin Gilbert and his Family, 1780–83* (1904); and *A Short Biography of John Leeth* (1904). Zadock Steele's narrative appeared in print two times in the first decade of the twentieth century: Dunklee, *Burning of Royalton* (1906), and Steele, *The Indian Captive* (1908).

4. See, for example, Derounian-Stodola, *Women's Indian Captivity Narratives*; Faery, *Cartographies of Desire*; and Kolodny, *The Land Before Her*.

5. For discussion of sex and its link to land acquisition, see Faery, *Cartographies of Desire*, and Namias, *White Captives*.

6. American Scenic and Historic Preservation Society, "Dedication," 244.

7. Ibid., 244–45.

8. Namias, *White Captives*, 29, 31, 36–37.

9. Ibid., 37.

10. Phelps, *Frances Slocum* (1905), 14.

11. Foster, "National Old Trails Road," 353.

12. Gentry, "National Old Trail Road Committee," 531.

13. For an in-depth discussion of Inkpaduta in all his complexity and contradiction, see Beck, *Inkpaduta: Dakota Leader*.

14. Gardner-Sharp, *History* (1910), 157. Her captors forced her to "trudge" through deep snow carrying a pack containing "eight bars of lead, one pint of lead-balls, one tepee cover made of the heaviest, thickest cloth, one blanket, one bed-comforter, one iron bar, one piece of wood several inches wide and four feet long, to keep the pack in shape."

15. Ibid., 333.

16. Ibid., 315–16.

17. Olson, "Tragedy, Tourism, and the Log Cabin," 69–71; Parvin, *Who Made Iowa*, 41.

18. Gardner-Sharp, *History* (1910), 351. Olson, "Tragedy, Tourism, and the Log Cabin," 69–71.

19. Gardner-Sharp, *History* (1910), 334–35.

20. Ibid., 397.

21. Byers, "Resting at Okoboji," 442–43.
22. Schuler, "Dear Brother John," 621–22.
23. W. H. Steele, *Memories of By-Gone Days*, 127–28.
24. Olson, "Tragedy," 69–71; Catherine W. Zipf argues in *Professional Pursuits* that the Arts and Crafts movement, with its dedication to anti-industrial production and work done at home, was singularly situated to allow women to enter the workplace because it allowed women to couch their work in traditional terms. For discussion of the uses of traditional ideals as an entrance for women into politics and reform movements in the Progressive Era, see Testi, "The Gender of Reform Politics," 1509–33.
25. Kimmel, *Manhood in America*, 43.
26. Kerber, "Women and Individualism," 587–92.
27. Ibid., 13–18; Rotundo, *American Manhood*, 10–18.
28. Kimmel, *Manhood in America*, 19–42; Rotundo, *American Manhood*, 19–30.
29. Kimmel, *Manhood in America*, 81; Calhoun, *The Gilded Age*, 2.
30. Kimmel, *Manhood in America*, 43.
31. Parvin, *Who Made Iowa*, 8, 50–51; *Theodore Roosevelt: An Autobiography*, 439.
32. Kimmel, *Manhood in America*, 82–84.
33. For a discussion of the male fear of feminization of culture, see Lears, *No Place of Grace*, 103–39.
34. Kerber, "Women and Individualism," 590. See also Pettigrew, *Brutes in Suits*.
35. Murphy, *Political Manhood*, 2.
36. Paine, "The Author of 'White Fang,'" 361.
37. Cook, "Nature-Books For the Holidays," 389.
38. Kimmel, *Manhood*, 87.
39. Ibid., 82.
40. Pettigrew, *Brutes in Suits*, 3.
41. Douglass, *The Feminization of American Culture*, 327.
42. Case, *The Masculine in Religion*, 25.
43. Ibid., 50.
44. Ibid., 78.
45. *Theodore Roosevelt*, 439, 487.
46. Ibid., 437.
47. Johnson, "A Home Talk with the Boys," 189.
48. It is important here to note that most captivity narratives republished, reissued, or written in the Progressive Era were not actually written

by the captives themselves. Those of Zadock Steele and Abbie Gardner-Sharp are the exceptions. While the 1906 *Burning of Royalton* was written by Ivah Dunklee, it included the unaltered text of Steele's narrative.

49. Dunklee, *Burning* (1906), 19.
50. Gardner-Sharp, *History* (1910), 73–83.
51. Phelps, *Frances Slocum* (1916), 11.
52. Lovejoy, *History of Royalton*, 601–603.
53. See in particular MacLeod, *Building Character in the American Boy*.
54. Quoted in Kett, *Rites of Passage*, 106.
55. Ibid., 107.
56. Greeley, "The Formation of Character," 94–95.
57. *Theodore Roosevelt*, 86, 27, 167.
58. Moore, "Society of the Army of the Tennessee," 67.
59. Phelps, *Frances Slocum* (1905), 70.
60. Dunklee, *Burning* (1907), 68–70.
61. Roosevelt, *The Strenuous Life*, 3–4.
62. Lovejoy, *History of Royalton*, 139.
63. Dunklee, *Burning* (1906), 27–28. Mrs. Hendee is called Hannah Handy in De Puy's *Ethan Allen and the Green Mountain Heroes of '76*.
64. Dunklee, *Burning* (1906), 29–32.
65. Ibid., 62.
66. Lovejoy, *History of Royalton*, 165–66. Lovejoy explained later in her account of Mrs. Hendee that she changed the spelling of her name to Handy because the family "wrote their name Handy, and the descendants continue to so write it, in distinction from another branch which has adopted the form 'Hendee.'"
67. Steele, *The Indian Captive*, xi.
68. Ibid., xi; Dunklee, *Burning of Royalton*, 68–71.
69. For a discussion of Roosevelt's sickly childhood and the development of his manly image as an adult, see McCullough, *Mornings on Horseback*.
70. *Theodore Roosevelt*, 27.
71. Ibid., 259.
72. Ibid.
73. Marsh, "From Separation to Togetherness," 513.
74. Buckley, *The Wrong and Peril of Woman*, 126.
75. See in particular Maynard, "'An Ideal Life in the Woods for Boys,'" 3–29; and Macleod, *Building Character in the American Boy*.
76. Behling, *The Masculine Woman in America*, 17. See also Chauncey, *Gay New York*, 113. Chauncey points out that men created The Knights

of King Arthur and the Sons of Daniel Boone as well as the Boy Scouts in order to provide their sons places to develop and exercise their masculinity. Middle- and upper-class men in the late nineteenth century began to idolize the masculine traits of the cowboy or rancher and the working-class man, signifying that they were concerned that their own lifestyles brought their sexuality and manliness into question.

77. Beveridge, *The Young Man and the World*, 20–32 and 57–58.

78. Rotundo, "Body and Soul," 32. See also Kimmel, "Men's Responses to Feminism," 269; and Maynard, "'An Ideal Life in the Woods for Boys,'" 3–29.

79. Anderson, *The Chief*, 131, 137–41.

80. Boy Scouts of America, *Handbook for Scoutmasters*, 105, 316, 315, 314.

81. Beard, *American Nervousness*, vi–ii, 77, 135.

82. Gulick, "The Girl's Branch," 416–18. For a discussion of the value of "playing by the rules," see Dudley, "Inside and Outside the Ring," 53–82.

83. Low, *How Girls can Help Their Country*, 11.

84. Rotundo, "Body and Soul," 1.

85. Boas, "Eugenics," 477.

86. Roosevelt, "The Strenuous Life," 21.

87. Gardner-Sharp, *History* (1910), 362–63.

88. Phelps, *Frances Slocum* (1905), 5.

89. *A Narrative of the Captivity of Nehemiah How*, 8.

90. Roosevelt, *The Winning of the West*, 108; Roosevelt, *The Winning of the West*, 99.

91. Turner, "Significance of the Frontier in American History," 111.

Epilogue

1. Scanlan, *Indian Creek Massacre*, 95–96.

2. Ibid, 97–98.

3. Ibid., 104–105.

4. Illinois State Historical Society, "Monument Unveiled," 333.

5. Ibid.

6. Phelps, *Frances Slocum* (1916), 147; Dunklee, *Burning of Royalton* (1906), 101.

7. American Scenic and Historic Preservation Society, "Dedication," 249.

8. Illinois State Historical Society, "Monument Unveiled," 335.

NOTES TO PAGES 175–78 207

9. Scanlan, *Indian Creek Massacre*, 95, 98.
10. Ibid, 3–4.
11. Hall, *Uncommon Defense*, 136–37. Shabbona's name, although Scanlan spells it Shabona and many of the places named after him in Illinois spell it Shabbona, is more commonly spelled Shaubena. I am referring to him as Shabbona here because that was the spelling chosen for Shabbona Park where the Indian Creek Massacre monument was erected.
12. Illinois State Historical Society, "Monument Unveiled," 333.
13. Gross, *Past and Present*, 20.
14. Illinois State Historical Society, "Monument Unveiled," 334.
15. Wood, *Lives of the Famous Indian Chiefs*, 438.
16. Gross, *Past and Present*, 20.
17. Illinois State Historical Society, "Monument Unveiled," 334–35. Shabbona, then, literally helped build the homes of those people who destroyed his traditional life, although he remained enough the "savage" to always prefer sleeping outdoors. In the 1840s, Shabbona and his family suffered from poverty and deprivation, and the settlers, in recognition of his service to them, built him a cabin of his own. He accepted the cabin, but slept always in a teepee beside it, using the building for storage. Gross, *Past and Present*, 21.

Bibliography

Adams, David Wallace. *Education for Extinction: American Indians and the Boarding School Experience, 1875–1928.* Lawrence: University Press of Kansas, 1995.

Allen, Phoebe A. "The Double Exposure of the Texas Captives," *Western Folklore* 32.4 (October 1973): 249–61.

American Numismatic Society. *Catalogue of the International Exhibition of Contemporary Medals, March 1910.* New York: American Numismatic Society, 1911.

American Scenic and Historic Preservation Society. "Dedication of the Statue of Mary Jemison, the White Woman of the Genesee." In *Sixteenth Annual Report of the Scenic and Historic Preservation Society, 1911,* 244–61. Albany: J. B. Lyon Co., 1911.

———. "Letchworth Park and Arboretum." In *Seventeenth Annual Report of the Scenic and Historic Preservation Society, 1912,* 70–75. Albany: The Argus Company Printers, 1912.

Anderson, H. Allen. *The Chief: Ernest Thompson Seton and the Changing West.* College Station: Texas A&M University Press, 1986.

Andover Theological Seminary. *Necrology, 1911–1914.* Cambridge, Mass.: Andover Theological Seminary, 1914.

Axtell, James. "The White Indians of Colonial America," *The William and Mary Quarterly* 32.1 (January 1975): 55–88.

Babb, Theodore Adolphus. *In the Bosom of the Comanches*. Dallas: Press of John F. Worley, 1912.

Bailey, L. H. *The Country Life Movement in the United States*. New York: The Macmillan Company, 1913.

Baillargeon, Morgan. *Legends of Our Times: Native Cowboy Life*. Seattle: University of Washington Press, 1998.

Barsh, Russel Lawrence. "Progressive Era Bureaucrats and the Unity of Twentieth Century Indian Policy," *American Indian Quarterly* 15.1 (Winter 1991): 1–17.

Barth, Gunther. *City People: The Rise of Modern City Culture in Nineteenth-Century America*. New York: Oxford University Press, 1982.

Bass, Florence. *Stories of Pioneer Life: for Young Readers*. New York: D. C. Heath & Co., 1900.

Beard, George Miller. *American Nervousness: Its Causes and Consequences*. New York: G. P. Putnam's Sons, 1881.

Beck, Paul Norman. *Inkpaduta: Dakota Leader*. Norman: University of Oklahoma Press, 2008.

Behling, Linda L. *The Masculine Woman in America, 1890–1935*. Urbana: University of Illinois Press, 2001.

Berkhofer, Robert F. *The White Man's Indian: Images of the American Indian from Columbus to the Present*. New York: Knopf, 1978.

Beveridge, Albert J. *The Young Man and the World*. New York: D. Appleton and Company, 1908.

Boas, Franz. "Eugenics," *The Scientific Monthly* 3.5 (November 1916): 471–78.

Boy Scouts of America. *Handbook for Scoutmasters*. New York: The Boy Scouts of America, 1913.

Brinkley, Douglas. *The Wilderness Warrior: Theodore Roosevelt and the Crusade for America*. New York: Harper Collins, 2009.

Brooks, James. *Captives and Cousins: Slavery, Kinship, and Community in the Southwest Borderlands*. Chapel Hill: The University of North Carolina Press, 2001.

Brown, Samuel J. *In Captivity: The Experience, Privations and Dangers of Samuel J. Brown and Others while Prisoners of the Hostile Sioux*. Washington, D.C.: Government Printing Office, 1900.

Bryan, William Jennings. *Speeches*. New York: Funk and Wagnalls Co., 1909.

Buckley, James M. *The Wrong and Peril of Woman Suffrage*. New York: Fleming H. Revell Company, 1909.

Burnham, Michelle. *Captivity and Sentiment: Cultural Exchange in American Literature, 1682–1861*. New York: Dartmouth, 1997.

BIBLIOGRAPHY

Bush-Brown, H. K. "Sculpture in Washington." In *Papers Relating to the Improvement of the City of Washington, District of Columbia.* Edited by Glenn Brown, 70–78. Washington, D.C.: Government Printing Office, 1901.

Byers, S. H. M. "Resting at Okoboji," *The Midland Monthly* 3, no. 5 (May 1895): 438–45.

Calhoun, Charles William, ed. *The Gilded Age: Perspectives on the Origins of Modern America.* Lanham, Md.: Rowland & Littlefield, 2007.

Calloway, Colin G. *North Country Captives: Selected Narratives of Indian Captivity from Vermont and New Hampshire.* Hanover: University Press of New England, 1992.

Carrigan, Wilhelmina Buce. *Captured by the Indians: Reminiscences of Pioneer Life in Minnesota.* Forest City, S.Dak.: Forest City Press, 1907.

Carroll, Lorrayne. *Rhetorical Drag: Gender Impersonation, Captivity, and the Writing of History.* Kent, Ohio: Kent State University Press, 2007.

Case, Carl Delos. *The Masculine in Religion.* New York: American Baptists Publication Society, 1906.

Castiglia, Christopher. *Bound and Determined: Captivity, Culture-Crossing and White Womanhood from Mary Rowlandson to Patty Hearst.* Chicago: University of Chicago Press, 1996.

Chauncey, George. *Gay New York: Gender, Urban Culture, and the Making of the Gay Male World.* New York: Basic Books, 1994.

Cook, May Estelle. "Nature-Books For the Holidays." *The Dial* 41, no. 491 (December 1, 1906): 387–90.

Cooper, Jr., John Milton. *Pivotal Decades: The United States, 1900–1920.* New York: Norton, 1990.

Daughters of the American Revolution. "Historic Preservation." http://www.ildar.org/historical.html (accessed December 10, 2013).

Dean, Bradley P. "Natural History, Romanticism, and Thoreau." In *American Wilderness: A New History.* Edited by Michael Lewis, 73–90. New York: Oxford University Press, 2007.

Deloria, Philip J. *Playing Indian.* New Haven, Conn.: Yale University Press, 1998.

Demos, John. *The Unredeemed Captive: A Family Story from Early America.* New York: Alfred A. Knopf, 1994.

Densmore, Christopher. *Red Jacket: Iroquois Diplomat and Orator.* Syracuse, N.Y.: Syracuse University Press, 1999.

De Puy, Henry W. *Ethan Allen and the Green Mountain Heroes of '76.* New York: Phinney & Co., 1861.

Derounian-Stodola, Kathryn Zabelle. *The War in Words: Reading the Dakota Conflict through the Captivity Literature*. Lincoln: University of Nebraska Press, 2009.

———, ed. *Women's Indian Captivity Narratives*. New York: Penguin Books, 1998.

———, and James Arthur Levernier. *The Indian Captivity Narrative, 1550–1900*. New York: Twayne Publishers, 1993.

DeShields, James T. *Cynthia Ann Parker: The Story of Her Capture at the Massacre of the Inmates of Parker's Fort*. St. Louis: Printed for the Author, 1886.

Diner, Steven J. *A Very Different Age: Americans of the Progressive Era*. New York: Hill and Wang, 1998.

Dippie, Brian W., ed. *Charlie Russell Roundup: Essays on America's Favorite Cowboy Artist*. Helena: Montana Historical Society Press, 1999.

———. *The Vanishing American: White Attitudes and U.S. Indian Policy*. Middletown, Conn.: Wesleyan University Press, 1982.

Dixon, Joseph K., and Rodman Wanamaker. *The Vanishing Race: The Last Great Indian Council*. New York: Doubleday, Page & Co, 1913.

Douglass, Ann. *The Feminization of American Culture*. New York: The Noonday Press, 1997.

Dudley, John. "Inside and Outside the Ring: Manhood, Race and Art in American Literary Naturalism," *College Literature* 29.1 (Winter 2002): 53–82.

Dunklee, Ivah. *Burning of Royalton, Vermont, by the Indians: A Careful Research of all that Pertains to the Subject, Including a reprint of Zadock Steele's Narrative*. Boston: Geo H. Ellis Co., 1906.

Dye, Nancy S., and Noralee Frankle. *Gender, Class, Race and Reform in the Progressive Era*. Lexington: University Press of Kentucky, 1991.

Eastburn, Robert. *The Dangers and Sufferings of Robert Eastburn And His Deliverance from Indian Captivity: Reprinted from the Original Edition of 1758 with Introduction and Notes by John R. Spears*. Cleveland: The Burrows Brothers Company, 1904.

Eastman, Charles. *From The Deep Woods to Civilization: Chapters in the Autobiography of an Indian*. Boston: Little, Brown & Co., 1916.

Ebersole, Gary. *Captured by Texts: Puritan to Postmodern Images of Captivity*. Charlottesville: University of Virginia Press, 1995.

Ellis, George W. "The Psychology of American Race Prejudice," *The Journal of Race Development* 5.3 (January, 1915): 297–315.

Emerson, Ralph Waldo. *Nature*. Boston: James Munroe & Company, 1849.

Engels, Frederick. *The Origin of the Family, Private Property, and the State.* Translated by Ernest Untermann. Chicago: Charles H. Kerr & Company, 1902.

Exley, Jo Ella Powell. *Frontier Blood: The Saga of the Parker Family.* College Station, Texas: Texas A&M University Press, 2001.

Faery, Rebecca Blevins. *Cartographies of Desire: Captivity, Race, and Sex in the Shaping of an American Nation.* Norman: University of Oklahoma Press, 1999.

Faragher, John Mack. *Rereading Frederick Jackson Turner: "The Significance of the Frontier in American History" and Other Essays.* New York: H. Holt and Co., 1994.

Farmer, Jared. *On Zion's Mount: Mormons, Indians, and the American Landscape.* Cambridge: Harvard University Press, 2008.

Fink, Leon, ed. *Major Problems in the Gilded Age and Progressive Era.* 2nd ed. New York: Houghton Mifflin, 2001.

First Report of the Park and Outdoor Art Association. Louisville, Ky., 1897.

Fish, Carl Russell. *The Development of American Nationality.* New York: American Book Company, 1913.

Foot, Katharine B. "The Heroism of Mrs. Hendee," *Wide Awake* 23.1 (June 1886): 300–305.

Foster, Sheppard, Mrs. "National Old Trails Road." In *Proceedings of the Fourth American Road Congress under the Auspices of American Highway Association, American Automobile Association,* 354–56. Baltimore: Waverly Press, 1915.

Franz, William C. "The Colossus of Staten Island: A Ponderous Memorial to a People Who Refused to Vanish." *American Heritage* 30.3 (April/May 1979).

Gangi, Rayna M. *Mary Jemison: White Woman of the Seneca.* Santa Fe: Clear Light Books, 1996.

Gardner-Sharp, Abbie. *History of the Spirit Lake Massacre and the Captivity of Miss Abbie Gardner.* Des Moines: Iowa Printing Company, 1895.

———. *History of the Spirit Lake Massacre and Captivity of Miss Abbie Gardner.* Des Moines: Kenyon Printing Company, 1910.

Gentry, Elizabeth Butler. "National Old Trail Road Committee," *Daughters of the American Revolution Magazine,* September 1913, 531.

Glassberg, David. *American Historical Pageantry: The Uses of Tradition in the Early Twentieth Century.* Chapel Hill: University of North Carolina Press, 1990.

Grant, Madison. *The Passing of the Great Race, Or The Racial Basis of European History*. New York: Charles Scribner's Sons, 1916.

Greeley, Horace. "The Formation of Character." In *Hints Toward Reforms, in Lectures, Addresses, and Other Writings*. 2nd ed., 85–111. New York: Fowlers and Wells, 1857.

Grese, Robert E. "Jens Jensen: The Landscape Architect as Conservationist." In *Midwestern Landscape Architecture*. Edited by William H. Tishler, 117–41. Urbana: University of Illinois Press, 2004.

Grinde, Jr., Donald A. "Iroquois Political Theory and the Roots of American Democracy." In *Exiled in the Land of the Free: Democracy, Indian Nations, and the U.S. Constitution*. Edited by Oren Lyons, et al., 228–80. Santa Fe: Clear Light Publishers, 1992.

Gross, Lewis M. *Past and Present of DeKalb County, Illinois*. Vol. 1 (of 2). Chicago: The Pioneer Publishing Company, 1907.

Guglielmo, Thomas A. *White on Arrival: Italians, Race, Color, and Power in Chicago, 1890–1945*. New York: Oxford University Press, 2003.

Gulick, Luther H. "The Girl's Branch of the Public Schools Athletic League of New York City." In *Proceedings of the Second Annual Playground Congress and Year Book*, 416–29. New York: Playground Association of America, 1908.

Haberly, David T. "Women and Indians: The Last of the Mohicans and the Captivity Tradition." *American Quarterly* 28.4 (Autumn 1976): 431–44.

Hagan, William T. *Quanah Parker: Comanche Chief*. Norman: University of Oklahoma Press, 1993.

Hall, John W. *Uncommon Defense: Indian Allies in the Black Hawk War*. Cambridge, Mass.: Harvard University Press, 2009.

History of Wyoming County, N.Y. New York: F. W. Beers & Co., 1880.

Hofsteader, Richard. *The Age of Reform: From Bryan to F.D.R.* New York: Alfred A. Knopf, 1972.

Holm, Tom. *Great Confusion in Indian Affairs: Native Americans and Whites in the Progressive Era*. Austin: University of Texas Press, 2005.

How, Nehemiah. *A Narrative of the Captivity of Nehemiah How in 1745–1747*. Cleveland: The Burrows Brothers, 1904.

Howland, Henry Raymond, ed. *Voices of the Glen*. New York: The Knickerbocker Press, 1911.

Hoxie, Frederick E. *A Final Promise: The Campaign to Assimilate the Indians, 1880–1920*. Lincoln: University of Nebraska Press, 2001.

———. ed. *Talking Back to Civilization: Indian Voices from the Progressive Era*. Boston: Bedford/St. Martins, 2001.

Huhndorf, Shari M. *Going Native: Indians in the American Cultural Imagination.* Ithaca, N.Y.: Cornell University Press, 2001.

Hunter, John Dunn. *Memoirs of a Captivity Among the Indians of North America.* London: Longman, Hurst, Rees, Orme, Brown and Green, 1823.

Illinois State Historical Society. "Monument Unveiled." In *Transactions of the Illinois State Historical Society for the Year 1907,* 332–41. Springfield: Phillips Bros., State Printers, 1908.

Johnson, R. W. "A Home Talk with the Boys." *The Midland Monthly* 3.2, (February 1895): 189.

Kelly, Fanny. *Narrative of My Captivity Among the Sioux Indians.* Chicago: R. R. Donnelley & Sons, 1891.

Kerber, Linda K. "Women and Individualism in American History," *The Massachusetts Review* 30.4 (Winter 1989): 589–609.

Kestler, Frances Roe. *The Indian Captivity Narrative: A Woman's View.* New York: Garland Pub., 1990.

Kett, Joseph F. *Rites of Passage: Adolescence in America, 1790 to the Present.* New York: Basic Books, Inc. 1977.

Kimmel, Michael. *Manhood in America: A Cultural History.* New York: The Free Press, 1996.

———. "Men's Responses to Feminism at the Turn of the Century," *Gender and Society* 1.3 (September 1987): 261–83.

King, John H. . *Three Hundred Days in a Yankee Prison.* Atlanta: J. P. Daves, 1904.

Knight, Louise W. *Citizen: Jane Addams and the Struggle for Democracy.* Chicago: University of Chicago Press, 2005.

Kolodny, Annette. *The Land Before Her: Fantasy and Experience of the American Frontiers. 1630–1860.* Chapel Hill: University of North Carolina Press, 1984.

Krech, Shepard. *The Ecological Indian: Myth and History.* New York: W. W. Norton & Co, 1999.

Laderman, Scott. "'It is Cheaper and Better to Teach a Young Indian Than to Fight an Old One': Thaddeus Pound and the Logic of Assimilation," *American Indian Culture and Research Journal* 26.3 (2002): 85–111.

Landsberg, Max. "Address of the President." In *Proceedings of the Twelfth New York State Conference of Charities and Correction,* 9–20. Albany: J. B. Lyon Company, State Printers, 1911.

Larned, Joseph Nelson. *The Life and Work of William Pryor Letchworth, Student and Minister of Public Benevolence.* New York: Houghton Mifflin Company, 1912.

Larson, Erik. *The Devil in the White City: Murder Magic and Madness at the Fair that Changed America.* New York: Crown, 2003.

Laut, Agnes C. "Pioneer Women of the West: The Heroines of Spirit Lake, Iowa," *The Outing Magazine,* October 1907–March 1908, 686–98.

Lears, T. J. Jackson. *No Place of Grace: Antimodernism and the Transformation of American Culture, 1880–1920.* Chicago: University of Chicago Press, 1981.

Leeth, John, and Ewel Jeffries. *A Short Biography of John Leeth, with an Account of His Life Among the Indians: Reprinted from the Original Edition of 1831, with Introduction by Reuben Gold Thwaites.* Cleveland: Burrows Brothers Company, 1904.

Letchworth, William Pryor. "Address by Hon. William Pryor Letchworth." In *Proceedings of the New York State Conference of Charities and Correction,* 24– 25. Albany: J. B. Lyon Company, State Printers, 1902.

———. *Care and Treatment of Epileptics.* New York: G. P. Putnam's Sons, 1900.

———. *The Insane in Foreign Countries.* New York: G. P. Putnam's Sons, 1889.

Levernier, James, and Hennig Cohen, eds. *The Indians and Their Captives.* Westport, Conn.: Greenwood Press, 1977.

Limerick, Patricia Nelson. *The Legacy of Conquest: The Unbroken Past of the American West.* New York: W. W. Norton, 1987.

Livingston County Historical Society. "An Address Delivered by Mr. J. D. Lewis." In *Thirty-sixth Annual Meeting, 1911,* 29–41. Nunda, N.Y.: W.B. Sanders, Publisher, 1913.

———. *Thirty-sixth Annual Meeting, 1911.* Nunda, N.Y.: W.B. Sanders, Publisher, 1913.

Lovejoy, Evelyn M. Wood. *History of Royalton, Vermont, with Family Genealogies, 1769–1911.* Burlington, Vt.: Free Press Printing Company, 1911.

Low, Juliette Gordon. *How Girls can Help Their Country: Adapted from Agnes Baden Powell and Sir Robert Baden-Powell's Handbook.* New York: Girl Scout National Headquarters, 1916.

Lutz, John Sutton. *Myth and Memory: Stories of Indigenous–European Contact.* Vancouver: University of British Columbia Press, 2007.

MacLeod, David I. *Building Character in the American Boy: The Boy Scouts, YMCA and Their Forefunners, 1870–1920.* Madison: University of Wisconsin Press, 1983.

Mann, Charles C. "1491," *The Atlantic Monthly* 289.3 (March 2002): 41–53.

Marsh, Margaret. "From Separation to Togetherness: The Social Construction of Domestic Space in American Suburbs, 1840–1915," *The Journal of American History* 76.2 (September, 1989): 506–27.

Mason, Randall. "Historic Preservation, Public Memory, and the Making of Modern New York City." In *Giving Preservation a History: Histories of Historic Preservation in the United States*. Edited by Max Page and Randall Mason, 131–62. New York: Routledge, 2004.

———. *The Once and Future New York: Historic Preservation and the Modern City*. Minneapolis: University of Minnesota Press, 2009.

Mattson, Kevin. *Creating a Democratic Public: The Struggle for Urban Participatory Democracy During the Progressive Era*. University Park, Pa.: The Pennsylvania State University Press, 1998.

Maynard, W. Barksdale. "'An Ideal Life in the Woods for Boys': Architecture and Culture in the Earliest Summer Camps," *Winterthur Portfolio* 34.1 (Spring 1999): 3–29.

McCullough, David G. *Mornings on Horseback: The Story of an Extraordinary Family, a Vanished Way of Life, and the Unique Child who Became Theodore Roosevelt*. New York: Simon & Schuster, 2001.

McGee, W. J. "Current Questions in Anthropology." *Science* 14.365 (December 1901).

Meginness, John F. *Biography of Frances Slocum, the Lost Sister of Wyoming A Complete Narrative of her Captivity and Wanderings Among the Indians*. Williamsport, Pa.: Heller Bros. Printing House, 1891.

———. *Otzinachson: A History of the Western Branch Valley of the Susquehanna*, revised edition. Williamsport, Pa.: Gazette and Bulletin Printing House, 1889.

Moore, W. S. "Society of the Army of the Tennessee: Sketches of Prominent Members of that Organization." *The Midland Monthly* 3.1, (January 1895): 66–78.

Morgan, Lewis H. *Ancient Society: Researches in the Lines of Human Progress from Savagery through Barbarism to Civilization*. New York: Henry Holt & Co., 1877.

Muir, John. *My First Summer in the Sierra*. New York: Houghton Mifflin Company, 1911.

———. *Our National Parks*. New York: Houghton Mifflin Company, 1901.

Murphy, Kevin P. *Political Manhood: Red Bloods, Mollycoddles, and the Politics of Progressive Era Reform*. New York: Columbia University Press, 2008.

Namias, June. *White Captives: Gender and Ethnicity on the American Frontier*, Chapel Hill: University of North Carolina Press, 1993.

———, and Sarah F. Wakefield. *Six Weeks in the Sioux Tepees: A Narrative of Indian Captivity*. Norman: University of Oklahoma Press, 1997.

New York State Museum. "The Mary Jemison Monument." In *Seventh Report of the Director of the Science Division*. Albany: University of the State of New York, 1911.

Olmsted, John C. "The True Purpose of a Large Public Park." *First Report of the Park and Outdoor Art Association*. Louisville, Ky., 1897.

Olson, Greg. "Tragedy, Tourism, and the Log Cabin: How Abbie Gardner Sharp and Charlotte Kirchner Butler Preserved and Promoted the Past." *Iowa Heritage Illustrated* 82.2 (Summer, 2001): 69–71.

Olster, Jeffrey. "Empire and Liberty: Contradictions and Conflicts in Nineteenth-Century Western Political History." In *A Companion to the American West*. Edited by William Deverell, 200–20. Malden, Mass.: Blackwell Publishing, 2004.

Operé, Fernando. *Indian Captivity in Spanish America*. Translated by Gustavo Pellón. Charlottesville: University of Virginia Press, 2008.

Paine, Ralph D. "The Author of 'White Fang.'" *Outing Magazine* 48.3, (June 1906): 360–66.

Paltsits, Victor Hugo. *A Narrative of the Captivity of Nehemiah How in 1745–1747*. Cleveland: The Burrows Brothers Company, 1904.

Parvin, Theodore Sutton. *Who Made Iowa, or, Who are the 'Pioneers and Old Settlers' of Iowa*. Davenport, Iowa; Egbert, Fidlar, and Chambers, Printers, 1896.

Pearce, Roy Harvey. "The Significances of the Captivity Narrative," *American Literature* 19 (March 1947): 1–20.

Peck, George. *Wyoming: Its History, Stirring Incidents, and Romantic Adventures*. New York: Harper & Brothers, 1858.

Pellow, Thomas. *The Adventures of Thomas Pellow, of Penryn, Mariner: Three and Twenty Years in Captivity Among the Moors*. New York: Macmillan & Co., 1890.

Pettigrew, John. *Brutes in Suits: Male Sensibility in America, 1890–1920*. Baltimore: Johns Hopkins University Press, 2007.

Phelps, Martha Bennett. *Frances Slocum: The Lost Sister of Wyoming; Compiled and Written by Her Grandniece, for Her Children and Grandchildren*. New York: The Knickerbocker Press, 1905.

———. *Frances Slocum: The Lost Sister of Wyoming*. Wilkes-Barre, Pa.: Published by the Author, 1906.

———. *Frances Slocum: The Lost Sister of Wyoming*. Wilkes-Barre, Pa.: Published by the Author, 1916.

Prucha, Francis Paul. *The Great Father: The United States Government and the American Indians*. Lincoln: University of Nebraska Press, 1984.

Ranney, Victoria Post. "Frederick Law Olmstead: Designing for Democracy in the Midwest." In *Midwestern Landscape Architecture*. Edited by William H. Tishler, 41–56. Urbana: University of Illinois Press, 2004.

Recchiuti, John Louis. *Civic Engagement: Social Science and Progressive Era Reform in New York City*. Philadelphia: University of Pennsylvania Press, 2006.

Renan, Ernest. "What is a Nation?" In *Nationalism in Europe, 1815 to the Present*. Edited by Stuart Woolf, 51–60. New York: Rutledge, 1995.

Roediger, David R. *The Wages of Whiteness: Race and the Making of the American Working Class*. New York: Verso, 1991.

Roosevelt, Theodore. *Americanism and Preparedness: Speeches of Theodore Roosevelt, July to November 1916*. New York: The Mail and Express, 1917.

———. *The Great Adventure: Present-Day Studies in American Nationalism*. New York: Charles Scribner's Sons, 1918.

———. *The Strenuous Life: Essays and Addresses*. New York: Century Co., 1902.

———. *Theodore Roosevelt: An Autobiography*. New York: Macmillan, 1916.

———. *The Winning of the West: An Account of the Exploration and Settlement of Our Country from the Alleghenies to the Pacific*. Vol. 2 (of 4). New York: G. P. Putnam's Sons, 1917.

———. *The Winning of the West: From the Alleghenies to the Mississippi, 1769–1776*. Vol. 1 (of 4). New York: G. P. Putnam's Sons, 1889.

———. *The Winning of the West: Louisiana and the Northwest, 1791–1807*. Vol. 4 (of 4). New York: G. P. Putnam's Sons, 1896.

Rotundo, E. Anthony. *American Manhood: Transformations in Masculinity from the Revolution to the Modern Era*. New York: Basic Books, 1993.

———. "Body and Soul: Changing Ideals of American Middle-Class Manhood, 1770 1920." *Journal of Social History* 16.4 (Summer 1983): 23–38.

Rowlandson, Mary White. *The Narrative of the Captivity and Removes of Mrs. Rowlandson*. Lancaster: Carter, Andrews and Co., 1828.

Sayre, Gordon M., ed. *American Captivity Narratives: Selected Narratives with Introduction*. Boston: Houghton Mifflin, 2000.

Scanlan, Charles M. *Indian Creek Massacre and Captivity of Hall Girls*. 2nd ed. Milwaukee: Reic Publishing Company, 1916.

Scheckel, Susan. *The Insistence of the Indian: Race and Nationalism in Nineteenth Century American Culture*. Princeton, N.J.: Princeton University Press, 1998.

Schuler, F. "Dear Brother John." *The Railway Conductor* 36.11, (November 1919): 621–22.

Seaver, James E. *A Narrative of the Life of Mrs. Mary Jemison.* Edited by June Namias. Norman: University of Oklahoma Press, 1992.

Seaver, James Everett. *Mary Jemison, The White Woman of the Genesee.* Edited by Charles Delamater Vail. New York: The American Scenic and Historic Preservation Society, 1918.

———. *A Narrative of the Life of Mary Jemison.* 6th ed. Edited by William Pryor Letchworth. New York: G. P. Putnam's Sons, 1898.

———. *A Narrative of the Life of Mary Jemison, De-he-wa-mis, the White Woman of the Genesee.* 7th ed. With notes by Wm Pryor Letchworth. New York: The Knickerbocker Press, 1910.

Seton, Ernest Thompson. *The Book of Woodcraft and Indian Lore.* Garden City, NY: Doubleday, Page & Co., 1912.

Seventeenth Annual Report, 1912, of the American Scenic and Historic Preservation Society. Albany: The Argus Company Printers, 1912.

Shifflett, Crandall. *Victorian America, 1876–1913.* New York: Facts on File, 1996.

Sieminski, Greg. "The Puritan Captivity Narrative and the Politics of the American Revolution." *American Quarterly* 42.1 (March 1990): 35–57.

Slocum, Charles Elihu. *The Slocums, Slocumbs, and Slocombs of America.* Vol. 2 (of 2). Defiance, Ohio: Published by the Author, 1908.

Slotkin, Richard. *Gunfighter Nation: The Myth of the Frontier in the Twentieth-Century.* New York: Macmillan, 1992.

———. *Regeneration Through Violence: The Mythology of the American Frontier, 1600–1860.* Middletown, Conn.: Wesleyan University Press, 1973.

Smith, Sidonie, and Julia Watson, eds. *Before They Could Vote: American Women's Autobiographical Writing, 1819–1919.* Madison: University of Wisconsin Press, 2006.

Snow, Dean R. *The Iroquois.* Cambridge, Mass.: Blackwell, 1994.

Society of American Indian. *Report of the Executive Council on the Proceedings of the First Annual Conference of the Society of American Indians.* Washington, D.C., 1912.

Spence, Mark David. *Dispossessing the Wilderness: Indian Removal and the Making of the National Parks.* New York: Oxford University Press, 1999.

Spiro, Jonathan Peter. *Defending the Master Race: Conservation, Eugenics, and the Legacy of Madison Grant.* Burlington: University of Vermont Press, 2009.

Steele, W. H. *Memories of By-Gone Days.* Omaha: The Beacon Press, 1912.

Steele, Zadock. *The Indian Captive: Or, A Narrative of the Captivity and Sufferings of Zadock Steele*. Springfield, Mass.: The H. R. Huntting Company, 1908.

Stratton, Royal B. *Captivity of the Oatman Girls: A True Story of the Early Emigration to the West*. Salem, Ore.: Oregon Teachers Monthly, 1909.

Taft, Grace Ellis. "The White Woman of Genesee." *The American Antiquarian and Oriental Journal* 35 (1913): 237–40.

Testi, Arnaldo. "The Gender of Reform Politics: Theodore Roosevelt and the Culture of Masculinity," *The Journal of American History* 81.4 (March 1995): 1509–33.

Tinnemeyer, Andrea. *Identity Politics of the Captivity Narrative After 1848*. Lincoln: University of Nebraska Press, 2006.

Trachtenberg, Alan. *Shades of Hiawatha: Staging Indian, Making American, 1880–1930*. New York: Hill and Wang, 2004.

Turner, Frederick Jackson. "The Significance of the Frontier in American History." In *Proceedings of the State Historical Society of Wisconsin at its Forty-First Annual Meeting*, 79–112. Madison, Wis.: Democrat Printing Company, 1894.

Turner-Strong, Pauline. *Captive Selves, Captivating Others: The Politics and Poetics of Colonial American Captivity Narratives*. Boulder: Westview, 1999.

U. S. Congress. Joint. *Report of the Country Life Commission*. 60th Cong., 2d Sess., 1909. S. Doc. 705.

VanDerBeets, Richard, ed. *Held Captive By Indians: Selected Narratives, 1642–1836*. Knoxville: University of Tennessee Press, 1973.

———. *Indian Captivity Narratives: An American Genre*. Lanham, Md.: University Press of America, 1984.

———. "The Indian Captivity Narrative as Ritual." *American Literature* 43.4 (January 1972): 548–62.

Vanderhoof, Elisha Woodward. *Historical Sketches of Western New York*. Buffalo, N.Y.: The Matthews Northrup Works, 1907.

Vaughan, Alden T., and Edward W. Clark. *Puritans Among the Indians: Accounts of Captivity and Redemption, 1676–1724*. Cambridge, Mass: Belknap Press, 1981.

Venebles, Robert W. "American Indian Influences on the America of the Founding Fathers." In *Exiled in the Land of the Free: Democracy, Indian Nations and the U.S. Constitution*. Edited by Oren Lyons, 73–124. Santa Fe: Clear Light Publishers, 1992.

Walton, William. *The Captivity and Sufferings of Benjamin Gilbert and his Family, 1780–83: Reprinted from the Original Ed. of 1784, with introduction*

and Notes by Frank H. Severance. Cleveland: The Burrows Brothers Company, 1904.
Water Supply Commission. "River Improvement." In *Annual Report of the State Water Supply Commission of New York for the Year Ending December 31, 1910.* Vol. 6. Albany: J. B. Lyon Company, 1911, 21–31.
Webster, William. "An Ornamental Farm," *Moore's Rural New Yorker,* March 16, 1861: http://www.letchworthparkhistory.com/ornfarm.html (accessed January 16, 2011).
Wellman, Paul I. "Cynthia Ann Parker," *Chronicles of Oklahoma* 12.2 (June 1934): 163–70.
White, Richard. "Frederick Jackson Turner and Buffalo Bill." In *The Frontier in American Culture: An Exhibition at the Newberry Library, August 26 1994 January 7 1995.* Edited by James R. Grossman, 7–65. Chicago: University of Chicago Press, 1994.
"William Pryor Letchworth." Western New York Heritage Press. http://wnyheritagepress.org/photos_week_2010/letchworth/letchworth_part2.htm (accessed January 15, 2011).
Williams, Daniel E., Christina Riley Brown, Salita S. Bryant, Dixon Bynum, and Randy Jasmine, eds. *Liberty's Captives: Narratives of Confinement in the Print Culture of the Early Republic.* Athens: University of Georgia Press, 2006.
Wood, Norman B. *Lives of the Famous Indian Chiefs From Cofachiqui, the Indian Princess and Powhatan down to and Including Chief Joseph and Geronimo.* Aurora, Ill.: American Indian Historical Publishing Company, 1906.
Wrobel, David M. *The End of American Exceptionalism: Frontier Anxiety from the Old West to the New Deal.* Lawrence: University Press of Kansas, 1993.
Zipf, Catherine W. *Professional Pursuits: Women and the Arts and Crafts Movement.* Knoxville: University of Tennessee Press, 2007.

Index

Addams, Jane, 37
allotment: to Jemison, 101–102, 200n26; to Slocum, 101, 106–107; support in captivity narratives for, 101–103
"Amazon" archetype, 132–33
Americanism: captivity narratives and, 4–5, 6, 22, 34–35; Indians and, 17–19, 112–13, 122–24, 128, 178; Roosevelt on, 3, 4
American Park and Outdoor Art Association (APOAA), 70–71
American Scenic and Historic Preservation Society (ASHPS), 47, 59, 64, 67–68
Ancient Society (Morgan), 104–105
APOAA. *See* American Park and Outdoor Art Association (APOAA)
Armstrong, M. N., 172, 174, 176–77, 178
Arts and Crafts movement, 204n24
ASHPS. *See* American Scenic and Historic Preservation Society (ASHPS)
assimilation: Gardner-Sharp's support for, 92–93, 96–99, 134; hybrid culture produced by captives, 16–17,

80, 91–92, 95, 107–11; Progressive Era and, 92–93, 96, 101–108, 111–12, 122–23, 126

Baden-Powell, Robert, 166
Bailey, L. H., 39–40, 51, 82–83, 87, 194n37
Beard, George M., 165
Beard, "Uncle Dan," 18, 19
Belknap, Simeon, 152
Bennett, George Slocum, 51
Beveridge, Albert J., 163–64
Black Hawk, 170, 171, 176
Bliss, Max, 44
Boas, Franz, 99, 100–101, 109, 167
Bonda, Peter, 128
Boone and Crockett Club, 73, 88, 161
Boy Scouts, 164, 206n76
Breid, Jacob, 93
Brinkley, Douglas, 61
Brooks, James, 16–17
Broughton, F. W., 93
Brouillette, Jean Baptiste, 128
Brown, Jonathan, 152
Bryan, William Jennings, 146

223

224 INDEX

Buckley, James M., 163
Buffalo Bill Cody, 13, 14
Bundy, Judson, 128
Burning of Royalton (Dunklee), 151
Burrows Brothers Company, 130, 152
Bush-Brown, Henry Kirk, 30, 38–39, 47, 59–60, 74–76
Button, Elias, 152

Caghnewaga Indians, 202n1
Call of the Wild, The (London), 148
captives. *See* female captives; Indian captives
Captive Selves, Captivating Others (Turner-Strong), 191n23
captivity monuments. *See* monuments, captivity
captivity narratives: categorization of, 6–7, 28; Christianity and, 6, 7, 28, 45, 125–26; cultural purposes of, 9, 49; historical accuracy of, 8, 28, 46–47; national identity and, 4–10, 16–20, 22–24, 28, 29, 179; Progressive Era (*See* Progressive Era captivity narratives); Puritan, 5–7, 24, 28, 45, 190n13; renewing of white frontier qualities through, 14–15, 19–20, 36–38, 48–49; Revolutionary-era, 28, 178–79; rural life and, 38–41; stages in development of genre of, 45–47. *See also* female captives; Indian captives
Care and Treatment of Epileptics (Letchworth), 55
Carlisle Indian School, 123
Carrigan, Minnie Buce, 33, 108, 124
Cartographies of Desire (Faery), 191n34
Case, Carl Delos, 149
census of 1890, 12, 28
Chaplin, Charlie, 37
character: community and, 157; development of, 154–56, 164–66, 168, 175–76; Manly Mothers and, 157–61, 168–69; physical education classes and, 166
Chauncey, George, 205n76
Chicago, Ill., 13
Children of the American Revolution, 29

Christianity: captivity narratives and, 5–7, 28, 45, 125–26; gender and, 149; Shabonna and, 175–76, 177; Slocum family and, 125
Church of Jesus Christ of Latter Day Saints, 12–13
cities, modernization of, 36–39
City Beautiful movement, 70
"Civilized Heredity Stronger Than a Savage Environment, A" (Slocum), 98
Clark, Mr., 153
Cole, Alphonso A., 106–107
Colonial Dames of America, 29
Comanche Indians, 31
Cooper, James Fenimore, 8
Cornplanter, 86
Country Life Commission, 40
cultural anthropology: practical consequences of, 102–103; race and, 99, 100–101
cultural hybrids. *See* hybrid culture produced by captives
culture and race, 109–11
Curtis, Edward, 93
Curtis, Elias, 152

Dakota people, 136, 153
Darwin, Charles, 99
Daughters of the American Revolution (DAR), 29, 134–35, 159
Davis, William, 175
Dawes Allotment Act, 47, 105, 117
Deerfield Massacre, 191n34
DeHart, Richard, 50
Dehgewanus. *See* Jemison, Mary
Deloria, Philip, 15
Demos, John, 191n34
Dewey, Gertrude, 44
Dewey, Helen, 44
Dial, The, 148
Diner, Steven J., 40
Dippie, Brian, 103
Dixon, Joseph Kossuth, 94, 95, 126–27
Dow, Charles M., 56, 57, 68, 79, 85
Dreiser, Theodore, 149
Dunklee, Ivah, 47–48, 151, 153, 159

INDEX

Eastman, Charles, 78–79, 80
Ebersole, Gary, 49
economic individualism, 144–45
Edison, Thomas, 37
Edison Electric, 148–49
Emerson, Ralph Waldo, 61
End of American Exceptionalism, The (Wrobel), 191n32
Engels, Frederick, 122
eugenics, 99–103
evolution, 99
evolutionary model of social development, 104
Ewing, George W., 25–26, 51, 110–11

Faery, Rebecca Blevins, 49, 191n34
family genealogy, 33–34, 42–45
Farmer, Jared, 55
farmers, 40–41
female captives: decision to remain with captors, 191n34; distinct place in American literature, 8; focus of captivity narratives on, 20–21, 130–32; "Indianized," 21; as Manly Mothers, 21, 133–34, 143–44, 157–59, 168–69; on types of, 132–33. *See also* Indian captives
Fish, Carl Russell, 35, 36, 38
Forest Reserve Act, 61
Fort Parker, 31
Foster, John, 154
"Frail Flower" archetype, 133, 134, 137, 139–40
Frances Slocum (Phelps), 21, 125, 167; on allotment to Frances, 101; on "Americanizing" of descendants, 33–34, 107–108; on assimilation into Miami culture, 118; first chapter of, 46; on Frances' hiding from white relatives, 106, 116; on Frances' separation from tribe, 135–36; on "moral dignity," 156; on Slocum genealogy, 33
Franklin, Benjamin, 114
"From Inspiration Point, June 8th, 1909" (Letchworth), 84

frontier: 1890 census on end of, 12, 28; Progressive Era's preoccupation with, 36–38, 48–49; role of captivity narratives in joining present to, 28–30, 33–34

Galton, Francis, 99
Gardeau Reservation, 58, 59
Gardner-Sharp, Abbie, 10, 42, 49, 102, 113, 115, 167; captivity narrative of, 45–47, 97, 136–38, 153, 203n14; as "Frail Flower" archetype, 134, 137, 139–40; health of, 138–39, 175; as Manly Mother, 21, 133–34, 168–69; promotion of self and cabin as tourist attraction, 138, 140–42, 174; support for "civilizing" of Indians, 92–93, 96–99, 134
gender: character and, 155–61, 174–75; Christianity and, 149; individualism and, 142–48, 165–67; Iroquois Indians and, 95; male domesticity and, 162–63; sexuality and, 163–64. *See also* female captives; women
genealogy, 33–34, 42–45
General Electric, 149
Genesee River Company, 63, 196nn21–22
Gentry, Elizabeth Butler, 135
Gibb, Giles, 152
Girl Scouts, 166
Glassberg, David, 113
Glen Iris: American Scenic and Historic Preservation Society and, 64, 67, 68; design of, 69, 75; Jemison's remains at, 50, 59, 65, 81–82, 114, 173; Letchworth's efforts to protect, 11–12, 22, 53–57, 60–68, 70–74, 82–88, 174; naming of, 54, 57
Godfroy, Francis, 127
Godfroy, Gabriel, 127
Granger, Carl, 153
Grant, Madison, 76, 99–101, 108
grants, land. *See* allotment
Gray, David, 77–78, 80, 83
Greeley, Horace, 146, 155
Green, Andrew Haswell, 64
Guglielmo, Thomas A., 193n17

226   INDEX

Gulick, Charlotte, 165
Gulick, Luther H., 165–66

Hall, Edward Hagaman, 29–30, 79, 94, 95
Hall, Rachel, 170–71, 172, 175, 178
Hall, Sylvia, 170, 175, 178
Handbook for Scout Masters (Boy Scouts of America), 164
Harriot, Dr., 153
Havens, Daniel, 152
Hazen, William Skinner, 48–49, 169; on character, 161, 162; on manhood, 143, 157; speech at Royalton memorial, 129, 147, 151, 156
Hendee, Mrs., 158–59, 160, 166, 168
Henderson, John W., 174
Hiokatoo, 119–21
historical pageantry and monuments trend, 41–45
Historical Sketches of Western New York (Vanderhoof), 121
History of Royalton (Lovejoy), 160, 205n66
History of Vermont (Lovejoy), 44
Hofsteader, Richard, 32
Holm, Tom, 110
Homestead Act, 12
homesteading, 12
"Home Talk with the Boys, A" (Johnson), 150
homosexuality, 163–64
Houghton, Richard, 158–59, 160
How, Nehemiah, 23, 125–26, 152, 167
Huhndorf, Shari, 15
Hunkpapa Lakota, 13
Hunter, John Dunn, 114–15
Hutchinson, Abijah, 152
Hutchinson, John, 152
hybrid culture produced by captives, 16–17, 95, 110; Jemison and, 17, 80, 91–92, 95, 109–10, 177; Slocum and, 17, 95, 107–11, 124, 177

identity, national, 4–10, 16–20, 22–24, 28, 29, 179
immigrants: "Americanization" of, 34–35, 91, 112; Grant's arguments against, 99–100; settlement in cities rather, 35–36
Indian Appropriation Act, 102–103
Indian captives: choice to "go Indian," 114–19, 121–22; good character of, 167–68; hybrid culture produced by, 16–17, 80, 89–92, 95, 107–11, 125, 177; lack of control over captivity narratives, 22–23; linking of modern family or community to, 33–34, 42–45, 112, 172, 178; national identity and, 4–5, 179; as the ultimate frontiersman, 14–15. *See also* female captives
Indian Creek Massacre, 170–77
Indians: Americanism and, 17–19, 112–13, 122–24, 128, 178; captivity narratives' portrayal of, 45–46, 47; conservationists' view of, 78–81; contradictory Euro-American understanding of and relationship with, 94–96; emphasis of captivity narratives on "civilizing" of, 92–93, 96, 101–104, 107–108, 111–12; justification of violent extermination of, 9–10, 14, 28; nature and, 78–79, 80; population of, 89–94, 199n4; Progressive Era and, 92–93, 96–99, 102–107, 122–23, 126, 175–78; as "wards of the state," 102–103, 105
individualism: benefits of, 145, 147–48; dangers of, 144, 145–46, 148–51; gender and, 142–48, 165–67; physical education and, 166–67; types of, 144
Inkpaduta, 136
Iroquis Indians, 95

Jemison, Mary, 108, 123–24, 135, 179; allotment to, 101–102, 200n26; assimilation into Seneca culture, 10, 19, 58, 80, 113, 118–19, 178; captivity narrative of, 22, 54, 70–71, 85–86, 104, 119–21, 126; death of, 58–59; hybrid culture produced by, 17, 80, 91–92, 95, 109–10, 177; Letchworth Park and, 11–12, 22, 53–57, 62–67, 70–74, 86–88, 174; Letchworth's

INDEX 227

moving of remains of, 50, 59, 65, 81–82, 114, 173; memorial ceremony for, 22, 68, 92, 94–95, 111; refusal to return to white society, 30–32, 60, 95, 102, 113, 119, 124; struggle with identity, 113, 118–19, 124
Jemison, Thomas, 77
Jensen, Jens, 70
Johnson, R. W., 150
Johnston, James N., 84
Jones, Amanda T., 83–84
Joplin, Scott, 13

Kahnawake Indians, 129, 202n1
Ke-ke-nok-esh-wah, 128
Kellogg, Elizabeth Duty, 31
Kent, John, 152
Kerber, Linda K., 147
Kett, Joseph, 154–55
Kimmel, Michael, 148
Kneeland, Joseph, 152
Knights of King Arthur, 206n76
Krech, Shepard, 78
Kunz, George Frederick, 67–68, 75, 76, 132

Lakota. *See* Hunkpapa Lakota
land grants. *See* allotment
Langdon, William Chauncy, 42
Larned, Joseph, 77
"Last Indian Council on the Genesee," 77–78
Lears, T. J. Jackson, 195n59
Leeth, John, 23, 126
Letchworth, Sara Evans, 84
Letchworth, William Pryor, 69, 75, 83–85, 173; American Scenic and Historic Preservation Society and, 64, 68; background of, 53, 56, 60; *Care and Treatment of Epileptics*, 55; death of, 82, 85; efforts to protect Glen Iris, 11–12, 22, 53–57, 60–68, 70–74, 82–88, 174; moving of Jemison's remains, 50, 59, 65, 81–82, 114; role in Jemison's captivity narrative, 22, 54, 70–71, 85–86, 120, 126
Letchworth Park. *See* Glen Iris

Lewis, J. D., 71, 198n53
Limerick, Patricia Nelson, 193n27
Livingston County Historical Society, 65, 71
London, Jack, 147–48
Lovejoy, Mary Evelyn Wood, 44, 160, 205n66
Low, Juliette Gordon, 166
Luce, Mr., 153

Maconaquah. *See* Slocum, Frances
Madonna of the Trail, 134–35, 159
Manly Mothers, 143–44, 170, 175; description of, 21, 133–34; Madonna of the Trail as, 134–35; in Progressive Era captivity narratives, 133–34, 157–61, 168–69
Manning, Warren H., 73, 74
Marble, Mr., 153
Marsh, Margaret, 162
Marshall, John, 103
masculinity: in captivity narratives, 151–54; character and, 163–65; individualism and, 143–51, 165–66; as learned, 163–65, 206n76; male domesticity and, 162–63
Mason, Peter, 152
Mattock, Mr., 153
Mattson, Kevin, 39
Mayflower Society, 29
McFadden, Major, 50
McKinley, William, 145–46
Meginness, John, 107–108, 125; *Otzinachson*, 120; on Slocum's allotment, 101; on Slocum's refusal to return to white society, 108, 115–18
memorials, captivity. *See* monuments, captivity
Miami Indians: capture of Slocum, 11, 26, 153; in Indiana, 128; removal to Kansas, 106
Midland Monthly Magazine, The: "A Home Talk with the Boys," 150; on Gardner-Sharp's cabin, 141; "Sketches of Prominent Members of" the Society of the Army of the Tennessee," 156

Miller, Lurena King, 50
Miniconjou, 13
modernization of cities, 36–39
Mohawk Indians, 77, 153
monuments, captivity: gender and, 130; importance of, 132, 172–73; issues of character in, 156, 172–73; moral influence of, 74–75, 143, 162; naturalistic parks and, 70–74; public opinion and, 75–76; trend of, 41–45
Moore, W. S., 156
Morgan, John Pierpont, 64
Morgan, Lewis Henry, 86, 104–105, 122
Muir, John, 78, 80–81, 88
Munson, William, 170–71, 172, 173, 175, 177
Murphy, Kevin P., 147
Muybridge, Eadweard, 13

Namias, June, 88; on Hiokatoo, 119; on types of white female captives, 132–33; *White Captives*, 190n13
Narrative of the Life of Mrs. Mary Jemison, A, 8
national identity, 4–10, 16–20, 22–24, 28, 29, 179
National Old Trails Road Association, 134
Nature (Emerson), 61
"New Woman," 37, 146–47
New York Times, 91, 93
Norris, Frank, 149
Norris, Philetus, 79

Olmsted, Frederick Law, 69
Olmsted, John, 69–70, 72–73, 75, 76
Olson, Greg, 140
Operé, Fernando, 189n6
Osawshequah, 111
Otzinachson (Meginness), 120
Our Young Folks, 155–56
Outing Magazine, 147–48
O-zah-shin-quah (Jane), 128

Pacific Railway Acts, 61
pageantry trend, historical, 41–45, 112–13
Paine, Ralph D., 147–48
Paltsits, Victor Hugo, 125–26

Parker, Arthur C., 47, 59, 65–67, 77, 79, 94–95, 111
Parker, Cynthia Ann, 30–32, 86
Parker, Ely S., 77, 86, 94
Parker, John Richard, 31
Parker, Nicholas H., 77
Parker, Quanah, 30, 31, 86
Parker family (of Texas), 32, 33
Parkhurst, Joseph, 152–53
park movement, 69
Parvin, Theodore, 138, 145–46
Passing of the Great Race, The (Grant), 99–100, 101
Pearce, Roy Harvey, 45–46, 47
Peck, George, 116–17, 118
Pember, Thomas, 152
Percival, Mary, 83
Peru Evening Journal, 127
Phelps, Martha Bennett: on Frances Slocum memorial, 50–51; on Slocum and Ewing, 25, 26. See also *Frances Slocum* (Phelps)
physical education, 165–67
Pillsbury, Samuel, 138
Pinchot, Gifford, 40, 41
Plummer, James Pratt, 31
Plummer, Rachel, 31
Pocahontas, 13
political individualism, 144
polygamy, 12–13
population, urban, 35, 148–49
poverty, 37–38
Pratt, Richard H., 123
Progressive Era captivity narratives, 171–72; allotment and, 101–103; conservative nature of, 48–49, 51; genealogy and geography in, 33–34, 46–47; historical pageantry and monuments trend and, 41–45; immigrants and, 34–35; individualism and, 142–48; issues of character in, 156; justification of violent extermination of Indians, 9–10, 14; Manly Mother in, 133–34, 143–44, 157–61, 168–69; masculinity in, 151–54; national identity and, 9, 23–24, 28–30, 33–34, 48–49;

INDEX

preference for female *versus* male captives in, 130–32; race and, 89–90; small towns and, 22, 30–33, 50–52, 112–13; support for "civilizing" of Indians, 92–93, 96, 101–104, 107–108, 111–12. *See also* female captives; Indian captives
"Puritan Captivity Narrative, The" (Sieminski), 190n13
Puritan captivity narratives, 5–7, 24, 28, 45, 190n13

race: Boas and Grant on, 99–101; culture and, 109–11
racism, scientific, 99–100, 101
ragtime, 13
railroad, 145
rape of female captives, 20
Redeemed Captive, Returning to Zion, The (William), 7
religion. *See* Christianity
Renan, Ernest, 3–4
Revolutionary-era captivity narratives, 28, 178–79
Rix, Deacon, 152
Rockefeller, John D., 64
Roediger, David R., 193n17
Roosevelt, Theodore, 15, 17, 24, 90, 122, 169; on character, 155–56, 157, 162, 167; on corporations, 146; Country Life Commission and, 40–41; on dangers of individualism, 149–50; on early permanent settlers, 36, 42–43, 44, 45, 172; as a "manly" man, 145, 161–62; *The Strenuous Life*, 157; "True Americanism and National Defense" speech, 3; *The Winning of the West*, 30, 34, 168
Rowlandson, Mary, 7, 115
Royalton, Raid of (1780): captivity narrative on, 33, 129, 151–54, 158–61, 202n1; commemoration of, 44, 48, 129, 153, 156, 173; Manly Mothers during, 158–61, 205n66
Rusoe d'Eres, Charles Dennis, 114
Russell, Charlie, 29

Sample, Samuel C., 107
Sauk Indians, 170, 171
Scanlan, Charles, 170–72, 174–75
scientific racism, 99–100, 101
Seaver, James Everett: on Jemison at reservation, 200n26; on Jemison's conversion before death, 126; on moving of Jemison's remains, 65; publication of Jemison's narrative, 82, 85–86, 120
Seneca Indians, 58, 77
Seton, Ernest Thompson, 17–18, 164
sexuality and gender, 163–64
Shabbona, 175–78, 207n17
Shabbona Park, 174, 176
Shongo, James, 77, 81–82
Sieminski, Greg, 190n13
"Significance of the Frontier in American History, The" (Turner), 12, 14, 34
Sitting Bull, 13
Slocum, Arthur Gaylord, 51
Slocum, Charles Elihu, 98
Slocum, Charles F., 51
Slocum, Frances, 135, 172, 173; allotment to, 101, 106–107; assimilation into Miami culture, 10, 19, 108, 110, 116–18, 178; Charles Elihu Slocum on, 98; curiosity about history of, 27–28; Ewing and, 25–26; genealogy and, 11, 27, 47, 91, 128, 152; hybrid culture produced by, 17, 95, 107–11, 124, 177; Meginness on, 115–16, 117, 118; memorial ceremony for, 22, 27, 50–51, 91, 127–28; Miami Indians' capture of, 11, 25–26, 119, 133, 153; as a notable figure in Indiana and Pennsylvania, 51–52; parents of, 124; Peck on, 116–17, 118; polygamy and, 131; refusal to participate in captivity narrative, 23, 113, 125, 192n36; refusal to return to white society, 26–27, 30–32, 52, 95, 102, 104, 108–109, 115, 116, 124, 125. *See also Frances Slocum* (Phelps)
Slocum, George, 125

Slocum, William F., 50
Slotkin, Richard, 14
small towns: celebration of link between captives and, 11, 27–38, 51–52; historical pageantry and monuments trend of, 41–45, 51–52, 112–13; use of captives to justify existence and cultural status, 10–11, 22, 32–33, 38–41, 50–52
Smith, John, 13
Smith, R. A., 42, 113
Snyder, Mr., 153
Social Darwinism, 99–100
social development, evolutionary model of, 104
social individualism, 144
Sons of Daniel Boone, 206n76
Sons of the American Revolution, 29
Sovereignty and Goodness of God, The (Rowlandson), 7
Spanish colonies, 190n6
Spence, Mark, 80
Spencer, Herbert, 99
Spirit Lake Massacre, 42, 113, 136, 139, 153, 173
Steele, Alice, 141–42
Steele, W. H., 141–42
Steele, Zadock, 21, 23, 33, 46–48, 129–30, 151–54, 160
steel production, 145
Stevens, Elias, 152, 153
Strenuous Life, The (Roosevelt), 157
Stutesman, James F., 127
Sunday, Billy, 149
"Survivor" archetype, 132

Taft, Grace, 121
Taylor Grazing Act, 12
Theodoric the Great, 76
Thoreau, Henry David, 61
Thwaites, Reuben Gold, 23, 126
"To Glen Iris" (Johnston), 84
Tracthenberg, Alan, 121–22
Truman, Harry S., 134

Trustees of Scenic and Historic Places and Objects, 64
Turner, Frederick Jackson, 4, 12, 14, 34, 122, 123, 202n65
Turner-Strong, Pauline, 191n23, 195n61

United Confederate Veterans, 29
Unredeemed Captive, The (Demos), 191n34
urban population, 35, 148–49

Vail, Charles D., 30, 35
Vanderhoof, Elisha, 121, 126
Vanishing Race, The (Wanamaker), 126

Wabash Times, 127–28
Wages of Whiteness, The (Roediger), 193n17
Wanamaker, John, 94
Wanamaker, Rodman, 94, 95–96, 126, 127
Webster, William, 69, 75
White, Richard, 14
White Captives (Namias), 190n13
White Fang (London), 147–48
"white Indians," 114, 115
whiteness studies, 193n17
White on Arrival (Guglielmo), 193n17
Wild, David, 44
wilderness, American concept of, 80–81
William, John, 7
Williams, Eunice, 191n34
Winning of the West, The (Roosevelt), 30, 34, 168
Wister, Owen, 162
women: character and, 157, 166, 174–76; Iroquis, 95; Progressive Era and the "New Woman," 37, 146–47; public life and the "mannish woman," 163; in the workforce, 146–47. *See also* female captives; gender
World's Columbian Exposition, 13
Wounded Knee Massacre, 13, 103, 117
Wright, Orville, 37
Wright, Wilbur, 37
Wrobel, David M., 191n32
Wyoming Benevolent Institute, 62, 63, 86

www.ingramcontent.com/pod-product-compliance
Lightning Source LLC
Chambersburg PA
CBHW020811230426
43666CB00007B/954